Let God Be GOD

A Study of the Attributes of God | Student Workbook | Revised Edition

Mark Eckel

Purposeful Design Publications is the publishing division of the Association of Christian Schools International (ACSI) and is committed to the ministry of Christian school education, to enable Christian educators and schools worldwide to effectively prepare students for life. As the publisher of textbooks, trade books, and other educational resources within ACSI, Purposeful Design Publications strives to produce biblically sound materials that reflect Christian scholarship and stewardship and that address the identified needs of Christian schools around the world.

Unless otherwise identified, all Scripture quotations are taken from the Holy Bible, New International Version® (NIV®). Copyright © 1973, 1978, 1984 by Biblica. All rights reserved worldwide. Used by permission.

Printed in the United States of America
25 24 23 22 21 20   5 6 7 8 9 10

Eckel, Mark
     Let God be God: A study of the attributes of God
     Revised edition
     ISBN 978-1-58331-275-9   Student workbook Catalog #HBLGS

Designer: Mike Riester
Editor: John Conaway

Purposeful Design Publications
A Division of ACSI
731 Chapel Hills Dr. • Colorado Springs, CO 80920
Care Team: 800-367-0798 • www.purposefuldesign.com

Contents

Introduction

A teenager passed out tracts in a park one summer. He was fifteen. The boy tried witnessing to a man whose idea of hell was "my job washing dishes at the neighborhood grill." All the young Christian knew was the basic gospel message contained in the pamphlets he was handing out. One morning the following fall during high school announcements, this young man was questioned by an atheist friend, who whispered, "How can you believe in something you can't see?"

Later that year the Christian teen became heavily involved in the political process. He worked hard for a regional candidate, but something was missing. He later resigned from the organization, writing, "I'm frustrated because I'm not addressing the root issues of our society. I feel as if I'm spraying water at the flames instead of at the coals."

These incidents and others led to a turning point in this young man's life. He was desperately searching for answers to questions that were not being adequately addressed in his home, school, or church. It was then that he encountered the writings of Francis Schaeffer. By high school graduation he had read all Dr. Schaeffer's books.

Schaeffer's philosophy, which focused on the personal development of a Christian worldview, revolutionized this teenager's thinking. Knowing God, he discovered, was more important than any other issue in the Scriptures—and in life. Dr. Schaeffer answered the questions all young people ask: *Why should I study this? So what? Who cares?* The founder of L'Abri made theology a reality to that student and to thousands of others.

I was that student over thirty years ago. Now my passionate desire is to prepare young people to know God and to make Him known to others. I want to help prepare teenagers to answer the inquiries of others about Christianity and their own Christian faith.

In this twenty-first century, how people think about the issues of life has changed little from the first century. They still ask the same questions: *Does God exist? If so, why does He matter?* Christian young people are taught that God exists, but they are often left asking, *So what?* May this course help to instruct the next generation of Christians about what they believe, and why.

May another Christian teenager give an atheist friend a better answer than I was able to give.

With passion for the subject and compassion for the student,

—Mark Eckel
Wheaton, Illinois

Part I
The Knowledge of GOD

Yahweh

Power and might are in your hand. (2 Chronicles 20:6)

The Lord is gracious and compassionate, slow to anger and rich in love. (Psalm 145:8)

Holy, holy, holy is the Lord God Almighty, who was, and is, and is to come. (Revelation 4:8)

God is love. (1 John 4:16)

I am the first and the last. (Isaiah 44:6)

Just and true are your ways. (Revelation 15:3)

The Lord reigns (Psalm 93:1)

My ways are higher than your ways and my thoughts than your thoughts. (Isaiah 55:9)

Christ of God (Luke 9:20)

Where can I flee from your presence? (Psalm 139:7)

He does not treat us as our sins deserve. (Psalm 103:10)

The Lord do not change (Malachi 3:6)

Ever-present

Great is your faithfulness. (Lamentations 3:23)

...knowledge of God! How unsearchable his judgments, and his paths beyond tracing out! (Romans 11:33)

Lord of the sabbath (Mark 2:28)

Oh, the depth of the riches of the wisdom and knowledge of God!

Righteousness and justice are the foundation of your throne; love and faithfulness go before you. (Psalm 89:14)

I am with you always (Matthew 28:20)

He is the true God. (1 John 5:20)

I am the Alpha and the Omega, the First and the Last, the Beginning and the End. (Revelation 22:13)

Nothing in all creation is hidden from God's sight. (Hebrews 4:13)

Give thanks to the Lord, for he is good; his love endures forever. (Psalm 118:1)

You alone are holy. (Revelation 15:4)

I AM (John 8:58)

The Lord is gracious and righteous; our God is full of compassion. (Psalm 116:5)

Holy, holy, holy is the Lord Almighty. (Isaiah 6:3)

No one comes to the Father except through me. (John 14:6)

I am the living bread that came down from heaven. (John 6:51)

The Lord works righteousness and justice for all the oppressed. (Psalm 103:6)

I am the way and the truth and the life. (John 14:6)

and the Word was God. (John 1:1)

The Lord is good and his love endures forever. (Psalm 100:5)

Taste and see that the Lord is good. (Psalm 34:8)

In the beginning was the Word, and the Word was with God

and he will be called Wonderful Counselor, Mighty God, Everlasting Father, Prince of Peace. (Isaiah 9:6)

Jesus, the pioneer and perfecter of faith. (Hebrews 12:2)

To God belong wisdom and power. (Job 12:13)

He is the Lord of both the dead and the living. (Romans 14:9)

He is the atoning sacrifice for our sins, and not only for ours but also for the sins of the whole world. (1 John 2:2)

the Lamb of God (John 1:29)

the Majesty in heaven. (Hebrews 1:3)

Your righteousness is everlasting. (Psalm 119:142)

For to us a child is born, to us a son is given, and the government will be on his shoulders. (Isaiah 9:6)

Christ died and returned to life so that he might be the Lord of both the dead and the living.

The Son is the radiance of God's glory and the exact representation of his being, sustaining all things by his powerful word. After he had provided purification for sins, he sat down at the right hand of the Majesty in heaven. (Hebrews 1:3)

we have a great high priest who has ascended into heaven, Jesus the Son of God, let us hold firmly to the faith we profess. (Hebrews 4:14)

Rose of Sharon (Song of Songs 2:1)

Let them know that you, whose name is the LORD—that you alone are the Most High over all the earth. (Psalm 83:18)

That which was from the beginning, which we have heard, which we have seen with our eyes, which we have looked at and our hands have touched... (Zechariah 14:9)

We have this hope as an anchor for the soul, firm and secure. It enters the inner sanctuary behind the curtain, where our forerunner, Jesus, has entered on our behalf. He has become a high priest forever, in the order of Melchizedek. (Hebrews 6:19-20)

God, the blessed and only Ruler, the King of kings and Lord of lords (1 Timothy 6:15)

The Son of Man came eating and drinking, and they say, 'Here is a glutton and a drunkard, a friend of tax collectors and sinners.' (Matthew 11:19)

the Father has sent his Son to be the Savior of the world. (1 John 4:14)

And we have seen and testify that

Desire of all nations

Bridegroom (Matthew 9:15)

Chosen of God (1 Peter 2:4)

See, I lay a stone in Zion, a tested stone, a precious cornerstone for a sure foundation. (Isaiah 28:16)

David, a righteous Branch, a King who will reign wisely and do what is just and right in the land. (Jeremiah 23:5)

Thanks be to God for his indescribable gift! (2 Corinthians 9:15)

God will be king over the whole earth. On that day there will be one LORD, and his name the only name. (Zechariah 14:9)

The LORD will be king over the whole earth. (Psalm 90:2)

From everlasting to everlasting you are God.

The virgin will conceive and give birth to a son, and will call him Immanuel. (Isaiah 7:14)

(O)ur Lord Jesus, that great Shepherd of the sheep (Hebrews 13:20)

The Lord is enthroned as King forever. (Psalm 29:10)

I am the true vine, and my Father is the gardener. (John 15:1)

(T)he Shepherd and Overseer of your souls (1 Peter 2:25)

(W)e have an advocate with the Father—Jesus Christ, the Righteous One. (1 John 2:1)

I am the Root and the Offspring of David, and the bright Morning Star. (Revelation 22:16)

As for God, his way is perfect. (Psalm 18:30)

Chief Shepherd (1 Peter 5:4)

Heir of all things (Hebrews 1:2)

Sceptre

Judge (Acts 10:42)

Yahweh

1

Knowing GOD

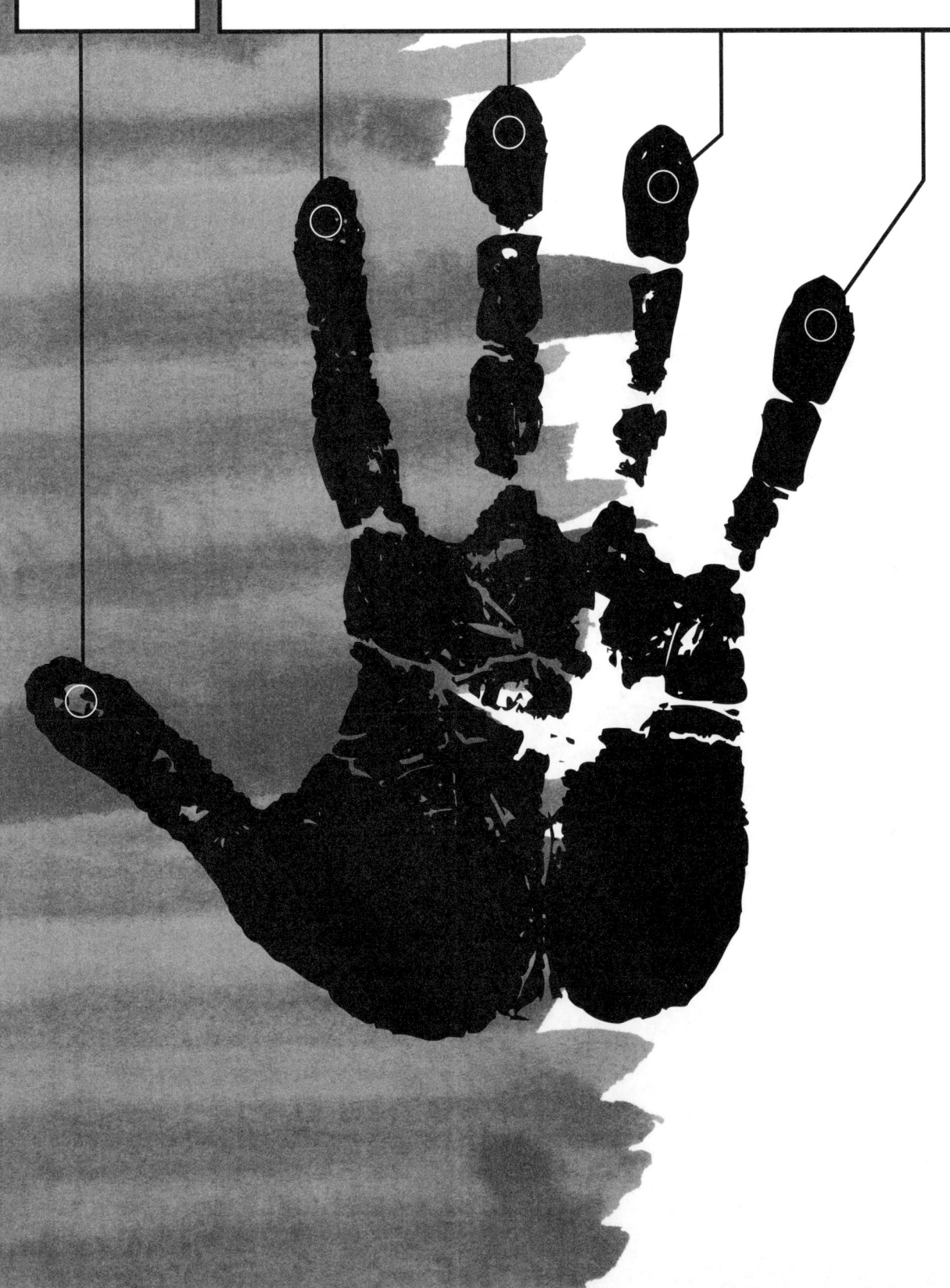

Interact 1.1
Labeling God

Write about the kind of God each label suggests.

Town Sheriff

Store Manager

Santa Claus or Aladdin's Genie

Party Animal

Grandfather

God-in-a-Box

Yahweh

Power and might are in your hand. (2 Chronicles 20:6)

The Lord is gracious and compassionate, slow to anger and rich in love. (Psalm 145:8)

Holy, holy, holy is the Lord God Almighty, who was, and is, and is to come. (Revelation 4:8)

God is love. (1 John 4:16)

I am the first and the last. (Isaiah 44:6)

Just and true are your ways. (Revelation 15:3)

The Lord reigns (Psalm 93:1)

My ways are higher than your ways and my thoughts than your thoughts. (Isaiah 55:9)

He does not treat us as our sins deserve. (Psalm 103:10)

I am with you always. (Matthew 28:20)

Christ of God (Luke 9:20)

Ever-present—Where can I flee from your presence? (Psalm 139:7)

Great is your faithfulness. (Lamentations 3:23)

Oh, the depth of the riches of the wisdom and knowledge of God! How unsearchable his judgments, and his paths beyond tracing out! (Romans 11:33)

Lord of the sabbath (Mark 2:28)

I am the living bread that came down from heaven. (John 6:51)

Righteousness and justice are the foundation of your throne; love and faithfulness go before you. (Psalm 89:14)

I am the Alpha and the Omega, the First and the Last, the Beginning and the End. (Revelation 22:13)

Nothing in all creation is hidden from God's sight. (Hebrews 4:13)

He is the true God. (1 John 5:20)

Give thanks to the Lord, for he is good; his love endures forever. (Psalm 118:1)

Holy, holy, holy is the Lord Almighty. (Isaiah 6:3)

No one comes to the Father except through me. (John 14:6)

You alone are holy. (Revelation 15:4)

I AM (John 8:58)

The Lord is gracious and righteous; our God is full of compassion. (Psalm 116:5)

I am the way and the truth and the life. (John 14:6)

In the beginning was the Word, and the Word was with God, and the Word was God. (John 1:1)

Taste and see that the Lord is good. (Psalm 34:8)

The Lord works righteousness and justice for all the oppressed. (Psalm 103:6)

And he will be called Wonderful Counselor, Mighty God, Everlasting Father, Prince of Peace. (Isaiah 9:6)

The Lord is good and his love endures forever. (Psalm 100:5)

To God belong wisdom and power. (Job 12:13)

Your righteousness is everlasting. (Psalm 119:142)

For to us a child is born, to us a son is given, and the government will be on his shoulders. (Isaiah 9:6)

And returned to life so that he might be the Lord of both the dead and the living. (Romans 14:9)

Jesus the Son of God, let us hold firmly to the faith we profess. (Hebrews 4:14)

After he had provided purification for sins, he sat down at the right hand of the Majesty in heaven. (Hebrews 1:3)

Jesus, the pioneer and perfecter of faith. (Hebrews 12:2)

Christ died and returned to life. (Romans 14:9)

He is the atoning sacrifice for our sins, and not only for ours but also for the sins of the whole world. (1 John 2:2)

God, the blessed and only Ruler, the King of kings and Lord of lords. (1 Timothy 6:15)

him who is and who was, and who is to come (Revelation 1:4)

that you alone are the Most High over all the earth. (Psalm 83:18)

sustaining all things by his powerful word. (Hebrews 1:3)

the Lamb of God (John 1:29)

the faithful witness, the firstborn from the dead and the ruler of the kings of the earth. (Revelation 1:5)

whose name is the LORD—that you alone are the Most High over all the earth. (Psalm 83:18)

which we have as an anchor for the soul, firm and secure. It enters the inner sanctuary behind the curtain, where our forerunner, Jesus, has entered on our behalf. He has become a high priest forever, in the order of Melchizedek. (Hebrews 6:19-20)

the LORD will be king over the whole earth. On that day there will be one LORD and his name the only name. (Zechariah 14:9)

The Son of Man came eating and drinking, and they say, 'Here is a glutton and a drunkard, a friend of tax collectors and sinners.' (Matthew 11:19)

the Morning Star (Revelation 22:16)

And we have seen and testify that the Father has sent his Son to be the Savior of the world. (1 John 4:14)

Desire of all nations (Haggai 2:7)

Branch, a king who will reign wisely (Jeremiah 23:5)

See, I lay a stone in Zion, a tested stone, a precious cornerstone for a sure foundation. (Isaiah 28:16)

Chosen of God (1 Peter 2:4)

Thanks be to God for his indescribable gift! (2 Corinthians 9:15)

Let them know that you, whose name is the LORD (Psalm 83:18)

The virgin will conceive and give birth to a son, and will call him Immanuel. (Isaiah 7:14)

The Son is the radiance of God's glory and the exact representation of his being. (Hebrews 1:3)

Rose of Sharon (Song of Songs 2:1)

That which was from the beginning, which we have heard. (1 John 1:1)

We have this hope as an anchor for the soul. (Hebrews 6:19)

God the blessed and only Ruler (1 Timothy 6:15)

From everlasting to everlasting you are God. (Psalm 90:2)

(O)ur Lord Jesus, that great Shepherd of the sheep (Hebrews 13:20)

The LORD will be king over the whole earth.

The Lord is enthroned as King forever. (Psalm 29:10)

I am the true vine, and my Father is the gardener. (John 15:1)

(T)he Shepherd and Overseer of your souls. (1 Peter 2:25)

(W)e have an advocate with the Father—Jesus Christ, the Righteous One. (1 John 2:1)

I am the Root and the Offspring of David, and the bright Morning Star. (Revelation 22:16)

As for God, his way is perfect. (Psalm 18:30)

Heir of all things (Hebrews 1:2)

Judge (Acts 10:42)

Yahweh

Sceptre (Numbers 24:17)

(C)hief Shepherd (1 Peter 5:4)

Interact 1.2
Can We Define God?

Read Job 38–41, and answer these questions.

1. What is the problem with treating God like one of the titles on Interact 1.1?

2. According to God, how does the Creator compare with the creature? Give three specific statements from Job 38–41 in which God compares himself with Job.

Follow-up question to #2: Why is it important for us to have an accurate concept of God?

3. How is God's description of Himself in Job 38–41 different from popular ideas about God?

4. What happens to our view of God when we make up our own ideas about God?

Follow-up question to #4: Which idea of God is more satisfying to people—the one they come up with themselves or the one presented in the Bible?

5. Is it possible to define God? Give reasons for your answer.

6. How would you summarize, in one sentence, the message of Job 38–41?

Yahweh

Power and might are in your hand (2 Chronicles 20:6)

The Lord is gracious and compassionate, slow to anger and rich in love. (2 Chronicles 20:6)

Holy, holy, holy is the Lord God Almighty, who was, and is, and is to come. (Revelation 4:8)

God is love. (1 John 4:16)   I am the first and the last (Isaiah 44:6)   Just and true are your ways. (Revelation 15:3)

The Lord reigns (Psalm 93:1)   My ways are higher than your ways and my thoughts than your thoughts. (Isaiah 55:9)

He does not treat us as our sins deserve. (Psalm 103:10)   The Lord do not change (Malachi 3:6)

Christ of God (Luke 9:20)   Ever-present—Where can I flee from your presence? (Psalm 139:7)

Great is your faithfulness. (Lamentations 3:23)   knowledge of God! How unsearchable his judgments, and his paths beyond tracing out! (Romans 11:33)   Lord of the Sabbath (Mark 2:28)

Oh, the depth of the riches of the wisdom and knowledge of God!

Righteousness and justice are the foundation of your throne; love and faithfulness go before you. (Psalm 89:14)

He is the true God. (1 John 5:20)

I am the Alpha and the Omega, the First and the Last, the Beginning and the End. (Revelation 22:13)

Nothing in all creation is hidden from God's sight. (Hebrews 4:13)

The Lord is gracious and righteous; our God is full of compassion. (Psalm 116:5)   Give thanks to the Lord, for he is good; his love endures forever. (Psalm 118:1)   You alone are holy (Revelation 15:4)

The Lord works righteousness and justice for all the oppressed. (Psalm 103:6)   I am the way and the truth and the life. No one comes to the Father except through me. (John 14:6)   Holy, holy, holy is the Lord Almighty (Isaiah 6:3)   Taste and see that the Lord is good (Psalm 34:8)   I AM (John 8:58)

To God belong wisdom and power. (Job 12:13)

In the beginning was the Word, and the Word was with God, and the Word was God. (John 1:1)   And he will be called Wonderful Counselor, Mighty God, Everlasting Father, Prince of Peace. (Isaiah 9:6)   The Lord is good and his love endures forever. (Psalm 100:5)

Your righteousness is everlasting. (Psalm 119:142)   And he will be the Lord of both the dead and the living. (Romans 14:9)   Jesus, the pioneer and perfecter of faith. (Hebrews 12:2)

He is the atoning sacrifice for our sins, and not only for ours but also for the sins of the whole world. (1 John 2:2)

who has provided purification for sins, he sat down at the right hand of the Majesty in heaven. (Hebrews 1:3)

Christ died and returned to life so that he might be the Lord of both the dead and the living. (Romans 14:9)

For to us a child is born, to us a son is given, and the government will be on his shoulders.

we have a great high priest who has ascended into heaven, Jesus the Son of God, let us hold firmly to the faith we profess. (Hebrews 4:14)

God, the exact representation of his being, sustaining all things by his powerful word.

The Son is the radiance of God's glory and the exact representation of his being. (Hebrews 1:3)

the blessed and only Ruler, the King of kings and Lord of lords (1 Timothy 6:15)

Rose of Sharon (Song of Songs 2:1)

(H)im who is and who was, and who is to come, and from the seven spirits before his throne (Revelation 1:4)

We have this hope as an anchor for the soul, firm and secure. It enters the inner sanctuary behind the curtain, where our forerunner, Jesus, has entered on our behalf. He has become a high priest forever, in the order of Melchizedek. (Hebrews 6:19-20)

Let them know that you, whose name is the LORD—that you alone are the Most High over all the earth. (Psalm 83:18)

That which was from the beginning, which we have heard, which we have seen with our eyes, which we have looked at and our hands have touched (1 John 1:1)

God, the blessed and only Ruler, the King of kings and Lord of lords (1 Timothy 6:15)

He is the firstborn from the dead, and the ruler of the kings of the earth. (Revelation 1:5)

the Lamb of God (John 1:29)

I will raise up for David a righteous Branch, a King who will reign (Jeremiah 23:5)

"Here is a glutton and a drunkard, a friend of tax collectors and sinners." (Matthew 11:19)

And we have seen and testify that the Father has sent his Son to be the Savior of the world. (1 John 4:14)

Desire of all nations (Haggai 2:7)

See, I lay a stone in Zion, a tested stone, a precious cornerstone for a sure foundation (Isaiah 28:16)

The LORD will be king over the whole earth. On that day there will be one LORD, and his name the only name. (Zechariah 14:9)

The Son of Man came eating and drinking (Matthew 9:15)

Chosen of God (1 Peter 2:4)

the bridegroom (Matthew 9:15)

from everlasting to everlasting you are God. (Psalm 90:2)

The virgin will conceive and give birth to a son, and will call him Immanuel. (Isaiah 7:14)

Thanks be to God for his indescribable gift! (2 Corinthians 9:15)

(O)ur Lord Jesus, that great Shepherd of the sheep (Hebrews 13:20)

The Lord is enthroned as King forever. (Psalm 29:10)

I am the true vine, and my Father is the gardener. (John 15:1)

(T)he Shepherd and Overseer of your souls (1 Peter 2:25)

(W)e have an advocate with the Father—Jesus Christ, the Righteous One. (1 John 2:1)

the Root and the Offspring of David, and the bright Morning Star. (Revelation 22:16)

As for God, his way is perfect. (Psalm 18:30)

I am the Root

Chief Shepherd (1 Peter 5:4)   Heir of all things (Hebrews 1:2)   Judge (Acts 10:42)

Sceptre (Numbers 24:17)   Yahweh

Interact 1.3
God Makes Himself Known

God has deliberately revealed Himself in ways that human beings can understand.

Definitions

Revelation is the disclosure of something previously unknown. Bible scholars divide the means of revelation into two categories:
- *general* or *unlimited revelation*—available to all people everywhere
- *specific* or *limited revelation*—available only to certain people at certain times

Research

Look up the references listed in the left-hand column to match them to the means of revelation listed on the right. (Some references will have two correct answers. Give both answers.)

Reference		Means
1. Exodus 10:1–2		A. Scripture
2. Numbers 12:6–8	and	B. Christ (the Incarnation)
3. Psalm 19:1, 7	and	C. conscience
4. John 1:1, 14, 18		D. history/miracles
5. Romans 2:14–15		E. face-to-face (theophany)
6. Colossians 1:15		F. nature
7. 2 Timothy 3:16		G. the prophets (including visions and dreams)
8. Hebrews 1:1–2	and	
9. 2 Peter 1:19–21		
10. Romans 1:20		

Which two means of revelation listed above are in the *general revelation* category?

What is our main source for special revelation?

Yahweh Power and might are in your hand. (2 Chronicles 20:6)

The Lord is gracious and compassionate, slow to anger and rich in love. (Psalm 145:8)

Holy, holy, holy is the Lord God Almighty, who was, and is, and is to come. (Revelation 4:8)

Just and true are your ways. (Revelation 15:3)

God is love. (1 John 4:16) I am the first and the last. (Isaiah 44:6)

The Lord reigns (Psalm 93:1) My ways are higher than your ways and my thoughts than your thoughts. (Isaiah 55:9) He does not treat us as our sins deserve. (Psalm 103:10) The Lord do not change (Malachi 3:6)

Christ of God (Luke 9:20) Ever-present—Where can I flee from your presence? (Psalm 139:7)

Great is your faithfulness. (Lamentations 3:23) Oh, the depth of the riches of the wisdom and knowledge of God! How unsearchable his judgments, and his paths beyond tracing out! (Romans) Lord of the Sabbath (Mark 2:28)

Righteousness and justice are the foundation of your throne; love and faithfulness go before you. (Revelation 22:13) You alone are holy. (Revelation 15:4) I AM (John 8:58)

I am the Alpha and the Omega, the First and the Last, the Beginning and the End. (Hebrews 4:13)

Nothing in all creation is hidden from God's sight. (Psalm 116:5) Give thanks to the Lord, for he is good; his love endures forever. (Psalm 118:1)

I am the way and the truth and the life. No one comes to the Father except through me. (John 14:6) Taste and see that the Lord is good and his love endures forever. (Psalm 34:8)

Holy, holy, holy is the Lord Almighty. (Isaiah 6:3)

In the beginning was the Word, and the Word was with God, and the Word was God. (John 1:1) The Lord is good (Psalm 100:5)

Wonderful Counselor, Mighty God, Everlasting Father, Prince of Peace. (Isaiah 9:6)

He is the true God (1 John 5:20)

He is the atoning sacrifice for our sins, and not only for ours but also for the sins of the whole world. (1 John 2:2)

The Lord works righteousness and justice for all the oppressed. (Psalm 103:6) Jesus, the pioneer and perfecter of faith. (Hebrews 12:2)

Your righteousness is everlasting. (Psalm 119:142) To God belong wisdom and power (Job 12:13)

Christ died and returned to life so that he might be the Lord of both the dead and the living. (Romans 14:9)

The Son is the radiance of God's glory and the exact representation of his being, sustaining all things by his powerful word. After he had provided purification for sins, he sat down at the right hand of the Majesty in heaven. (Hebrews 1:3)

Rose of Sharon (Song of Songs 2:1) whose name is the LORD—that you alone are the Most High over all the earth. (Psalm 83:18)

the Father has sent his Son to be the Savior of the world. (1 John 4:14)

The LORD will be king over the whole earth. On that day there will be one LORD, and his name the only name. (Zechariah 14:9)

Chosen of God (1 Peter 2:4) Thanks be to God for his indescribable gift! (2 Corinthians 9:15)

From everlasting to everlasting you are God. (Psalm 90:2) The virgin will conceive and give birth to a son, and will call him Immanuel. (Isaiah 7:14)

(O)ur Lord Jesus, that great Shepherd of the sheep (Hebrews 13:20) The Lord is enthroned as King forever. (Psalm 29:10)

I am the true vine, and my Father is the gardener. (John 15:1) The Shepherd and Overseer of your souls. (1 Peter 2:25)

(W)e have an advocate with the Father—Jesus Christ, the Righteous One. (1 John 2:1)

I am the Root and the Offspring of David, and the bright Morning Star. (Revelation 22:16) As for God, his way is perfect. (Psalm 18:30)

Heir of all things (Hebrews 1:2) Judge (Acts 10:42) Yahweh

Interact 1.4
The O–I–C–A Method

Examine Genesis 1:1 closely. Answerithe questions for the O-I-C-A method of Bible study.

Observation: What does the verse say?

Interpretation: What did the verse mean *for the first readers, then*?

Correlation: How does the verse fit in with other Scripture?

Application: What does the verse mean for *us, now*?

O

I

C

A

Yahweh   Power and might are in your hand. (2 Chronicles 20:6)

The Lord is gracious and compassionate, slow to anger and rich in love. (Psalm 145:8)

Holy, holy, holy is the Lord God Almighty, who was, and is, and is to come. (Revelation 4:8)

God is love. (1 John 4:16)   I am the first and the last. (Isaiah 44:6)   Just and true are your ways. (Revelation 15:3)

The Lord reigns (Psalm 93:1)   My ways are higher than your ways and my thoughts than your thoughts. (Isaiah 55:9)   the Lord do not change (Malachi 3:6)

Christ of God (Luke 9:20)   Where can I flee from your presence? (Psalm 139:7)   He does not treat us as our sins deserve. (Psalm 103:10)   I am with you always. (Matthew 28:20)

Ever-present. (Lamentations 3:23)   How unsearchable his judgments, and his paths beyond tracing out! (Romans 11:33)   Lord of the Sabbath. (Matt. 12:8)

Great is your faithfulness. (Lamentations 3:23)   love and faithfulness go before you. (Psalm 89:14)

Oh, the depth of the riches of the wisdom and knowledge of God! How unsearchable his judgments, and his paths beyond tracing out! (Romans 11:33)

Righteousness and justice are the foundation of your throne; love and faithfulness go before you. (Psalm 89:14)   I AM (John 8:58)

He is the true God. (1 John 5:20)   the First and the Last, the Beginning and the End. (Revelation 22:13)   You alone are holy. (Revelation 15:4)

I am the Alpha and the Omega, the First and the Last, the Beginning and the End. (Revelation 22:13)   his love endures forever. (Psalm 118:1)

creation is hidden from God's sight. (Hebrews 4:13)   Give thanks to the Lord, for he is good; his love endures forever. (Psalm 118:1)

The Lord is gracious and righteous; our God is full of compassion. (Psalm 116:5)   Holy, holy, holy is the Lord Almighty. (Isaiah 6:3)   No one comes to the Father except through me. (John 14:6)   Taste and see that the Lord is good. (Psalm 34:8)

Nothing in all creation is hidden from God's sight. (Hebrews 4:13)   I am the way and the truth and the life. (John 14:6)   The Lord is good and his love endures forever. (Psalm 100:5)

To God belong wisdom and power. (Job 12:13)   In the beginning was the Word, and the Word was with God, and the Word was God. (John 1:1)   Wonderful Counselor, Mighty God, Everlasting Father, Prince of Peace. (Isaiah 9:6)

The Lord works righteousness and justice for all the oppressed. (Psalm 103:6)   And he will be called Wonderful Counselor, Mighty God, Everlasting Father, Prince of Peace. (Isaiah 9:6)

Your righteousness is everlasting. (Psalm 119:142)   I am the Lord of both the dead and the living. (Romans 14:9)   After he had provided purification for sins, he sat down at the right hand of the Majesty in heaven. (Hebrews 1:3)

For to us a child is born, to us a son is given, and the government will be on his shoulders. (Isaiah 9:6)   He is the atoning sacrifice for our sins, and not only for ours but also for the sins of the whole world. (1 John 2:2)

Christ died and returned to life so that he might be the Lord of both the dead and the living. (Romans 14:9)   let us hold firmly to the faith we profess. (Hebrews 4:14)   the Lamb of God (John 1:29)   Jesus, the pioneer and perfecter of faith. (Hebrews 12:2)

The Son is the radiance of God's glory and the exact representation of his being, sustaining all things by his powerful word. (Hebrews 1:3)   who is the faithful witness, the firstborn from the dead, and the ruler of the kings of the earth. (Revelation 1:5)

Therefore, since we have a great high priest who has ascended into heaven, Jesus the Son of God, let us hold firmly to the faith we profess. (Hebrews 4:14)

Let them know that you, whose name is the LORD—that you alone are the Most High over all the earth. (Psalm 83:18)   that you may have the freedom to enter the Most Holy Place by the blood of Jesus. (Hebrews 10:19)

We have this hope as an anchor for the soul, firm and secure. It enters the inner sanctuary behind the curtain, where our forerunner, Jesus, has entered on our behalf. He has become a high priest forever, in the order of Melchizedek. (Hebrews 6:19-20)

God, the blessed and only Ruler, the King of kings and Lord of lords. (1 Timothy 6:15)   That which we have seen and heard we proclaim also to you. (1 John 1:3)

That which was from the beginning, which we have heard, which we have seen with our eyes, which we have looked at and our hands have touched—this we proclaim concerning the Word of life. (1 John 1:1)

Rose of Sharon (Song of Solomon 2:1)   The Son of Man came eating and drinking, and they say, 'Here is a glutton and a drunkard, a friend of tax collectors and sinners.' (Matthew 11:19)   the Father has sent his Son to be the Savior of the world. (1 John 4:14)

God the blessed and only Ruler, the King of kings. (1 Timothy 6:15)   the King of kings and Lord of lords. (1 Timothy 6:15)   And we have seen and testify that the Father has sent his Son to be the Savior of the world. (1 John 4:14)

The LORD will be king over the whole earth. (Zechariah 14:9)   Chosen of God (1 Peter 2:4)   Bridegroom (Matthew 6:12)   Thanks be to God for his indescribable gift! (2 Corinthians 9:15)

From everlasting to everlasting you are God. (Psalm 90:2)   On that day there will be one LORD, and his name the only name. (Zechariah 14:9)   the righteous Branch, a King who will reign wisely and do what is just and right in the land. (Jeremiah 23:5)

The virgin will conceive and give birth to a son, and will call him Immanuel. (Isaiah 7:14)   Desire of all nations. (Haggai 2:7)   I lay a stone in Zion, a tested stone, a precious cornerstone for a sure foundation. (Isaiah 28:16)

(O)ur Lord Jesus, that great Shepherd of the sheep (Hebrews 13:20)   The Lord is enthroned as King forever. (Psalm 29:10)

I am the true vine, and my Father is the gardener. (John 15:1)

(T)he Shepherd and Overseer of your souls (1 Peter 2:25)   the Righteous One. (1 John 2:1)

(W)e have an advocate with the Father—Jesus Christ, the Righteous One. (1 John 2:1)   I am the Root and the Offspring of David, and the bright Morning Star. (Revelation 22:16)

As for God, his way is perfect. (Psalm 18:30)

I am the Root and the Offspring of David, and the bright Morning Star (Revelation 22:16)

Heir of all things (Hebrews 1:2)   Judge (Acts 10:42)

I am the Chief Shepherd (1 Peter 5:4)   Scepter (Numbers 24:17)   Yahweh

2

Describing GOD

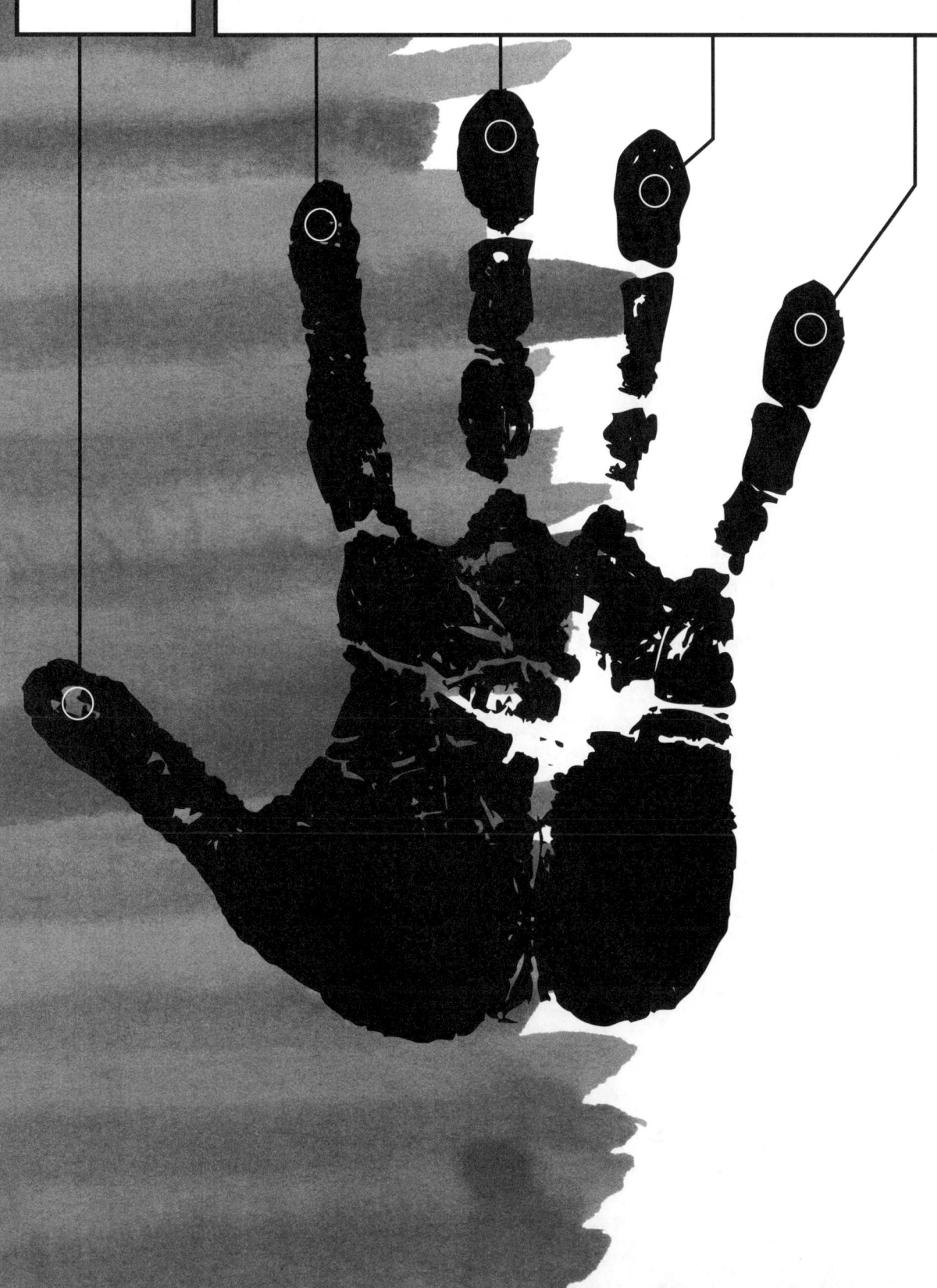

Interact 2.1

God's Attributes

You will be completing this chart throughout the course.

Attribute	Meaning	Symbol	Reference(s)
Supreme	The only God, above all "gods"	○↑	Isaiah 40:18, 25
Self-existent			
Sovereign	Has absolute authority	♔○	Isaiah 40:10
Infinite			
Immutable			
Eternal			
Incomprehensible			
Ineffable			
Omniscient			
Omnipresent			

Continued on back →

Let God Be GOD

Attribute	Meaning	Symbol	Reference(s)
Omnipotent			
Good			
Wise			
Truthful			
Holy			
Righteous			
Merciful			
Just			
Long-Suffering			
Loving			

Let God Be GOD

Interact 2.2
God and People

Read Acts 17:22–31, and answer the first question.

1. What do these verses tell us about God and people?

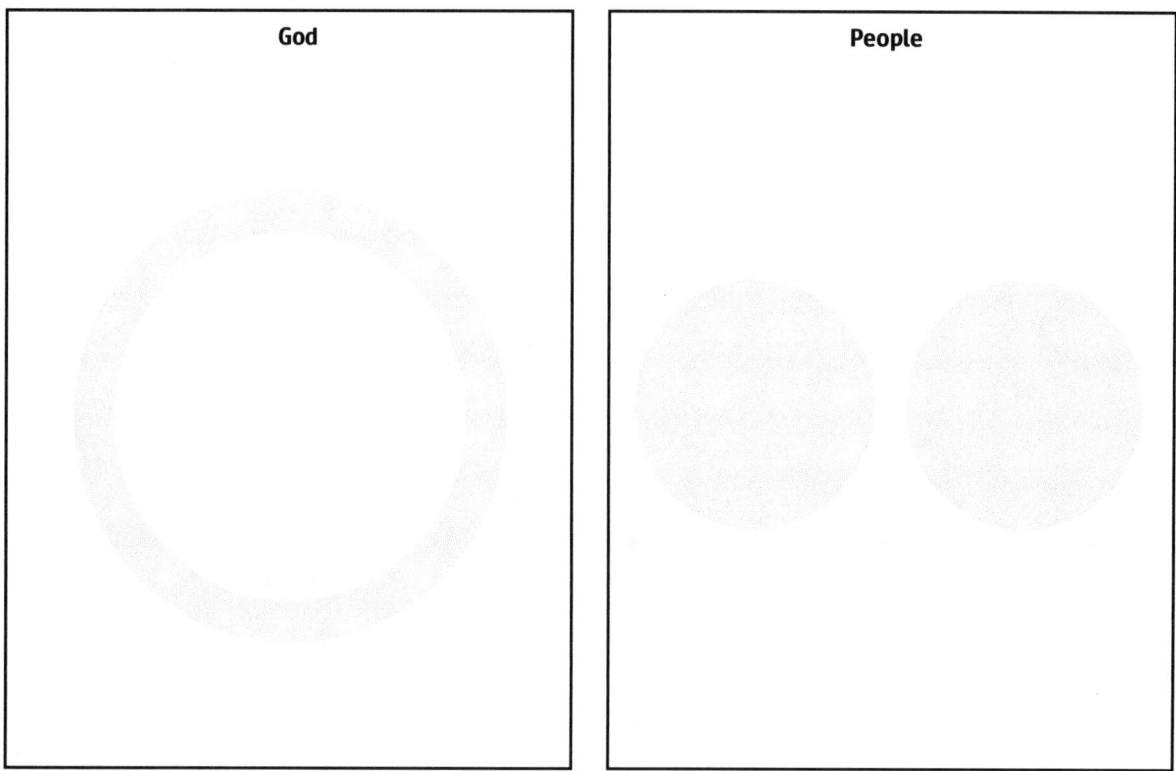

God	People

2. With knowledge comes responsibility, and Paul gave information about God to the people in Athens. According to Paul, what did God want the people to do with that knowledge?

Let God Be GOD

Part II
The Trinity

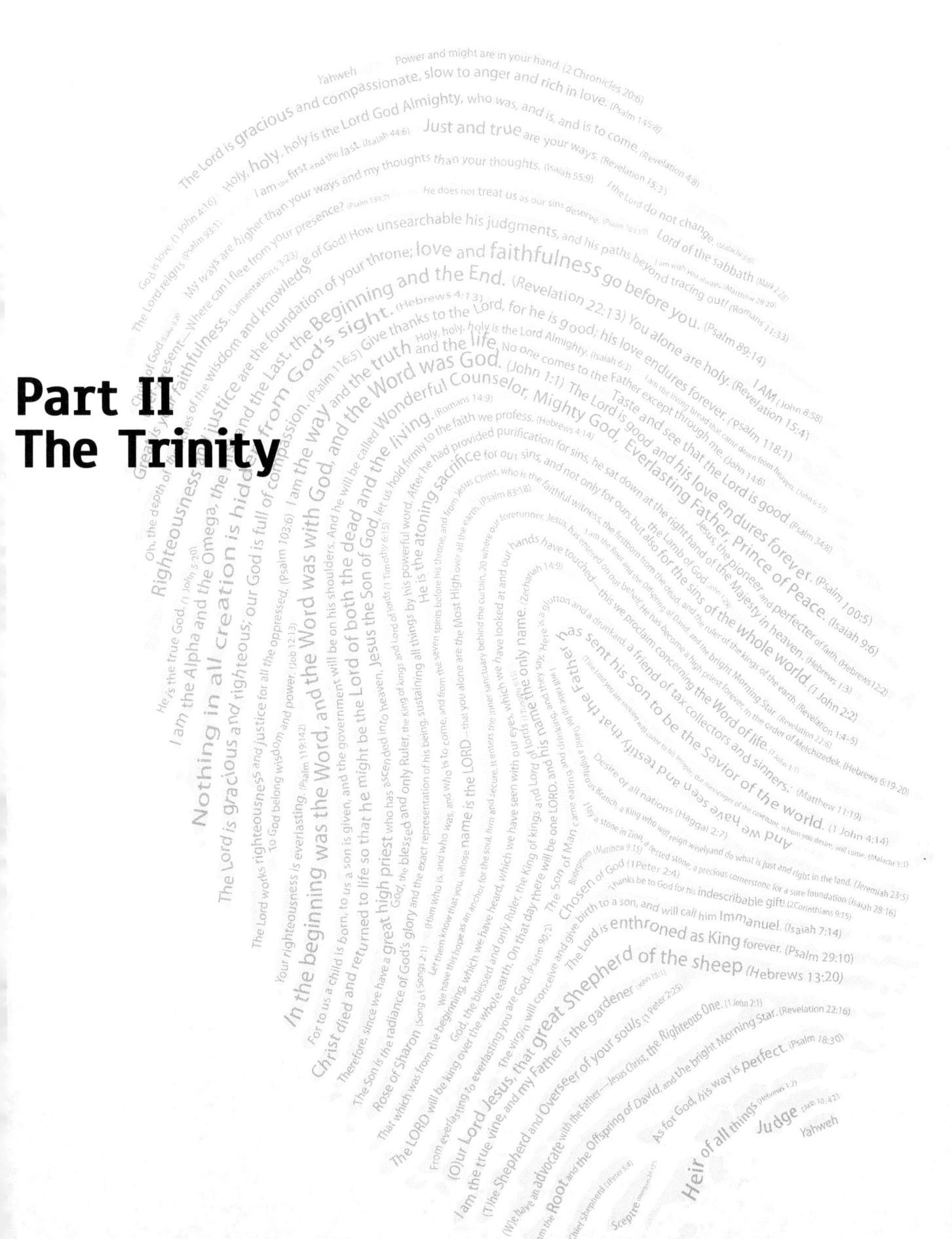

Yahweh

Power and might are in your hand. (2 Chronicles 20:6)

The Lord is gracious and compassionate, slow to anger and rich in love. (Psalm 145:8)

Holy, holy, holy is the Lord God Almighty, who was, and is, and is to come. (Revelation 4:8)

God is love. (1 John 4:16)

I am the first and the last. (Isaiah 44:6)

Just and true are your ways. (Revelation 15:3)

The Lord reigns (Psalm 93:1)

My ways are higher than your ways and my thoughts than your thoughts. (Isaiah 55:9)

He does not treat us as our sins deserve. (Psalm 103:10)

Christ of God (Luke 9:20)

Ever-present—Where can I flee from your presence? (Psalm 139:7)

(I the Lord do not change. (Malachi 3:6)

Great is your faithfulness. (Lamentations 3:23)

On the depth of the riches of the wisdom and knowledge of God! How unsearchable his judgments, and his paths beyond tracing out! (Romans 28:20)

Lord of the sabbath. (Mark 2:28)

Righteousness and justice are the foundation of your throne; love and faithfulness go before you. (Psalm 89:14)

I am the Alpha and the Omega, the First and the Last, the Beginning and the End. (Revelation 22:13) You alone are holy. (Revelation 15:4)

He is the true God. (1 John 5:20)

Nothing in all creation is hidden from God's sight. (Hebrews 4:13)

Give thanks to the Lord, for he is good; his love endures forever. (Psalm 118:1)

I AM (John 8:58)

Holy, holy, holy is the Lord Almighty. (Isaiah 6:3)

I am the living bread that came down from heaven. (John 6:51)

The Lord is gracious and righteous; our God is full of compassion. (Psalm 116:5)

I am the way and the truth and the life. No one comes to the Father except through me. (John 14:6)

Taste and see that the Lord is good and his love endures forever. (Psalm 34:8)

I AM (John 14:6)

To God belong wisdom and power. (Job 12:13)

In the beginning was the Word, and the Word was with God, and the Word was God. (John 1:1)

The Lord is good and his love endures forever. (Psalm 100:5)

And he will be called Wonderful Counselor, Mighty God, Everlasting Father, Prince of Peace. (Isaiah 9:6)

The Lord works righteousness and justice for all the oppressed. (Psalm 103:6)

Your righteousness is everlasting. (Psalm 119:142)

For us a child is born, to us a son is given, and the government will be on his shoulders. And he will be called Wonderful Counselor, Mighty God, Everlasting Father, Prince of Peace.

Jesus the pioneer and perfecter of faith. (Hebrews 12:2)

Let us hold firmly to the faith we profess. (Hebrews 4:14)

After he had provided purification for sins, he sat down at the right hand of the Majesty in heaven. (Hebrews 1:3)

He is the Lord of both the dead and the living. (Romans 14:9)

Jesus the Son of God, let us hold firmly to the faith we profess. (Hebrews 4:14)

the Lamb of God. (John 1:29)

the bright Morning Star. (Revelation 22:16)

in the order of Melchizedek. (Hebrews 6:20)

He is the atoning sacrifice for our sins, and not only for ours but also for the sins of the whole world. (1 John 2:2)

the Root and the Offspring of David, and the bright Morning Star. (Revelation 22:16)

For us a child is born, to us a son is given, and the government will be on his shoulders. (Isaiah 9:6)

Christ died and returned to life so that he might be the Lord of both the dead and the living. (Romans 14:9)

The Son is the radiance of God's glory and the exact representation of his being, sustaining all things by his powerful word. (Hebrews 1:3)

Rose of Sharon (Song of Songs 2:1)

(H)im who is and who was, and who is to come, and from the seven spirits before his throne. (Revelation 1:4)

He is the Most High over all the earth. (Psalm 83:18)

the King of kings and Lord of lords. (1 Timothy 6:15)

That which was from the beginning, which we have heard, which we have seen with our eyes, which we have looked at and our hands have touched—this we proclaim concerning the Word of life. (1 John 1:1)

the blessed and only Ruler, the King of kings and Lord of lords. (1 Timothy 6:15)

We have this hope as an anchor for the soul, firm and secure. It enters the inner sanctuary behind the curtain, where our forerunner, Jesus, has entered on our behalf. He has become a high priest forever, in the order of Melchizedek. (Hebrews 6:19-20)

God the blessed and only Ruler, the King of kings and Lord of lords. (1 Timothy 6:15)

Desire of all nations (Haggai 2:7)

I lay a stone in Zion, a tested stone, a precious cornerstone for a sure foundation. (Isaiah 28:16)

Here is a glutton and a drunkard, a friend of tax collectors and sinners. (Matthew 11:19)

the Father has sent his Son to be the Savior of the world. (1 John 4:14)

And we have seen and testify that the Father has sent his Son to be the Savior of the world. (1 John 4:14)

Let them know that you, whose name is the LORD—that you alone are the Most High over all the earth. (Psalm 83:18)

Jesus Christ is Lord. (Philippians 2:11)

The LORD will be king over the whole earth. (Zechariah 14:9)

For to us a child is born, to us a son is given, and the government will be on his shoulders. (Isaiah 9:6)

The Son of Man came eating and drinking, and they say, 'Here is a glutton and a drunkard, a friend of tax collectors and sinners.' (Matthew 11:19)

Chosen of God (1 Peter 2:4)

a righteous Branch, a King who will reign wisely and do what is just and right in the land. (Jeremiah 23:5)

The LORD will be king over the whole earth. (Zechariah 14:9)

From everlasting to everlasting you are God. (Psalm 90:2)

The virgin will conceive and give birth to a son, and will call him Immanuel. (Isaiah 7:14)

Bridegroom (Matthew 9:15)

Thanks be to God for his indescribable gift! (2 Corinthians 9:15)

(O)ur Lord Jesus, that great Shepherd of the sheep (Hebrews 13:20)

The Lord is enthroned as King forever. (Psalm 29:10)

I am the true vine, and my Father is the gardener (John 15:1)

(T)he Shepherd and Overseer of your souls (1 Peter 2:25)

(W)e have an advocate with the Father—Jesus Christ, the Righteous One. (1 John 2:1)

I am the Root and the Offspring of David, and the bright Morning Star. (Revelation 22:16)

As for God, his way is perfect. (Psalm 18:30)

Chief Shepherd (1 Peter 5:4)

Sceptre (Numbers 24:17)

Heir of all things (Hebrews 1:2)

Judge (Acts 10:42)

Yahweh

3

GOD Is One

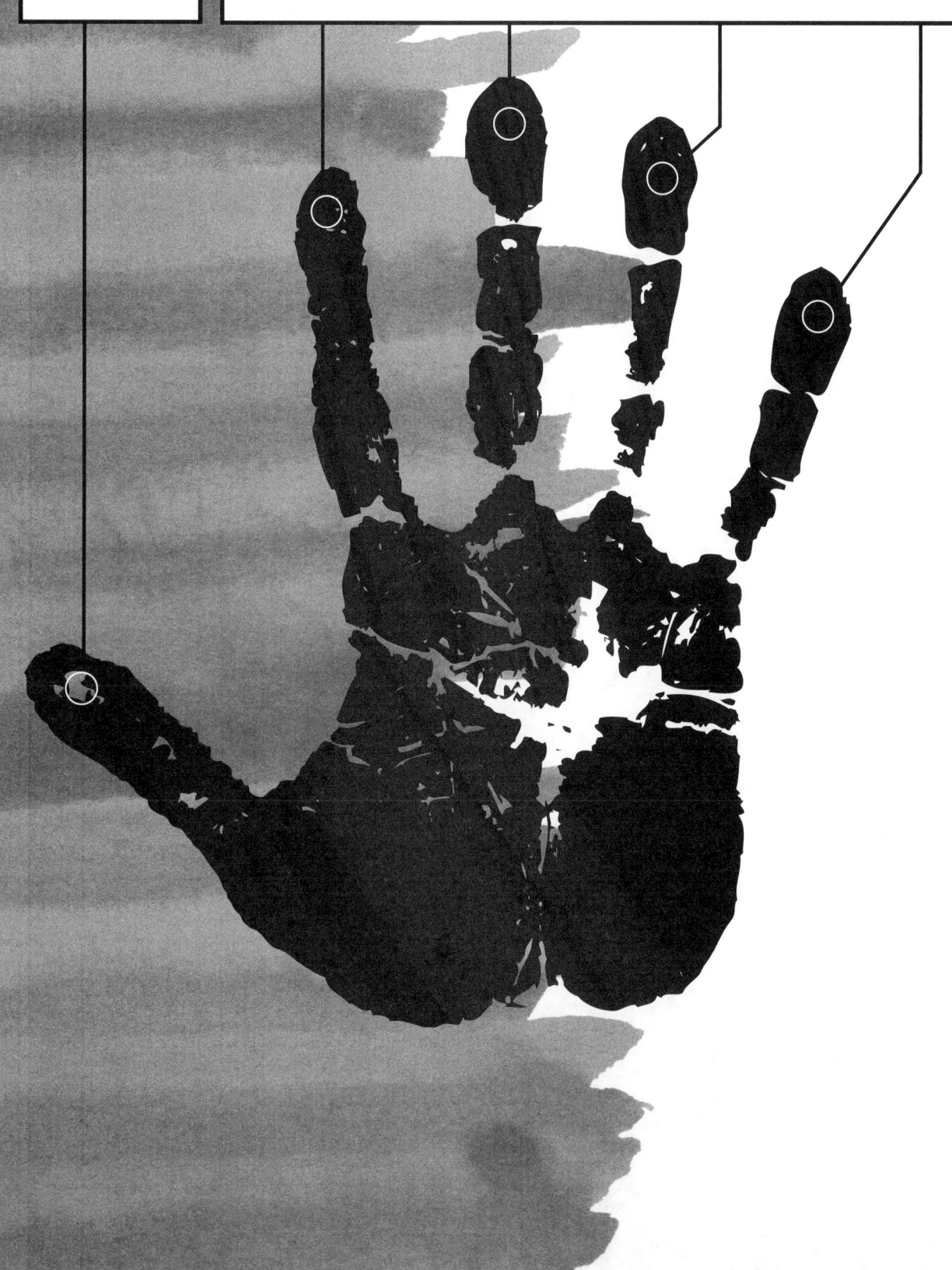

Monotheism vs. Polytheism

Monotheism		Polytheism
	Definition	
	Religions	
	Divine names	
	Divine character	
	Believers' attitudes	
	Effect on believers' lives	
	"Advantages" of this belief	
	"Disadvantages" of this belief	
	So what?	

Yahweh

Power and might are in your hand. (2 Chronicles 20:6)

The Lord is gracious and compassionate, slow to anger and rich in love. (Psalm 145:8)

Holy, holy, holy is the Lord God Almighty, who was, and is, and is to come. (Revelation 4:8)

Just and true are your ways. (Revelation 15:3)

God is love. (1 John 4:16)

The Lord reigns (Psalm 93:1)

I am the first and the last. (Isaiah 44:6)

Christ of God (Luke 9:20)

My ways are higher than your ways and my thoughts than your thoughts. (Isaiah 55:9)

He does not treat us as our sins deserve. (Psalm 103:10)

The Lord do not change (Malachi 3:6)

Ever-present—Where can I flee from your presence? (Psalm 139:7)

Great is your faithfulness. (Lamentations 3:23)

He is the true God. (1 John 5:20)

On the depth of the riches of the wisdom and knowledge of God! How unsearchable his judgments, and his paths beyond tracing out! (Romans 11:33)

Lord of the sabbath (Mark 2:28)

Righteousness and justice are the foundation of your throne; love and faithfulness go before you. (Psalm 89:14)

I am with you always. (Matthew 28:20)

I am the Alpha and the Omega, the First and the Last, the Beginning and the End. (Revelation 22:13)

Nothing in all creation is hidden from God's sight. (Hebrews 4:13)

You alone are holy. (Revelation 15:4)

The Lord is gracious and righteous; our God is full of compassion. (Psalm 116:5)

I AM (John 8:58)

Give thanks to the Lord, for he is good; his love endures forever. (Psalm 118:1)

Holy, holy, holy is the Lord Almighty. (Isaiah 6:3)

I am the living bread that came down from heaven. (John 6:51)

I am the way and the truth and the life. (John 14:6)

In the beginning was the Word, and the Word was with God, and the Word was God. (John 1:1)

No one comes to the Father except through me. (John 14:6)

Taste and see that the Lord is good (Psalm 34:8)

The Lord is good and his love endures forever. (Psalm 100:5)

Your righteousness is everlasting. (Psalm 119:142)

To God belong wisdom and power. (Job 12:13)

And he will be called Wonderful Counselor, Mighty God, Everlasting Father, Prince of Peace. (Isaiah 9:6)

The Lord works righteousness and justice for all the oppressed. (Psalm 103:6)

I am the Lord of both the dead and the living, Jesus the Son of God, let us hold firmly to the faith we profess. (Hebrews 4:14)

He is the atoning sacrifice for our sins, and not only for ours but also for the sins of the whole world. (1 John 2:2)

Jesus, the pioneer and perfecter of faith. (Hebrews 12:2)

For to us a child is born, to us a son is given, and the government will be on his shoulders. (Isaiah 9:6)

Christ died and returned to life so that he might be the Lord of both the dead and the living. (Romans 14:9)

Therefore, since we have a great high priest who has ascended into heaven, Jesus the Son of God (Hebrews 4:14)

The Son is the radiance of God's glory and the exact representation of his being, sustaining all things by his powerful word. After he had provided purification for sins, he sat down at the right hand of the Majesty in heaven. (Hebrews 1:3)

Rose of Sharon (Song of Songs 2:1)

God, the blessed and only Ruler, the King of kings and Lord of lords. (1 Timothy 6:15)

He is the Root and the Offspring of David, and the bright Morning Star. (Revelation 22:16)

the Lamb of God (John 1:29)

I am the Root and the Offspring of David, and the bright Morning Star. (Revelation 22:16)

Jesus, the Word of life in the order of Melchizedek. (Hebrews 6:19-20)

That which was from the beginning, which we have heard, which we have seen with our eyes, which we have looked at and our hands have touched—this we proclaim concerning the Word of life. (1 John 1:1)

whose name is the LORD—that you alone are the Most High over all the earth. (Psalm 83:18)

The LORD will be king over the whole earth. On that day there will be one LORD, and his name the only name. (Zechariah 14:9)

Let them now that you, whose name is the LORD

We have this hope as an anchor for the soul, firm and secure. It enters the inner sanctuary behind the curtain, where our forerunner, Jesus, has entered on our behalf. He has become a high priest forever, in the order of Melchizedek. (Hebrews 6:19-20)

God, the blessed and only Ruler, the King of kings and Lord of lords. (1 Timothy 6:15)

the Son of Man came eating and drinking, and they say, 'Here is a glutton and a drunkard, a friend of tax collectors and sinners.' (Matthew 11:19)

Rabbi (John 9:2)

See, I lay a stone in Zion, a tested stone, a precious cornerstone for a sure foundation. (Isaiah 28:16)

A stone in Zion, a chosen and precious cornerstone, and the one who trusts in him will never be put to shame. (1 Peter 2:4-6)

Chosen of God (1 Peter 2:4)

Desire of all nations (Haggai 2:7)

a righteous Branch, a King who will reign wisely and do what is just and right in the land. (Jeremiah 23:5)

Thanks be to God for his indescribable gift! (2 Corinthians 9:15)

And we have seen and testify that the Father has sent his Son to be the Savior of the world. (1 John 4:14)

and give birth to a son, and will call him Immanuel. (Isaiah 7:14)

The virgin will conceive and give birth to a son, and will call him Immanuel. (Isaiah 7:14)

The Lord is enthroned as King forever. (Psalm 29:10)

From everlasting to everlasting you are God. (Psalm 90:2)

(O)ur Lord Jesus, that great Shepherd of the sheep (Hebrews 13:20)

I am the true vine, and my Father is the gardener. (John 15:1)

(The) Shepherd and Overseer of your souls. (1 Peter 2:25)

(W)e have an advocate with the Father—Jesus Christ, the Righteous One. (1 John 2:1)

As for God, his way is perfect. (Psalm 18:30)

I am the Root and the Offspring of David, and the bright Morning Star. (Revelation 22:16)

(Chief Shepherd) (1 Peter 5:4)

Sceptre (Numbers 24:17)

Judge (Acts 10:42)

Heir of all things (Hebrews 1:2)

Yahweh

God vs. "Gods" in Ancient Israel

Canaanite "gods"		God
1 Chronicles 16:26, Isaiah 44:15	Creation	Genesis 1:1
Amos 5:26	Eternity	Psalm 90:2
1 Kings 18:25–29	Power	1 Kings 18:30–39
Deuteronomy 4:28, Isaiah 44:9	Knowledge	Psalm 19:14; 139:23
1 Samuel 7:3	Worship	1 Samuel 7:3
Isaiah 44:10	Provision	Psalm 50:15; 68:7–10; Deuteronomy 11:14–15
2 Kings 23:7	Morality	Leviticus 11:44

Let God Be GOD

Yahweh

Power and might are in your hand. (2 Chronicles 20:6)

The Lord is gracious and compassionate, slow to anger and rich in love. (Psalm 145:8)

Holy, holy, holy is the Lord God Almighty, who was, and is and is to come.

God is love. (1 John 4:16)

I am the first and the last. (Isaiah 44:6) Just and true are your ways. (Revelation 4:9)

The Lord reigns (Psalm 93:1) My ways are higher than your ways and my thoughts than your thoughts. (Isaiah 55:9)

He does not treat us as our sins deserve. (Psalm 103:10) The Lord do not change. (Malachi 3:6)

Christ of God (Luke 9:20) Ever-present... Where can I flee from your presence? (Psalm 139:7)

Great is your faithfulness. (Lamentations 3:23)

Oh, the depth of the riches of the wisdom and knowledge of God! How unsearchable his judgments, and his paths beyond tracing out! (Romans 11:33)

Lord of the sabbath (Mark 2:28)

Righteousness and justice are the foundation of your throne; love and faithfulness go before you. (Psalm 89:14)

I am the Alpha and the Omega, the First and the Last, the Beginning and the End. (Revelation 22:13) You alone are holy. (Revelation 15:4)

He is the true God. (1 John 5:20) (Hebrews 4:13) Give thanks to the Lord, for he is good; his love endures forever. (Psalm 118:1)

Nothing in all creation is hidden from God's sight. Holy, holy, holy is the Lord Almighty. I AM (John 8:58)

The Lord is gracious and righteous; our God is full of compassion. (Psalm 116:5) I am the way and the truth and the life. (Isaiah 6:3) No one comes to the Father except through me. (John 14:6)

In the beginning was the Word, and the Word was with God, and the Word was God. (John 1:1) The Lord is good and his love endures forever. (Psalm 100:5)

Your righteousness is everlasting. (Psalm 119:142) Taste and see that the Lord is good. (Psalm 34:8)

To God belong wisdom and power. (Job 12:13) and he will be called Wonderful Counselor, Mighty God, Everlasting Father, Prince of Peace. (Isaiah 9:6)

The Lord works righteousness and justice for all the oppressed. the pioneer and perfecter of faith. (Hebrews 12:2)

For to us a child is born, to us a son is given; and the government will be on his shoulders. And he will be the Lord of both the dead and the living. (Romans 14:9)

He is the atoning sacrifice for our sins, and not only for ours but also for the sins of the whole world. (1 John 2:2)

Christ died and returned to life so that he might be the great high priest who has ascended into heaven, Jesus the Son of God, let us hold firmly to the faith we profess. (Hebrews 4:14) the Lamb of God (John 1:29)

The Son is the radiance of God's glory and the exact representation of his being, sustaining all things by his powerful word. After he had provided purification for sins, he sat down at the right hand of the Majesty in heaven. (Hebrews 1:3)

God the blessed and only Ruler, the King of kings and Lord of lords (1 Timothy 6:15) who is the faithful witness, the firstborn from the dead, and the ruler of the kings of the earth. (Revelation 1:5)

Rose of Sharon (Song of Songs 2:1) (Him who) know that you, whose name is the LORD— that you alone are the Most High over all the earth. (Psalm 83:18) Jesus the Bright Morning Star. (Revelation 22:16) a high priest forever, in the order of Melchizedek. (Hebrews 7:17)

That which was from the beginning, which we have heard, which we have seen with our eyes, which we have looked at and our hands have touched. the King of kings and Lord of lords (Revelation 17:14) And we have seen

The LORD will be king over the whole earth. On that day there will be one LORD, and his name the only name. (Zechariah 14:9) The Son of Man came eating and drinking, and they say, 'Here is a glutton and a drunkard, a friend of tax collectors and sinners.' (Matthew 11:19)

From everlasting to everlasting you are God. (Psalm 90:2) Desire of all nations (Haggai 2:7) and we have seen his glory, the glory of the One and Only, who came from the Father, full of grace and truth. (John 1:14)

(O)ur Lord Jesus, that great Shepherd of the sheep (Hebrews 13:20) I lay a stone in Zion, a tested stone, a precious cornerstone for a sure foundation (Isaiah 28:16)

The virgin will conceive and give birth to a son, and will call him Immanuel. (Isaiah 7:14) Chosen of God (1 Peter 2:4)

The Lord is enthroned as King forever. (Psalm 29:10) Branch, a King who will reign wisely and do what is just and right in the land. (Jeremiah 23:5)

I am the true vine, and my Father is the gardener. (John 15:1) Thanks be to God for his indescribable gift! (2 Corinthians 9:15)

(T)he Shepherd and Overseer of your souls (1 Peter 2:25)

(W)e have an advocate with the Father—Jesus Christ, the Righteous One. (1 John 2:1) Root and the Offspring of David, and the bright Morning Star. (Revelation 22:16)

As for God, his way is perfect. (Psalm 18:30)

I am the Chief Shepherd (1 Peter 5:4) Heir of all things (Hebrews 1:2) Judge (Acts 10:42)

Sceptre (Numbers 24:17) Yahweh

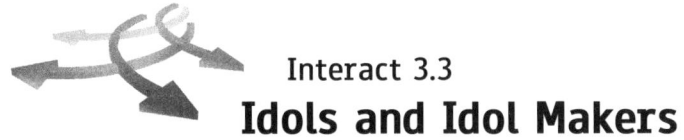

Interact 3.3
Idols and Idol Makers

God Challenges Idol Worshippers (Isaiah 44:6–8)

• What does God say about Himself?

• What challenge does He make to the readers of this chapter?

God's Opinion of Idol Makers (Isaiah 44:9–12)

• What does God say about those who make idols?

• Why do you think God was so harsh?

Why Idols Are Silly (Isaiah 44:13–20)

• Why does an idol make no sense?

• What is an idol—really?

• Why do people worship idols?

Let God Be GOD

Yahweh   Power and might are in your hand. (2 Chronicles 20:6)

The Lord is gracious and compassionate, slow to anger and rich in love.

Holy, holy, holy is the Lord God Almighty, who was, and is, and is to come. (Psalm 145:8)

God is love. (1 John 4:16)   I am the first and the last. (Isaiah 44:6)   Just and true are your ways. (Revelation 15:3)

The Lord reigns (Psalm 93:1)   My ways are higher than your ways and my thoughts than your thoughts. (Isaiah 55:9)   He does not treat us as our sins deserve. (Psalm 103:10)

Christ of God (Luke 9:20)   Ever-present—Where can I flee from your presence? (Psalm 139:7)   I the Lord do not change. (Malachi 3:6)

Great is your faithfulness. (Lamentations 3:23)   knowledge of God! How unsearchable his judgments and his paths beyond tracing out! (Romans 11:33)   Lord of the sabbath (Mark 2:28)

Righteousness and justice are the foundation of your throne; love and faithfulness go before you. (Psalm 89:14)   I AM (John 8:58)

Oh, the depth of the riches of the wisdom and   the First and the Last, the Beginning and the End. (Revelation 22:13) You alone are holy. (Revelation 15:4)

He is the true God. (1 John 5:20)   I am the Alpha and the Omega   is hidden from God's sight. (Hebrews 4:13)   Give thanks to the Lord, for he is good; his love endures forever. (Revelation 22:13)

Nothing in all creation   I am full of compassion. (Psalm 116:5)   Holy, holy, holy is the Lord Almighty. (Isaiah 6:3)   Taste and see that the Lord is good. (Psalm 34:8)

The Lord is gracious and righteous; our God is full of compassion. (Psalm 103:6)   I am the way and the truth and the life. No one comes to the Father except through me. (John 14:6)   the pioneer and perfecter of faith. (Hebrews 12:2)

The Lord works righteousness and justice for all the oppressed. (Psalm 103:6)   In the beginning was the Word, and the Word was with God, and the Word was God. (John 1:1) The Lord is good and his love endures forever. (Psalm 100:5)

Your righteousness is everlasting. (Psalm 119:142)   and he will be called Wonderful Counselor, Mighty God, Everlasting Father, Prince of Peace. (Isaiah 9:6)

To God belong wisdom and power. (Job 12:13)   He is the atoning sacrifice for our sins. (Romans 14:9)   Jesus the pioneer and perfecter of faith. (Hebrews 12:2)

For to us a child is born, to us a son is given, and the government will be on his shoulders. And he will be the Lord of both the dead and the living. (Romans 14:9)   Jesus Christ, who is the faithful witness. (Revelation 1:5)

Christ died and returned to life so that he might be the Lord of both the dead and the living. (Romans 14:9)   He is the Most High over all the earth. (Psalm 83:18)

Therefore, since we have a great high priest who has ascended into heaven, Jesus the Son of God, let us hold firmly to the faith we profess. (Hebrews 4:14)

The Son is the radiance of God's glory and the exact representation of his being, sustaining all things by his powerful word. After he had provided purification for sins, he sat down at the right hand of the Majesty in heaven. (Hebrews 1:3)

Rose of Sharon (Song of Songs 2:1)   Him who is, and who was, and who is to come. (Revelation 1:4)   name is the LORD—that you alone are the Most High over all the earth. (Psalm 83:18)   the Lamb of God. (John 1:36)

That which was from the beginning, which we have heard, which we have seen with our eyes, which we have looked at and our hands have touched—this we proclaim concerning the Word of life. (1 John 1:1)

God, the blessed and only Ruler, the King of kings and Lord of lords. (1 Timothy 6:15)   the Father has sent his Son to be the Savior of the world. (1 John 4:14)

Let them know that you, whose name is the LORD   a friend of tax collectors and sinners. (Matthew 11:19)

We have this hope as an anchor for the soul, firm and secure. It enters the inner sanctuary behind the curtain, where our forerunner, Jesus, has entered on our behalf. He has become a high priest forever, in the order of Melchizedek. (Hebrews 6:19-20)

The LORD will be king over the whole earth. On that day there will be one LORD, and his name the only name. (Zechariah 14:9)   Chosen of God (1 Peter 2:4)

God the blessed and only Ruler, the King of kings, and Lord of lords. (Psalm 99:2)   and will call him Immanuel. (Isaiah 7:14)

From everlasting to everlasting you are God.   The virgin will conceive and give birth to a son, and will call him Immanuel. (Isaiah 7:14)   Thanks be to God for his indescribable gift! (2 Corinthians 9:15)

(O)ur Lord Jesus, that great Shepherd of the sheep   The Lord is enthroned as King forever. (Psalm 29:10)

I am the true vine, and my Father is the gardener. (John 15:1)   (Hebrews 13:20)

(T)he Shepherd and Overseer of your souls. (1 Peter 2:25)

(W)e have an advocate with the Father—Jesus Christ, the Righteous One. (1 John 2:1)   Jesus Christ, the bright Morning Star. (Revelation 22:16)

I am the Root and the Offspring of David, and the bright Morning Star. (Revelation 22:16)   As for God, his way is perfect. (Psalm 18:30)

Chief Shepherd (1 Peter 5:4)   Heir of all things (Hebrews 1:2)   Judge (Acts 10:42)

Sceptre (Isaiah 24:23)   Yahweh

Interact 3.4
The Dangers of Idolatry

Find and read each verse or passage of Scripture, and answer the questions.

1. Read Romans 1:21–24 and Psalm 4:2. What is idolatry?

2. Read Exodus 20:2 and Revelation 21:8 and 22:15. What is God's attitude toward idolatry?

3. Idolatry has links to what other sins?

Colossians 3:5

1 Corinthians 6:9

Ephesians 5:5

Galatians 5:20

1 Corinthians 5:10

1 Samuel 15:23

4. Read 1 Corinthians 10:14. What is God's command concerning idolatry?

Let God Be GOD

Yahweh

Power and might are in your hand. (2 Chronicles 20:6)

The Lord is gracious and compassionate, slow to anger and rich in love.

Holy, holy, holy is the Lord God Almighty, who was, and is, and is to come. (Revelation 4:8)

God is love. (1 John 4:16)

I am the first and the last. (Isaiah 44:6)

Just and true are your ways. (Psalm 145:8)

The Lord reigns (Psalm 93:1)

My ways are higher than your ways and my thoughts than your thoughts. (Isaiah 55:9)

Where can I flee from your presence? (Psalm 139:7)

He does not treat us as our sins deserve. (Psalm 103:10)

I the Lord do not change. (Malachi 3:6)

Christ of God (Luke 9:20)

Ever-present. (Lamentations 3:23)

Great is your faithfulness. (Lamentations 3:23)

Oh, the depth of the riches of the wisdom and knowledge of God! How unsearchable his judgments, and his paths beyond tracing out! (Romans 11:33)

Lord of the sabbath (Mark 2:28)

He is the true God. (1 John 5:20)

Righteousness and justice are the foundation of your throne; love and faithfulness go before you. (Psalm 89:14)

I am the Alpha and the Omega, the First and the Last, the Beginning and the End. (Revelation 22:13)

Nothing in all creation is hidden from God's sight. (Hebrews 4:13)

You alone are holy. (Revelation 15:4)

I AM (John 8:58)

The Lord is gracious and righteous; our God is full of compassion. (Psalm 116:5)

Give thanks to the Lord, for he is good; his love endures forever. (Psalm 118:1)

I am the way and the truth and the life. No one comes to the Father except through me. (John 14:6)

Holy, holy, holy is the Lord Almighty. (Isaiah 6:3)

Taste and see that the Lord is good. (Psalm 34:8)

The Lord is good and his love endures forever. (Psalm 100:5)

In the beginning was the Word, and the Word was with God, and the Word was God. (John 1:1)

To God belong wisdom and power. (Job 12:13)

The Lord works righteousness and justice for all the oppressed. (Psalm 103:6)

Your righteousness is everlasting. (Psalm 119:142)

And he will be called Wonderful Counselor, Mighty God, Everlasting Father, Prince of Peace. (Isaiah 9:6)

Jesus the pioneer and perfecter of faith. (Hebrews 12:2)

For to us a child is born, to us a son is given, and the government will be on his shoulders.

He might be the Lord of both the dead and the living. (Romans 14:9)

Jesus the Son of God, let us hold firmly to the faith we profess. (Hebrews 4:14)

Christ died and returned to life so that he might be the Lord of both the dead and the living.

The Son is the radiance of God's glory and the exact representation of his being, sustaining all things by his powerful word. After he had provided purification for sins, he sat down at the right hand of the Majesty in heaven. (Hebrews 1:3)

Rose of Sharon (Song of Songs 2:1)

a great high priest who has ascended into heaven, Jesus the Son of God (Hebrews 4:14)

God, the blessed and only Ruler, the King of kings and Lord of lords (1 Timothy 6:15)

Him who is and who was, and who is to come, and from the seven spirits before his throne (Revelation 1:4)

Let them know that you, whose name is the LORD—that you alone are the Most High over all the earth. (Psalm 83:18)

it enters the inner sanctuary behind the curtain, where our forerunner, Jesus, has entered on our behalf. He has become a high priest forever, in the order of Melchizedek. (Hebrews 6:19-20)

We have this hope as an anchor for the soul, firm and secure. (Hebrews 6:19)

which we have heard, which we have seen with our eyes, which we have looked at and our hands have touched (1 John 1:1)

the LORD will be king over the whole earth. On that day there will be one LORD, and his name the only name (Zechariah 14:9)

Here is a glutton and a drunkard, a friend of tax collectors and sinners. (Matthew 11:19)

The Son of Man came eating and drinking, and they say (Matthew 11:19)

this we proclaim concerning the Word of life. (1 John 1:1)

the Lamb of God (John 1:29)

the messenger of the covenant, whom you desire, will come (Malachi 3:1)

that the Father has sent his Son to be the Savior of the world. (1 John 4:14)

Desire of all nations (Haggai 2:7)

a righteous Branch, a King who will reign wisely and do what is just and right in the land. (Jeremiah 23:5)

a stone in Zion, a tested stone, a precious cornerstone for a sure foundation (Isaiah 28:16)

Thanks be to God for his indescribable gift! (2 Corinthians 9:15)

Chosen of God (1 Peter 2:4)

The virgin will conceive and give birth to a son, and will call him Immanuel. (Isaiah 7:14)

That which was from the beginning (1 John 1:1)

God, the blessed and only Ruler

The LORD will be king over the whole earth.

From everlasting to everlasting you are God. (Psalm 90:2)

Our Lord Jesus, that great Shepherd of the sheep (Hebrews 13:20)

The Lord is enthroned as King forever. (Psalm 29:10)

I am the true vine, and my Father is the gardener. (John 15:1)

(T)he Shepherd and Overseer of your souls. (1 Peter 2:25)

(W)e have an advocate with the Father—Jesus Christ, the Righteous One. (1 John 2:1)

Root and the Offspring of David, and the bright Morning Star. (Revelation 22:16)

As for God, his way is perfect. (Psalm 18:30)

I am the Root

Chief Shepherd (1 Peter 5:4)

Sceptre (Numbers 24:17)

Heir of all things (Hebrews 1:2)

Judge (Acts 10:42)

Yahweh

4

GOD **Is Triune**

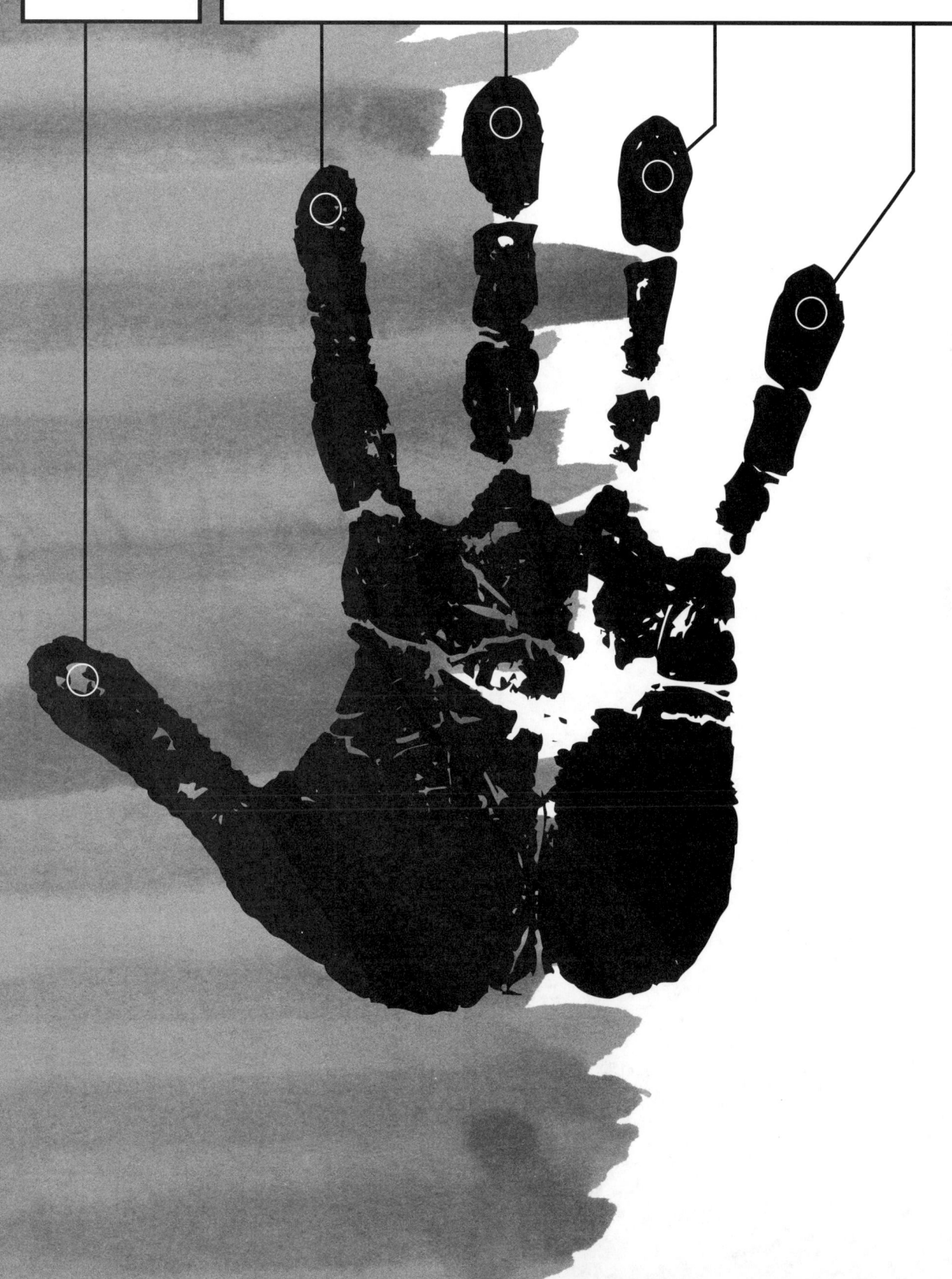

Interact 4.1
The Trinity

Look up each verse or passage and write what it tells you about one or more of the members of the Trinity—the Father, Son, and Holy Spirit. (Note: Sometimes the text says "God" instead of "Father.")

Matthew 3:16–17

Matthew 28:19

John 16:12–15

Acts 2:32–33

Acts 11:15–17

Acts 20:27–28

Romans 1:1–4

Romans 8:1–4

Continued on back →

Let God Be GOD

The Trinity continued

1 Corinthians 12:3–6

2 Corinthians 13:11, 14

Ephesians 4:4–6

2 Thessalonians 2:13–14

Titus 3:4–7

1 Peter 1:2

1 Peter 4:14

1 John 4:2–3

Interact 4.2
God the Father

In a concordance, find verses in the New Testament that contain the word *Father* or *God*. Write the references in the left-hand column. Look up each verse. Beside each reference, write an answer to the question in the right-hand column.

Verses about the Father	How do these verses show that the Father is God?

Let God Be GOD

Yahweh

Power and might are in your hand. (2 Chronicles 20:6)

The Lord is gracious and compassionate, slow to anger and rich in love. (Psalm 145:8)

Holy, holy, holy is the Lord God Almighty, who was, and is, and is to come. (Revelation 4:8)

Just and true are your ways. (Revelation 15:3)

God is love. (1 John 4:16)

I am the first and the last. (Isaiah 44:6)

The Lord reigns (Psalm 93:1)

My ways are higher than your ways and my thoughts than your thoughts. (Isaiah 55:9)

He does not treat us as our sins deserve. (Psalm 103:10)

The Lord do not change (Malachi 3:6)

Christ of God (Luke 9:20)

Ever-present— Where can I flee from your presence? (Psalm 139:7)

Great is your faithfulness. (Lamentations 3:23)

Righteousness and justice are the foundation of your throne; love and faithfulness go before you. (Psalm 89:14)

Oh, the depth of the riches of the wisdom and knowledge of God! How unsearchable his judgments, and his paths beyond tracing out! (Romans 11:33)

Lord of the sabbath (Mark 2:28)

I am the Alpha and the Omega, the First and the Last, the Beginning and the End. (Revelation 22:13)

Nothing in all creation is hidden from God's sight. (Hebrews 4:13)

He is the true God. (1 John 5:20)

The Lord is gracious and righteous; our God is full of compassion. (Psalm 116:5)

I am the way and the truth and the life. (John 14:6)

Holy, holy, holy is the Lord Almighty. (Isaiah 6:3)

No one comes to the Father except through me. (John 14:6)

You alone are holy. (Revelation 15:4)

I AM (John 8:58)

Give thanks to the Lord, for he is good; his love endures forever. (Psalm 118:1)

Taste and see that the Lord is good. (Psalm 34:8)

The Lord is good and his love endures forever. (Psalm 100:5)

In the beginning was the Word, and the Word was with God, and the Word was God. (John 1:1)

Your righteousness is everlasting (Psalm 119:142)

To God belong wisdom and power (Job 12:13)

The Lord works righteousness and justice for all the oppressed. (Psalm 103:6)

I am the living bread that came down from heaven. (John 6:51)

I am with you always. (Matthew 28:20)

And he will be called Wonderful Counselor, Mighty God, Everlasting Father, Prince of Peace. (Isaiah 9:6)

For to us a child is born, to us a son is given, and the government will be on his shoulders. (Isaiah 9:6)

the Lamb of God (John 1:29)

Jesus, the pioneer and perfecter of faith. (Hebrews 12:2)

He is the atoning sacrifice for our sins, and not only for ours but also for the sins of the whole world. (1 John 2:2)

Jesus Christ, who is the faithful witness, the firstborn from the dead, and the ruler of the kings of the earth. (Revelation 1:5)

Christ died and returned to life so that he might be the Lord of both the dead and the living. (Romans 14:9)

The Son is the radiance of God's glory and the exact representation of his being, sustaining all things by his powerful word. After he had provided purification for sins, he sat down at the right hand of the Majesty in heaven. (Hebrews 1:3)

Jesus the Son of God ... let us hold firmly to the faith we profess. (Hebrews 4:14)

and who is, and who was, and who is to come, and from the seven spirits before his throne, (Revelation 1:4)

We have a great high priest who has ascended into heaven, Jesus the Son of God (Hebrews 4:14)

God, the blessed and only Ruler, the King of kings and Lord of lords (1 Timothy 6:15)

He is the Most High over all the earth. (Psalm 83:18)

We have this hope as an anchor for the soul, firm and secure. It enters the inner sanctuary behind the curtain, where Jesus, who went before us, has entered on our behalf. He has become a high priest forever, in the order of Melchizedek. (Hebrews 6:19-20)

the Father has sent his Son to be the Savior of the world. (1 John 4:14)

And we have seen and we testify that

Here is a glutton and a drunkard, a friend of tax collectors and sinners. (Matthew 11:19)

Desire of all nations (Haggai 2:7)

Chosen of God (1 Peter 2:4)

See, I lay a stone in Zion, a tested stone, a precious cornerstone for a sure foundation (Isaiah 28:16)

Branch, a King who will reign (Jeremiah 23:5)

Thanks be to God for his indescribable gift! (2 Corinthians 9:15)

Desire of all nations ... Just and right in the land (Matthew 3:15)

The Son of Man came eating and drinking, and they say, 'Here is a glutton...'

God, the blessed and only Ruler, On that day there will be one LORD, and his name the only name. (Zechariah 14:9)

The LORD will be king over the whole earth. (Psalm 90:2)

From everlasting to everlasting you are God. (Psalm 90:2)

That which was from the beginning, which we have heard, which we have seen with our eyes, which we have looked at and our hands have touched. (1 John 1:1)

Rose of Sharon (Song of Songs 2:1)

The virgin will conceive and give birth to a son, and will call him Immanuel. (Isaiah 7:14)

The Lord is enthroned as King forever. (Psalm 29:10)

(O)ur Lord Jesus, that great Shepherd of the sheep (Hebrews 13:20)

I am the true vine, and my Father is the gardener. (John 15:1)

(T)he Shepherd and Overseer of your souls (1 Peter 2:25)

(W)e have an advocate with the Father—Jesus Christ, the Righteous One. (1 John 2:1)

As for God, his way is perfect. (Psalm 18:30)

I am the Root and the Offspring of David, and the bright Morning Star (Revelation 22:16)

I am the Chief Shepherd (1 Peter 5:4)

Sceptre (Numbers 24:17)

Heir of all things (Hebrews 1:2)

Judge (Acts 10:42)

Yahweh

Interact 4.3
God the Son

In a concordance, find verses in the New Testament that contain the word **Son** or **Jesus** or **Christ**. Write the references in the left-hand column. Look up each verse. Beside each reference, write an answer to the question in the right-hand column.

Verses about Jesus	How do these verses show that Jesus is God?

Let God Be GOD

Yahweh

Power and might are in your hand. (2 Chronicles 20:6)

The Lord is gracious and compassionate, slow to anger and rich in love. (2 Chronicles 30:9)

Holy, holy, holy is the Lord God Almighty, who was, and is, and is to come. (Revelation 4:8)

Just and true are your ways. (Revelation 15:3)

God is love. (1 John 4:16)

I am the first and the last. (Isaiah 44:6)

The Lord reigns. (Psalm 93:1)

My ways are higher than your ways and my thoughts than your thoughts. (Isaiah 55:9)

Where can I flee from your presence? (Psalm 139:7)

He does not treat us as our sins deserve. (Psalm 103:10)

I the Lord do not change. (Malachi 3:6)

Christ of God (Luke 9:20)

Ever-present

Great is your faithfulness. (Lamentations 3:23)

of God! How unsearchable his judgments, and his paths beyond tracing out! (Romans 11:33)

love and faithfulness go before you.

Lord of the sabbath (Mark 2:28)

I am with you always. (Matthew 28:20)

Righteousness and justice are the foundation of your throne; love and faithfulness go before you. (Psalm 89:14)

Oh, the depth of the riches of the wisdom and knowledge of God! (Romans 11:33)

He is the true God. (1 John 5:20)

I am the Alpha and the Omega, the First and the Last, the Beginning and the End. (Revelation 22:13)

Nothing in all creation is hidden from God's sight. (Hebrews 4:13)

The Lord is gracious and righteous; our God is full of compassion. (Psalm 116:5)

Give thanks to the Lord, for he is good; his love endures forever. (Psalm 118:1)

You alone are holy. (Revelation 15:4)

I AM (John 8:58)

The Lord works righteousness and justice for all the oppressed. (Psalm 103:6)

I am the way and the truth and the life. (John 14:6)

Holy, holy, holy is the Lord Almighty. (Isaiah 6:3)

No one comes to the Father except through me. (John 14:6)

Taste and see that the Lord is good. (Psalm 34:8)

To God belong wisdom and power. (Job 12:13)

Your righteousness is everlasting. (Psalm 119:142)

In the beginning was the Word, and the Word was with God, and the Word was God. (John 1:1)

The Lord is good and his love endures forever. (Psalm 100:5)

he will be called Wonderful Counselor, Mighty God, Everlasting Father, Prince of Peace. (Isaiah 9:6)

For to us a child is born, to us a son is given, and the government will be on his shoulders. And (Isaiah 9:6)

the pioneer and perfecter of faith. (Hebrews 12:2)

the Son of God, let us hold firmly to the faith we profess. (Hebrews 4:14)

He is the Lord of both the dead and the living. (Romans 14:9)

He is the atoning sacrifice for our sins, and not only for ours but also for the sins of the whole world. (1 John 2:2)

Christ died and returned to life so that he might be the Lord of both the dead and the living. (Romans 14:9)

God, the blessed and only Ruler, the King of kings and Lord of lords. (1 Timothy 6:15)

let us hold firmly to the faith we profess. (Hebrews 4:14)

After he had provided purification for sins, he sat down at the right hand of the Majesty in heaven. (Hebrews 1:3)

The Son is the radiance of God's glory and the exact representation of his being, sustaining all things by his powerful word. (Hebrews 1:3)

the Lamb of God. (John 1:29)

the faithful witness, the firstborn from the dead, and the ruler of the kings of the earth. (Revelation 1:5)

the bright Morning Star. (Revelation 22:16)

a high priest forever, in the order of Melchizedek. (Hebrews 6:20)

Rose of Sharon (Song of Songs 2:1)

Him who is and who was and who is to come. (Revelation 1:4)

That which was from the beginning, which we have heard, which we have seen with our eyes, which we have looked at and our hands have touched. (1 John 1:1)

we have this hope as an anchor for the soul, firm and secure. It enters the inner sanctuary behind the curtain, (Hebrews 6:19)

where our forerunner, Jesus, has entered on our behalf. He has become a high priest forever. (Hebrews 6:20)

the Word of life. (1 John 1:1)

we proclaim concerning the Word of life. (1 John 1:1)

I am the living bread that came down from heaven. (John 6:51)

"Here is a glutton and a drunkard, a friend of tax collectors and sinners." (Matthew 11:19)

And we have seen and testify that the Father has sent his Son to be the Savior of the world. (1 John 4:14)

you alone are the Most High over all the earth. (Psalm 83:18)

The LORD will be king over the whole earth. (Zechariah 14:9)

that you, whose name is the LORD—that you alone are the Most High over all the earth. (Psalm 83:18)

The Son of Man came eating and drinking, and they say ... (Matthew 11:19)

I will raise up to David a righteous Branch, a King who will reign wisely and do what is just and right in the land. (Jeremiah 23:5)

a stone in Zion, a tested stone, a precious cornerstone for a sure foundation. (Isaiah 28:16)

Chosen of God (1 Peter 2:4)

thanks be to God for his indescribable gift! (2 Corinthians 9:15)

Desire of all nations (Haggai 2:7)

Bridegroom (Matthew 9:15)

the messenger of the covenant, whom you desire, will come. (Malachi 3:1)

From everlasting to everlasting you are God. (Psalm 90:2)

The virgin will conceive and give birth to a son, and will call him Immanuel. (Isaiah 7:14)

The LORD will be king over the whole earth.

Our Lord Jesus, that great Shepherd of the sheep (Hebrews 13:20)

The Lord is enthroned as King forever. (Psalm 29:10)

I am the true vine, and my Father is the gardener. (John 15:1)

The Shepherd and Overseer of your souls. (1 Peter 2:25)

We have an advocate with the Father—Jesus Christ, the Righteous One. (1 John 2:1)

I am the Root and the Offspring of David, and the bright Morning Star. (Revelation 22:16)

As for God, his way is perfect. (Psalm 18:30)

Heir of all things (Hebrews 1:2)

Judge (Acts 10:42)

Yahweh

Chief Shepherd (1 Peter 5:4)

Sceptre

Interact 4.4
God the Holy Spirit

In a concordance, find verses in the New Testament that contain the words **_Holy Spirit_** or **_Spirit_**. Write the references in the left-hand column. Look up each verse. Beside each reference, write an answer to the question in the right-hand column.

Verses about the Holy Spirit	How do these verses show that the Holy Spirit is God?

Let God Be GOD

Part III
GOD's Unshared Attributes

Yahweh   Power and might are in your hand. (2 Chronicles 20:6)

The Lord is gracious and compassionate, slow to anger and rich in love. (Psalm 145:8)

Holy, holy, holy is the Lord God Almighty, who was, and is, and is to come. (Revelation 4:8)

God is love. (1 John 4:16)   I am the first and the last. (Isaiah 44:6)   Just and true are your ways. (Revelation 15:3)

The Lord reigns. (Psalm 93:1)

Christ of God (Luke 9:20)   My ways are higher than your ways and my thoughts than your thoughts. (Isaiah 55:9)   He does not treat us as our sins deserve. (Psalm 103:10)   I the Lord do not change. (Malachi 3:6)

Ever-present—Where can I flee from your presence? (Psalm 139:7)

Great is your faithfulness. (Lamentations 3:23)   Lord of the sabbath (Mark 2:28)

Oh, the depth of the riches of the wisdom and knowledge of God! How unsearchable his judgments, and his paths beyond tracing out! (Romans 11:33)

Righteousness and justice are the foundation of your throne; love and faithfulness go before you. (Psalm 89:14)

Nothing in all creation is hidden from God's sight. (Hebrews 4:13) You alone are holy. (Revelation 15:4)

I am the Alpha and the Omega, the First and the Last, the Beginning and the End. (Revelation 22:13)

He is the true God. (1 John 5:20)   Give thanks to the Lord, for he is good; his love endures forever. (Psalm 118:1)

The Lord is gracious and righteous; our God is full of compassion. (Psalm 116:5)   Holy, holy, holy is the Lord Almighty. (Isaiah 6:3)   I AM (John 8:58)

To God belong wisdom and power. (Job 12:13)   I am the way and the truth and the life. No one comes to the Father except through me. (John 14:6)   Taste and see that the Lord is good. (Psalm 34:8)

The Lord works righteousness and justice for all the oppressed. (Psalm 103:6)   In the beginning was the Word, and the Word was with God, and the Word was God. (John 1:1)   The Lord is good and his love endures forever. (Psalm 100:5)

Your righteousness is everlasting. (Psalm 119:142)   I am the living bread that came down from heaven. (John 6:51)   Everlasting Father, Prince of Peace. (Isaiah 9:6)

To us a child is born, to us a son is given, and the government will be on his shoulders. And he will be called Wonderful Counselor, Mighty God. (Isaiah 9:6)   I am with you always. (Matthew 28:20)

For to us a child is born, to us a son is given. (Isaiah 9:6)   Jesus, the pioneer and perfecter of faith. (Hebrews 12:2)

Christ died and returned to life so that he might be the Lord of both the dead and the living. (Romans 14:9)   Let us hold firmly to the faith we profess. (Hebrews 4:14)

The Son is the radiance of God's glory and the exact representation of his being, sustaining all things by his powerful word. After he had provided purification for sins, he sat down at the right hand of the Majesty in heaven. (Hebrews 1:3)

Rose of Sharon (Song of Songs 2:1)   (H)im who is and who was, and who is to come. (Revelation 1:4)   He is the atoning sacrifice for our sins, and not only for ours but also for the sins of the whole world. (1 John 2:2)

That which was from the beginning, which we have heard. (1 John 1:1)   Let them know that you, whose name is the LORD—that you alone are the Most High over all the earth. (Psalm 83:18)   the Lamb of God (John 1:36)   the ruler of the kings of the earth. (Revelation 1:5)

We have this hope as an anchor for the soul, firm and secure. It enters the inner sanctuary behind the curtain, where our forerunner, Jesus, has entered on our behalf. He has become a high priest forever, in the order of Melchizedek. (Hebrews 6:19-20)

God, the blessed and only Ruler, the King of kings and Lord of lords. (1 Timothy 6:15)   I am the Root and the Offspring of David, and the bright Morning Star. (Revelation 22:16)

The LORD will be king over the whole earth. (Zechariah 14:9)   I will pour out on the house of David... a spirit of grace. (Zechariah 12:10)   Desire of all nations (Haggai 2:7)

The Son of Man came eating and drinking, and they say, 'Here is a glutton and a drunkard, a friend of tax collectors and sinners.' (Matthew 11:19)

From everlasting to everlasting you are God. (Psalm 90:2)   On that day there will be one LORD, and his name the only name. (Zechariah 14:9)   the Father has sent his Son to be the Savior of the world. (1 John 4:14)

The virgin will conceive and give birth to a son, and will call him Immanuel. (Isaiah 7:14)   Chosen of God (1 Peter 2:4)   And we have seen and testify (1 John 4:14)

(O)ur Lord Jesus, that great Shepherd of the sheep (Hebrews 13:20)   Thanks be to God for his indescribable gift! (2 Corinthians 9:15)

The Lord is enthroned as King forever. (Psalm 29:10)   Righteous Branch, a King who will reign wisely and do what is just and right in the land. (Jeremiah 23:5)

I am the true vine, and my Father is the gardener. (John 15:1)   I lay a stone in Zion, a tested stone, a precious cornerstone for a sure foundation. (Isaiah 28:16)

(T)he Shepherd and Overseer of your souls (1 Peter 2:25)   Jesus Christ, the Righteous One. (1 John 2:1)

(W)e have an advocate with the Father—Jesus Christ, the Righteous One. (1 John 2:1)   and the Offspring of David, and the bright Morning Star. (Revelation 22:16)

As for God, his way is perfect. (Psalm 18:30)   Heir of all things (Hebrews 1:2)

I am the Root (Revelation 22:16)   Chief Shepherd (1 Peter 5:4)   Sceptre (Numbers 24:17)   Judge (Acts 10:42)   Yahweh

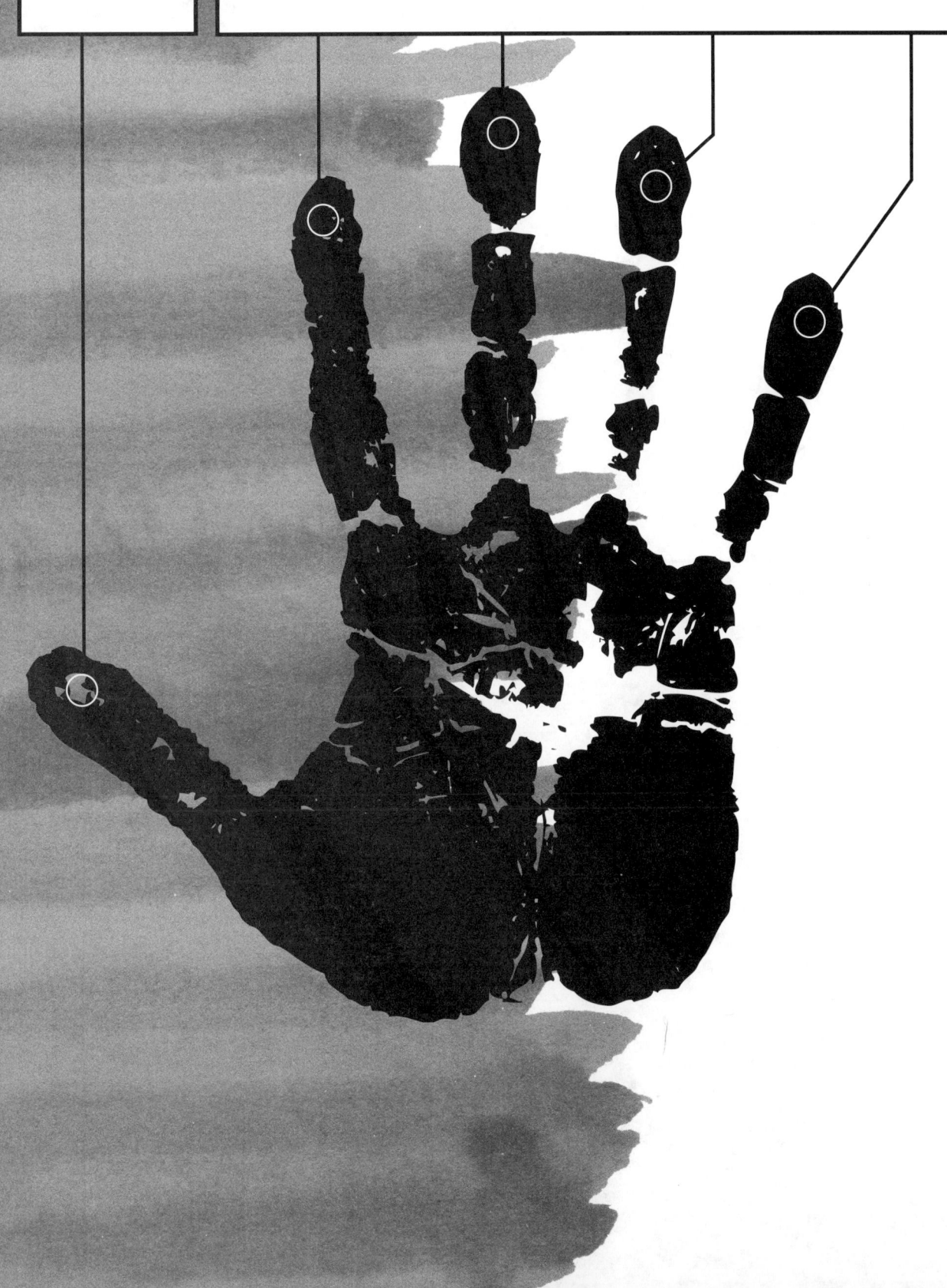

5

GOD Is Supreme and Self-Existent

Interact 5.1
God Is Supreme

1. The following Bible passages talk about the supremacy of God. As you read each passage, answer this question: Over what or whom is God supreme?

1 Chronicles 29:11–12   Isaiah 40:25

2 Chronicles 20:6   Isaiah 42:8

Job 42:1–6   Isaiah 44:6

Psalm 8:1   Isaiah 45:22

Psalm 9:1–2   Isaiah 46:5

Psalm 24:1–2   Isaiah 55:8–11

Psalm 93:1   Ephesians 1:20–21

Psalm 95:1–6   Philippians 2:9–11

Psalm 113:1–9   Colossians 1:15–20

Psalm 145:3–7   Hebrews 1:1–4

Continued on back →

Let God Be GOD

Interact 5.1

God Is Supreme Continued

Revelation 4:8–11

Revelation 5:11–14

Revelation 7:9–12

Revelation 15:1–4

2. What other attributes do the writers link to God's supremacy?

3. According to these passages, how should we respond to the fact that God is supreme? (You may have to look in the surrounding verses to find a response.)

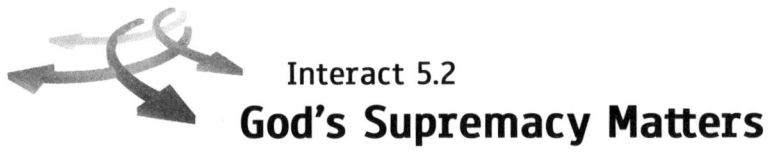

Interact 5.2
God's Supremacy Matters

Look up the following passages from Psalm 118. After reading each passage, answer the questions.

Psalm 118:5–7
• How did God show that He is supreme?

• What difference did God's action make in the life of this psalmist?

Psalm 118:8–9
• What are some things we trust in?

• Why is it better to trust in the Lord?

Psalm 118:13–14
• How did God show that He is supreme?

• What difference did God's action make in the life of this psalmist?

Psalm 118:15–16
• What are some "mighty things" you have seen God do?

• How do you respond when God helps you?

Psalm 118:19–21
• Why is the psalmist thankful?

• What do you have to be thankful for?

Continued on back →

Let God Be GOD

God's Supremacy Matters Continued

Psalm 118:22–24

• Who has rejected the Lord today?

• What reasons do we have for rejoicing anyway?

Psalm 118:25–27

• What New Testament event does this passage remind you of?

• Why do we have even more reasons to rejoice than this psalmist did?

Psalm 118:28

• How can you show your thanks to God?

• How can you exalt Him in your life?

Let God Be GOD

Interact 5.3
Before Genesis 1:1

Find and read each verse or passage of Scripture, and answer the questions.

1. Describe what reality was like before Genesis 1:1. You may use words, artwork, symbols, or anything else that you think will help communicate what you want to say. Be prepared to explain your work.

2. Look up the following verses: Psalm 90:2, Psalm 93:2, Isaiah 40:28, and Acts 17:24–25. How do these verses add to your knowledge of God's self-existence?

Let God Be GOD

Yahweh

Power and might are in your hand. (2 Chronicles 20:6)

The Lord is gracious and compassionate, slow to anger and rich in love. (Psalm 145:8)

Holy, holy, holy is the Lord God Almighty, who was, and is, and is to come. (Revelation 4:8)

God is love. (1 John 4:16)

I am the first and the last. (Isaiah 44:6)

Just and true are your ways. (Revelation 15:3)

The Lord reigns (Psalm 93:1)

My ways are higher than your ways and my thoughts than your thoughts. (Isaiah 55:9)

He does not treat us as our sins deserve. (Psalm 103:10)

(the Lord do not change (Malachi 3:6))

Christ of God (Luke 9:20)

Ever-present— Where can I flee from your presence? (Psalm 139:7)

Great is your faithfulness. (Lamentations 3:23)

Oh, the depth of the riches of the wisdom and knowledge of God! How unsearchable his judgments and his paths beyond tracing out! (Romans 11:33)

love and faithfulness go before you. (Psalm 89:14)

(I am with you always. (Matthew 28:20))

Lord of the sabbath (Mark 2:28)

Righteousness and justice are the foundation of your throne; love and faithfulness go before you. (Psalm 89:14)

I am the Alpha and the Omega, the First and the Last, the Beginning and the End. (Revelation 22:13)

Nothing in all creation is hidden from God's sight. (Hebrews 4:13)

Give thanks to the Lord, for he is good; his love endures forever. (Psalm 118:1)

I am the way and the truth and the life. (John 14:6)

Holy, holy, holy is the Lord Almighty. (Isaiah 6:3)

No one comes to the Father except through me. (John 14:6)

You alone are holy. (Revelation 15:4)

I AM (John 8:58)

I am the living bread that came down from heaven. (John 6:51)

The Lord is good and his love endures forever. (Psalm 100:5)

Taste and see that the Lord is good. (Psalm 34:8)

Everlasting Father, Prince of Peace. (Isaiah 9:6)

Wonderful Counselor, Mighty God, Everlasting Father

The Lord is gracious and righteous; our God is full of compassion. (Psalm 116:5)

He is the true God. (1 John 5:20)

The Lord works righteousness and justice for all the oppressed. (Psalm 103:6)

Your righteousness is everlasting. (Psalm 119:142)

To God belong wisdom and power. (Job 12:13)

In the beginning was the Word, and the Word was with God, and the Word was God. (John 1:1)

he might be the Lord of both the dead and the living. (Romans 14:9)

For to us a child is born, to us a son is given, and the government will be on his shoulders. And he will be called Wonderful Counselor, Mighty God, Everlasting Father, Prince of Peace. (Isaiah 9:6)

Christ died and returned to life so that he might be the Lord of both the dead and the living. (Romans 14:9)

Jesus the Son of God, let us hold firmly to the faith we profess. (Hebrews 4:14)

He is the atoning sacrifice for our sins, and not only for ours but also for the sins of the whole world. (1 John 2:2)

Therefore, since we have a great high priest who has ascended into heaven, Jesus the Son of God, let us hold firmly to the faith we profess. (Hebrews 4:14)

God, the blessed and only Ruler, the King of kings and Lord of lords (1 Timothy 6:15)

The Son is the radiance of God's glory and the exact representation of his being, sustaining all things by his powerful word. After he had provided purification for sins, he sat down at the right hand of the Majesty in heaven. (Hebrews 1:3)

the Lamb of God (John 1:29)

the Root of David, and the ruler of the kings of the earth. (Revelation 1:5)

a high priest forever, in the order of Melchizedek. (Hebrews 7:17)

Jesus, the pioneer and perfecter of faith. (Hebrews 12:2)

the bright Morning Star (Revelation 22:16)

the Father has sent his Son to be the Savior of the world. (1 John 4:14)

and his name the only name. (Zechariah 14:9)

Here is a glutton and a drunkard, a friend of tax collectors and sinners. (Matthew 11:19)

The Son of Man came eating and drinking, and they say, Here is a glutton and a drunkard, a friend of tax collectors and sinners. (Matthew 11:19)

Let them know that you, whose name is the LORD—that you alone are the Most High over all the earth. (Psalm 83:18)

We have this hope as an anchor for the soul, firm and secure. It enters the inner sanctuary behind the curtain, which we have seen with our eyes, which we have looked at and our hands have touched.

which we have heard, which we have seen with our eyes, which we have looked at and our hands have touched. (1 John 1:1)

(The Lord you are seeking will suddenly come to his temple.) (Malachi 3:1)

this we proclaim concerning the Word of life. (1 John 1:1)

The LORD will be king over the whole earth. On that day there will be one LORD, and his name the only name. (Zechariah 14:9)

Desire of all nations (Haggai 2:7)

a righteous Branch, a King who will reign wisely and do what is just and right in the land. (Jeremiah 23:5)

And a stone in Zion, a tested stone, a precious cornerstone for a sure foundation (Isaiah 28:16)

Thanks be to God for his indescribable gift! (2 Corinthians 9:15)

Chosen of God (1 Peter 2:4)

Bridegroom (Matthew 9:15)

The Son of Man (Matthew 9:6)

Rose of Sharon (Song of Songs 2:1)

Let them know this hope as an anchor for the soul

We have the exact representation of his being

That which was from the beginning (1 John 1:1)

God the blessed and only Ruler over the whole earth. (Psalm 90:2)

from everlasting to everlasting you are God. (Psalm 90:2)

The LORD will be king over the whole earth.

The virgin will conceive and give birth to a son, and will call him Immanuel. (Isaiah 7:14)

(O)ur Lord Jesus, that great Shepherd of the sheep (Hebrews 13:20)

The Lord is enthroned as King forever. (Psalm 29:10)

I am the true vine, and my Father is the gardener. (John 15:1)

(T)he Shepherd and Overseer of your souls. (1 Peter 2:25)

(W)e have an advocate with the Father—Jesus Christ, the Righteous One. (1 John 2:1)

(I) am the Root and the Offspring of David, and the bright Morning Star. (Revelation 22:16)

As for God, his way is perfect. (Psalm 18:30)

Heir of all things (Hebrews 1:2)

Judge (Acts 10:42)

Chief Shepherd (1 Peter 5:4)

Sceptre (Numbers 24:17)

Yahweh

6 GOD Is Sovereign

Interact 6.1
God Is Sovereign

Look up the following passages and jot down the main points about God's sovereignty in creation, in people's lives, and in events.

Genesis 50:20

Exodus 8:15, 32; 9:7, 12, 34–35; 10:1–2, 20, 27; 11:9–10; 14:1–4, 8

1 Kings 12:15

Psalm ll5:3

Psalm 139:16

Proverbs 16:1, 4, 9, 33; 19:21

Proverbs 21:30

Isaiah 45:1–7

Isaiah 46:9–11

Continued on back →

Let God Be GOD

Interact 6.1
God Is Sovereign continued

Lamentations 3:37–38

Matthew 10:29–31

Acts 2:22–23

Acts 17:24–31

Romans 8:28–39

Ephesians 1:9–12

Ephesians 2:4–10

7

GOD Is Infinite

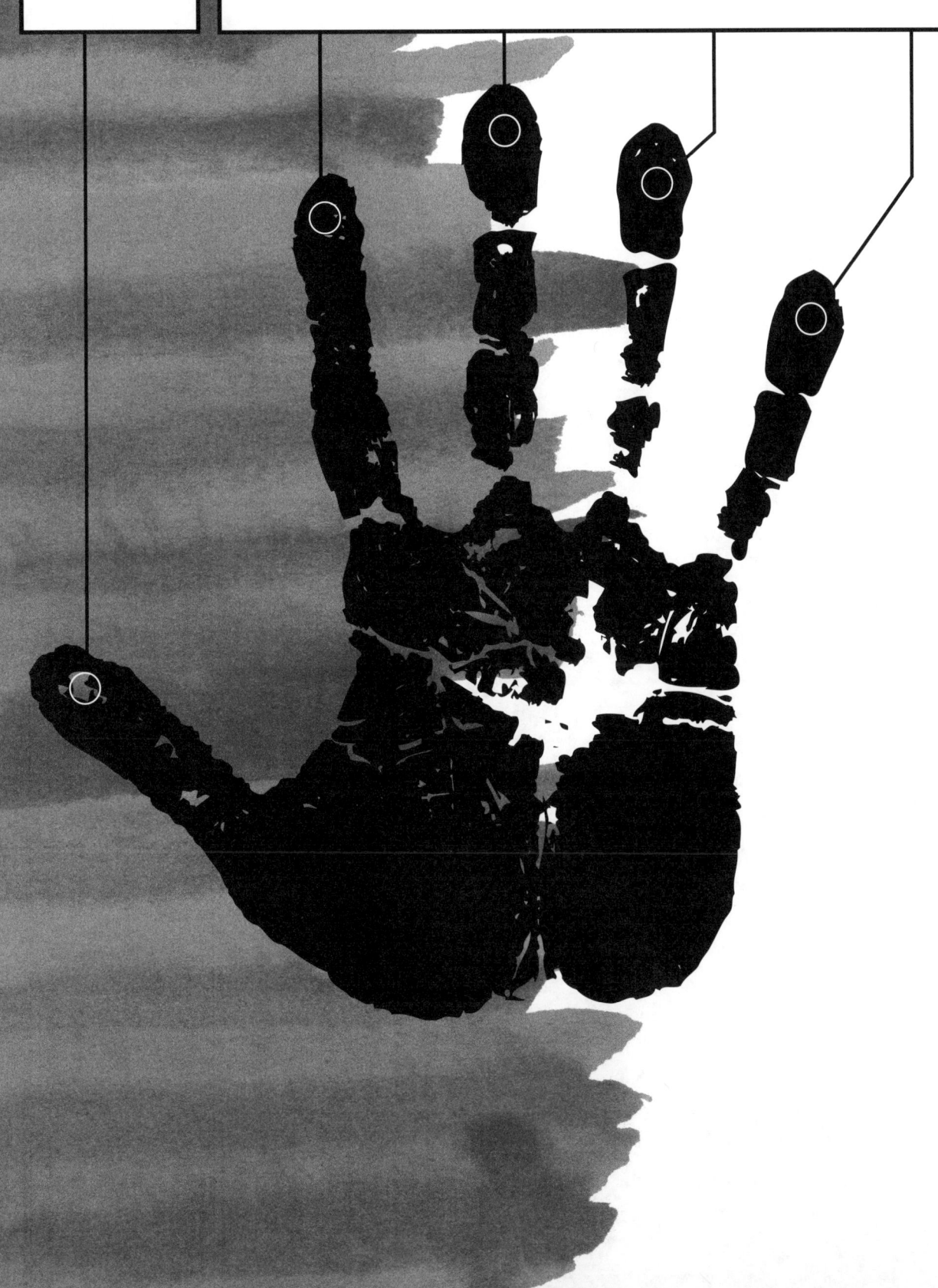

Interact 7.1
My Limitations

1. What things or forces limit your movements, your actions, your possibilities, and so on? List as many limitations as you can. The following questions might stimulate your thinking:

What keeps you from flying like Superman?

What keeps you from living in outer space or under the ocean?

What keeps you from knowing everything?

What keeps you from running at the speed of sound?

What keeps you from lifting a huge building?

What keeps you from bowling a perfect game every time?

2. Name one thing you would do if you had no limitations.

Let God Be GOD

Yahweh   Power and might are in your hand. (2 Chronicles 20:6)

The Lord is gracious and compassionate, slow to anger and rich in love.

Holy, holy, holy is the Lord God Almighty, who was, and is, and is to come. (Revelation 4:8)

God is love. (1 John 4:16)   I am the first and the last. (Isaiah 44:6)   Just and true are your ways. (Revelation 15:3)

The Lord reigns (Psalm 93:1)   My ways are higher than your ways and my thoughts than your thoughts. (Isaiah 55:9)

Christ of God (Luke 9:20)   Ever-present....Where can I flee from your presence? (Psalm 139:7)   He does not treat us as our sins deserve. (Psalm 103:10)   The Lord do not change. (Malachi 3:6)

Great is your faithfulness. (Lamentations 3:23)   Oh, the depth of the riches of the wisdom and knowledge of God! How unsearchable his judgments, and his paths beyond tracing out! (Romans 11:33)   Lord of the sabbath (Mark 2:28)

Righteousness and justice are the foundation of your throne; love and faithfulness go before you. (Psalm 89:14)   I am with you always. (Matthew 28:20)

I am the Alpha and the Omega, the First and the Last, the Beginning and the End. (Revelation 22:13) You alone are holy. (Revelation 15:4)

He is the true God. (1 John 5:20)   I am the way and the truth and the life. (John 14:6)   I am the living bread that came down from heaven. (John 6:51)

Nothing in all creation is hidden from God's sight. (Hebrews 4:13)   Give thanks to the Lord, for he is good; his love endures forever. (Psalm 118:1)   I AM (John 8:58)

The Lord is gracious and righteous; our God is full of compassion. (Psalm 116:5)   Holy, holy, holy is the Lord Almighty. (Isaiah 6:3)   Taste and see that the Lord is good. (Psalm 34:8)

To God belong wisdom and power. (Job 12:13)   In the beginning was the Word, and the Word was with God, and the Word was God. (John 1:1)   The Lord is good and his love endures forever. (Psalm 100:5)

Your righteousness is everlasting. (Psalm 119:142)   No one comes to the Father except through me. (John 14:6)   And he will be called Wonderful Counselor, Mighty God, Everlasting Father, Prince of Peace. (Isaiah 9:6)

The Lord works righteousness and justice for all the oppressed. (Psalm 103:6)   I am the Lord of both the dead and the living. (Romans 14:9)   Jesus, the pioneer and perfecter of faith. (Hebrews 12:2)

For to us a child is born, to us a son is given, and the government will be on his shoulders. (Isaiah 9:6)   He is the atoning sacrifice for our sins, and not only for ours but also for the sins of the whole world. (1 John 2:2)

Christ died and returned to life so that he might be the Lord of both the dead and the living. (Romans 14:9)   Jesus the Son of God, let us hold firmly to the faith we profess. (Hebrews 4:14)   the Lamb of God (John 1:29)   Jesus, the pioneer and perfecter of faith. (Hebrews 12:2)

The Son is the radiance of God's glory and the exact representation of his being, sustaining all things by his powerful word. After he had provided purification for sins, he sat down at the right hand of the Majesty in heaven. (Hebrews 1:3)

Rose of Sharon (Song of Songs 2:1)   (H)im who is and who was, and who is to come. (1 Timothy 6:15)   After...Jesus Christ, who is the faithful witness, the firstborn from the dead, and the ruler of the kings of the earth. (Revelation 1:5)

That which was from the beginning, which we have heard, which we have seen with our eyes, which we have looked at and our hands have touched—this we proclaim concerning the Word of life. (1 John 1:1)   a high priest forever, in the order of Melchizedek. (Hebrews 6:20)

The LORD will be king over the whole earth. On that day there will be one LORD, and his name the only name. (Zechariah 14:9)   the Father has sent his Son to be the Savior of the world. (1 John 4:14)

God the blessed and only Ruler, the King of kings and Lord of lords. (1 Timothy 6:15)   Here is a glutton and a drunkard, a friend of tax collectors and sinners. (Matthew 11:19)

Let them know that you, whose name is the LORD—that you alone are the Most High over all the earth. (Psalm 83:18)   We have this hope as an anchor for the soul, firm and secure. It enters the inner sanctuary behind the curtain, where our forerunner, Jesus, has entered on our behalf. He has become a high priest forever, in the order of Melchizedek. (Hebrews 6:19-20)

The Son of Man came eating and drinking, and they say 'Here is a glutton and a drunkard, a friend of tax collectors and sinners.' (Matthew 11:19)   the Word of life. (1 John 1:1)   And we have seen and testify that the Father has sent his Son to be the Savior of the world. (1 John 4:14)

(H)e...a stone in Zion, a tested stone, a precious cornerstone for a sure foundation. (Isaiah 28:16)   Desire of all nations (Haggai 2:7)

The Son of Man (Matthew 9:6)   Chosen of God (1 Peter 2:4)   Branch, a King who will reign wisely and do what is just and right in the land. (Jeremiah 23:5)

from everlasting to everlasting you are God. (Psalm 90:2)   The virgin will conceive and give birth to a son, and will call him Immanuel. (Isaiah 7:14)   Thanks be to God for his indescribable gift! (2 Corinthians 9:15)

(O)ur Lord Jesus, that great Shepherd of the sheep (Hebrews 13:20)   The Lord is enthroned as King forever. (Psalm 29:10)

I am the true vine, and my Father is the gardener. (John 15:1)   (T)he Shepherd and Overseer of your souls. (1 Peter 2:25)

(W)e have an advocate with the Father—Jesus Christ, the Righteous One. (1 John 2:1)   (I am) the Root and the Offspring of David, and the bright Morning Star. (Revelation 22:16)   As for God, his way is perfect. (Psalm 18:30)

I am the Chief Shepherd (1 Peter 5:4)   Heir of all things (Hebrews 1:2)   Judge (Acts 10:42)

Scepter (Numbers 24:17)   Yahweh

Interact 7.2
God Is Infinite

1. When we say that God is infinite, we are saying something about what He is *not*. Since *finite* means "having limits," to describe God as infinite is to say that He has no limits.

According to these verses, what are some of the ways in which God is not limited?

Deuteronomy 4:39

1 Kings 8:27

Psalm 139:1–4

Isaiah 40:12–14

Isaiah 40:25–26

Isaiah 44:6–8

2. There is another meaning of *infinite*: "perfect." Something that is limited does not reach its potential. It falls short of what it could be. It is not perfect. But God is perfect in every way.

According to these verses, what are some of the ways in which God is perfect?

Exodus 33:19

Psalm 18:30–31

Psalm 103:8

Psalm 118:1

Isaiah 41:10

Let God Be GOD

Yahweh Power and might are in your hand. (2 Chronicles 20:6)

The Lord is gracious and compassionate, slow to anger and rich in love.

Holy, holy, holy is the Lord God Almighty, who was, and is, and is to come. (Revelation 1:8)

God is love. (1 John 4:16) I am the first and the last. (Isaiah 44:6) Just and true are your ways. (Revelation 15:3)

The Lord reigns (Psalm 93:1) My ways are higher than your ways and my thoughts than your thoughts. (Isaiah 55:9) He does not treat us as our sins deserve. (Psalm 103:10) the Lord do not change. (Malachi 3:6)

Christ of God (Luke 9:20) Ever-present—Where can I flee from your presence? (Psalm 139:7) Lord of the sabbath (Mark 2:28)

Great is your faithfulness. (Lamentations 3:23) Oh, the depth of the riches of the wisdom and knowledge of God! How unsearchable his judgments, and his paths beyond tracing out! (Romans 11:33)

Righteousness and justice are the foundation of your throne; love and faithfulness go before you. (Psalm 89:14) I AM (John 8:58)

I am the Alpha and the Omega, the First and the Last, the Beginning and the End. (Revelation 22:13) You alone are forever. (Revelation 15:4)

Nothing in all creation is hidden from God's sight. (Hebrews 4:13) Give thanks to the Lord, for he is good; his love endures forever. (Psalm 118:1)

The Lord is gracious and righteous; our God is full of compassion. (Psalm 116:5) Taste and see that the Lord is good (Psalm 34:8)

He is the true God. (1 John 5:20) Holy, holy, holy is the Lord Almighty. (Isaiah 6:3)

The Lord works righteousness and justice for all the oppressed. (Psalm 103:6) I am the way and the truth and the life. No one comes to the Father except through me. (John 14:6)

To God belong wisdom and power. (Job 12:13) In the beginning was the Word, and the Word was with God, and the Word was God. (John 1:1) The Lord is good and his love endures forever. (Psalm 100:5)

Your righteousness is everlasting. (Psalm 119:142) and he will be called Wonderful Counselor, Mighty God, Everlasting Father, Prince of Peace. (Isaiah 9:6)

For to us a child is born, to us a son is given, and the government will be on his shoulders. (Isaiah 9:6) the Lamb of God (John 1:29) Jesus, the pioneer and perfecter of faith. (Hebrews 12:2)

Christ died and returned to life so that he might be the Lord of both the dead and the living. (Romans 14:9) and see that the Lord is good (Psalm 34:8)

The Son is the radiance of God's glory and the exact representation of his being, sustaining all things by his powerful word. (Hebrews 1:3) Jesus, the Son of God, let us hold firmly to the faith we profess. (Hebrews 4:14) right hand of the Majesty in heaven. (Hebrews 1:3)

Therefore, since we have a great high priest who has ascended into heaven, Jesus the Son of God After he had provided purification for sins, he sat down at the Jesus, the Majesty in heaven. (Hebrews 1:3)

God, the blessed and only Ruler, the King of kings and Lord of lords. (1 Timothy 6:15) He is the atoning sacrifice for our sins, and not only for ours but also for the sins of the whole world. (1 John 2:2)

That which was from the beginning, which we have heard, which we have seen with our eyes, which we have looked at and our hands have touched—this we proclaim concerning the Word of life. (1 John 1:1) in the order of Melchizedek. (Hebrews 6:19-20)

God, the blessed and only Ruler name is the LORD—and rejoice before him. (Psalm 68:4) He has become a high priest forever, in the order of Melchizedek. (Hebrews 6:19-20)

The LORD will be king over the whole earth. On that day there will be one LORD, and his name the only name. (Zechariah 14:9) the Father has sent his Son to be the Savior of the world. (1 John 4:14)

From everlasting to everlasting you are God. (Psalm 90:2) The Son of Man came eating and drinking, and they say, 'Here is a glutton and a drunkard, a friend of tax collectors and sinners.' (Matthew 11:19) Desire of all nations (Haggai 2:7) And we have seen

(O)ur Lord Jesus, that great Shepherd of the sheep (Hebrews 13:20) The virgin will conceive and give birth to a son, and will call him Immanuel. (Isaiah 7:14) Chosen of God (1 Peter 2:4) Branch, a King who will reign wisely and do what is just and right in the land. (Jeremiah 23:5)

I am the true vine, and my Father is the gardener. (John 15:1) The Lord is enthroned as King forever. (Psalm 29:10) Thanks be to God for his indescribable gift! (2 Corinthians 9:15) a stone in Zion, a tested stone, a precious cornerstone for a sure foundation. (Isaiah 28:16)

Rose of Sharon (Song of Songs 2:1)

(T)he Shepherd and Overseer of your souls (1 Peter 2:25) (W)e have an advocate with the Father—Jesus Christ, the Righteous One. (1 John 2:1)

(T)he Root and the Offspring of David, and the bright Morning Star. (Revelation 22:16)

As for God, his way is perfect. (Psalm 18:30)

I am the Chief Shepherd (1 Peter 5:4) Heir of all things (Hebrews 1:2) Judge (Acts 10:42)

Sceptre (Numbers 24:17) Yahweh

God's Infinite Attributes

The following attributes are called God's "shared attributes" because we can use the same word to describe God and human beings. However, even though the word can be used for human beings, the meaning changes a lot when we use the word to describe God!

Choose an attribute from this list: *good*, *wise*, *truthful*, *holy*, *righteous*, *merciful*, *just*, *long-suffering*, or *loving*.

Attribute:_____

1. Give examples of things that *human beings* can do to show this attribute.

2. Give examples of things that *God* does to show this attribute. (Remember that God is infinite, so He has no limitations and does everything perfectly.) Give a Bible reference for every action of God that you mention.

Yahweh

Power and might are in your hand. (2 Chronicles 20:6)

The Lord is gracious and compassionate, slow to anger and rich in love. (Psalm 145:8)

Holy, holy, holy is the Lord God Almighty, who was, and is, and is to come. (Revelation 4:8)

God is love. (1 John 4:16)

I am the first and the last. (Isaiah 44:6)

Just and true are your ways. (Revelation 15:3)

The Lord reigns (Psalm 93:1)

My ways are higher than your ways and my thoughts than your thoughts. (Isaiah 55:9)

He does not treat us as our sins deserve. (Psalm 103:10)

the Lord do not change. (Malachi 3:6)

Christ of God (Luke 9:20)

Where can I flee from your presence? (Psalm 139:7)

Ever-present

Great is your faithfulness. (Lamentations 3:23)

Oh, the depth of the riches of the wisdom and knowledge of God! How unsearchable his judgments, and his paths beyond tracing out! (Romans 11:33)

Lord of the sabbath (Mark 2:28)

I am with you always. (Matthew 28:20)

Righteousness and justice are the foundation of your throne; love and faithfulness go before you. (Psalm 89:14)

I am the Alpha and the Omega, the First and the Last, the Beginning and the End. (Revelation 22:13)

Nothing in all creation is hidden from God's sight. (Hebrews 4:13)

Give thanks to the Lord, for he is good; his love endures forever. (Psalm 118:1)

You alone are holy. (Revelation 15:4)

He is the true God (1 John 5:20)

The Lord is gracious and righteous; our God is full of compassion. (Psalm 116:5)

I am the way and the truth and the life. (John 14:6)

Holy, holy, holy is the Lord Almighty. (Isaiah 6:3)

No one comes to the Father except through me. (John 14:6)

Taste and see that the Lord is good (Psalm 34:8)

In the beginning was the Word, and the Word was with God, and the Word was God. (John 1:1)

I AM (John 8:58)

I AM

The Lord works righteousness and justice for all the oppressed. (Psalm 103:6)

Wonderful Counselor, Mighty God, Everlasting Father, Prince of Peace. (Isaiah 9:6)

I am the living bread that came down from heaven. (John 6:51)

To God belong wisdom and power. (Job 12:13)

Your righteousness is everlasting. (Psalm 119:142)

For to us a child is born, to us a son is given, and the government will be on his shoulders. (Isaiah 9:6)

Therefore, since we have a great high priest who has ascended into heaven, let us hold firmly to the faith we profess. (Hebrews 4:14)

Christ died and returned to life so that he might be the Lord of both the dead and the living. (Romans 14:9)

He is the atoning sacrifice for our sins, and not only for ours but also for the sins of the whole world. (1 John 2:2)

the Lamb of God (John 1:29)

Jesus the pioneer and perfecter of faith. (Hebrews 12:2)

the bright Morning Star (Revelation 22:16)

the ruler of the kings of the earth. (Revelation 1:5)

After he had provided purification for sins, he sat down at the right hand of the Majesty in heaven. (Hebrews 1:3)

The Lord is good and his love endures forever. (Psalm 100:5)

The Son is the radiance of God's glory and the exact representation of his being, sustaining all things by his powerful word. (Hebrews 1:3)

God, the blessed and only Ruler, the King of kings and Lord of lords (1 Timothy 6:15)

whose name is the LORD—that you alone are the Most High over all the earth. (Psalm 83:18)

It enters the inner sanctuary behind the curtain, where our forerunner, Jesus, has entered on our behalf. He has become a high priest forever, in the order of Melchizedek. (Hebrews 6:19-20)

We have this hope as an anchor for the soul, firm and secure. (Hebrews 6:19)

Let them know that you, whose name is the LORD

which we have seen with our eyes, which we have looked at and our hands have touched. (1 John 1:1)

The LORD will be one LORD, and his name the only name. (Zechariah 14:9)

The Son of Man came eating and drinking, and they say, 'Here is a glutton and a drunkard, a friend of tax collectors and sinners.' (Matthew 11:19)

the Bridegroom (Matthew 9:15)

Desire of all nations (Haggai 2:7)

And we have seen and testify that the Father has sent his Son to be the Savior of the world. (1 John 4:14)

a stone in Zion, a tested stone, a precious cornerstone for a sure foundation (Isaiah 28:16)

a righteous Branch, a King who will reign wisely and do what is just and right in the land (Jeremiah 23:5)

Chosen of God (1 Peter 2:4)

thanks be to God for his indescribable gift! (2 Corinthians 9:15)

From everlasting to everlasting you are God. (Psalm 90:2)

The virgin will conceive and give birth to a son, and will call him Immanuel. (Isaiah 7:14)

God, the blessed and only Ruler. On that day there will be one LORD

The LORD will be king over the whole earth. (Psalm 90:2)

The Lord is enthroned as King forever. (Psalm 29:10)

Rose of Sharon (Song of Songs 2:1)

That which was from the beginning (1 John 1:1)

(O)ur Lord Jesus, that great Shepherd of the sheep (Hebrews 13:20)

The LORD is my shepherd (Psalm 23:1)

I am the true vine, and my Father is the gardener (John 15:1)

(T)he Shepherd and Overseer of your souls (1 Peter 2:25)

(W)e have an advocate with the Father—Jesus Christ, the Righteous One. (1 John 2:1)

I am the Root and the Offspring of David, and the bright Morning Star. (Revelation 22:16)

As for God, his way is perfect. (Psalm 18:30)

Heir of all things (Hebrews 1:2)

Chief Shepherd (1 Peter 5:4)

Sceptre (Numbers 24:17)

Judge (Acts 10:42)

Yahweh

8 GOD Is Immutable and Eternal

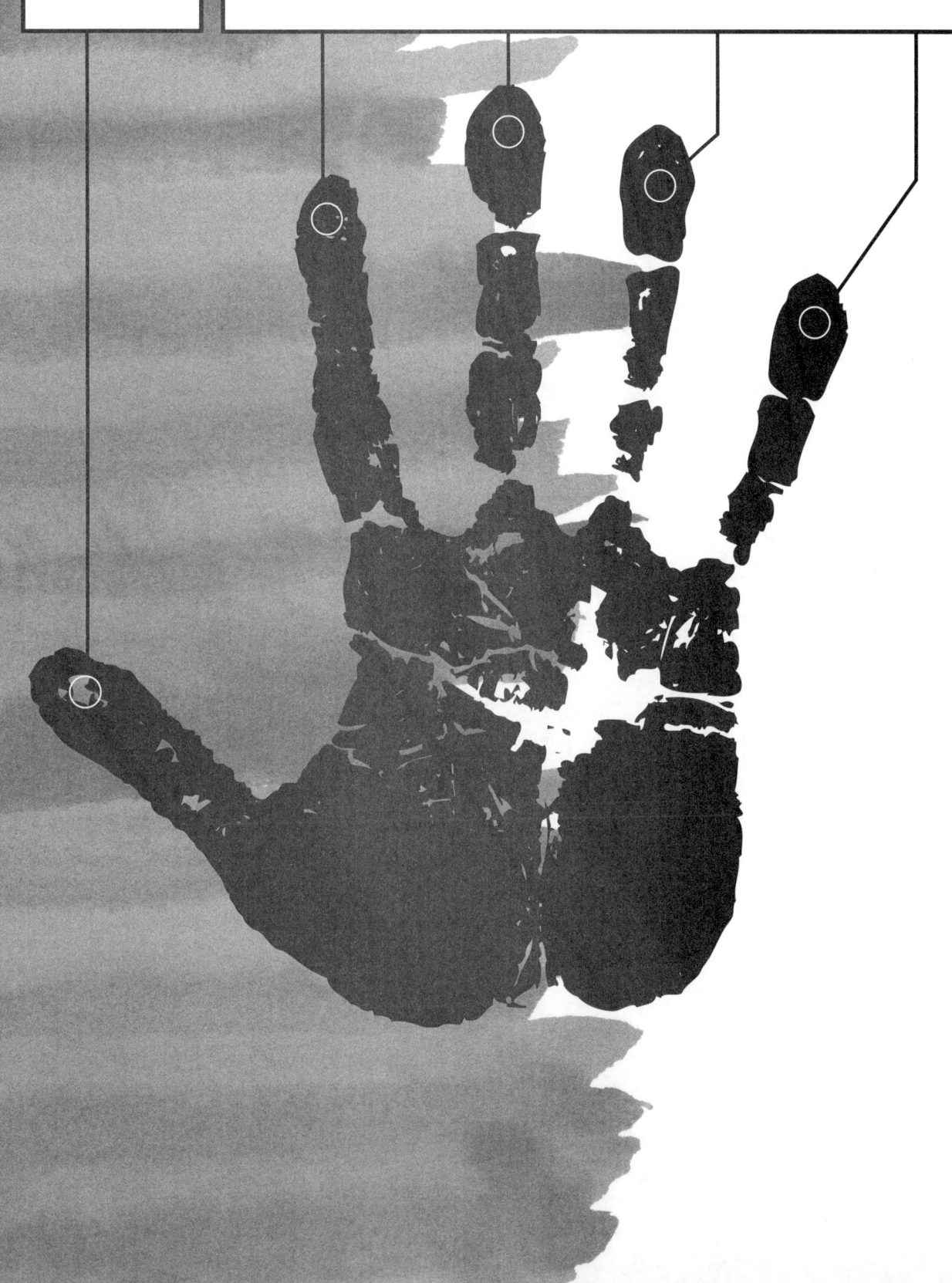

Interact 8.1
God Is Immutable

Explore what it means for us that God is immutable, or unchanging.

1. Record what these verses tell us about God, along with your own thoughts and questions.

Numbers 23:19–20

1 Samuel 15:29

Psalm 110:4

Isaiah 46:9–11

Malachi 3:6

Romans 2:1–11 (especially verse 11)

2. Answer the following questions and explain how the fact that God is immutable bears on these issues:
- What are some fads you have witnessed?
- When does something become "old-fashioned" or "outdated"?
- Does the fact that something is "new" make it right, good, or best?
- Does being "old" make something wrong or inferior?

Continued on back →

Let God Be GOD

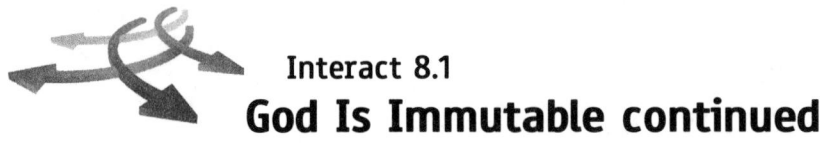

God Is Immutable continued

3. People cry for "equality" and "consistency" and "justice." How does God's immutability affect these issues?

4. Christians are supposed to reflect God's character. Select a characteristic from the list below, read the verse associated with it, and explain why it is especially important for Christians to show that characteristic.

Honesty. Proverbs 14:5

Trustworthiness. Titus 2:10

Sincerity. Romans 12:11

Integrity. Titus 2:7

Dependability. Proverbs 13:17

Good reputation. 3 John 12

Responsibility. Nehemiah 9:8

Truthfulness. Proverbs 12:22

Faithfulness. 1 Corinthians 4:2

Right intentions. Proverbs 14:22

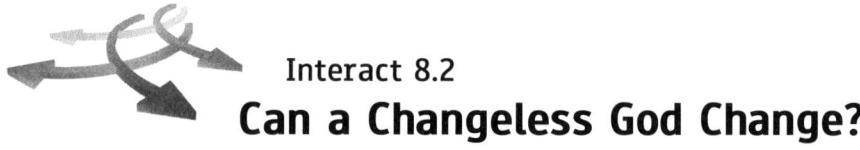

Interact 8.2
Can a Changeless God Change?

The verses listed in the chart below suggest that God may have changed His mind. Look up each passage, and in the first column describe the specific circumstances of God's actions. Then in the second column summarize how these verses might better be explained than by saying that God changed.

	Circumstances	God can't change, so ...
Genesis 6:5–8	The people of Noah's day have sinned so greatly that judgment must fall.	
Exodus 32:9–14		
Judges 2:17–18		
1 Samuel 15:1–11		
Jeremiah 18:7–10		
Amos 7:1–6		
Jonah 3:1–10		

Let God Be GOD

Yahweh

Power and might are in your hand. (2 Chronicles 20:6)

The Lord is gracious and compassionate, slow to anger and rich in love.

Holy, holy, holy is the Lord God Almighty, who was, and is, and is to come.

God is love. (1 John 4:16)

The Lord reigns (Psalm 93:1)

I am the first and the last. (Isaiah 44:6)

Just and true are your ways. (Revelation 15:3)

Christ of God (Luke 9:20)

My ways are higher than your ways and my thoughts than your thoughts. (Isaiah 55:9)

He does not treat us as our sins deserve. (Psalm 103:10)

Ever-present—Where can I flee from your presence? (Psalm 139:7)

[I] the Lord do not change. (Malachi 3:6)

Great is your faithfulness. (Lamentations 3:23)

On the depth of the riches of the wisdom and knowledge of God! How unsearchable his judgments, and his paths beyond tracing out! (Romans 11:33)

Lord of the sabbath. (Mark 2:28)

Righteousness and justice are the foundation of your throne; love and faithfulness go before you. (Psalm 89:14)

I am the Alpha and the Omega, the First and the Last, the Beginning and the End. (Revelation 22:13) You alone are holy. (Revelation 15:4)

He is the true God. (1 John 5:20)

Nothing in all creation is hidden from God's sight. (Hebrews 4:13) I am the way and the truth and the life. (John 14:6)

I am the living bread that came down from heaven. (John 6:51)

The Lord is gracious and righteous; our God is full of compassion. (Psalm 116:5) Give thanks to the Lord, for he is good; his love endures forever. (Psalm 118:1)

Holy, holy, holy is the Lord Almighty. (Isaiah 6:3)

I AM! (John 8:58)

The Lord works righteousness and justice for all the oppressed. (Psalm 103:6)

In the beginning was the Word, and the Word was with God, and the Word was God. (John 1:1) The Lord is good and see that the Lord is good. (Psalm 34:8)

To God belong wisdom and power. (Job 12:13)

No one comes to the Father except through me. (John 14:6)

Taste and see that the Lord is good. (Psalm 34:8)

Your righteousness is everlasting. (Psalm 119:142)

For to us a child is born, to us a son is given, and the government will be on his shoulders. And he will be called Wonderful Counselor, Mighty God, Everlasting Father, Prince of Peace. (Isaiah 9:6)

Jesus, the pioneer and perfecter of faith. (Hebrews 12:2)

Therefore, since we have a great high priest who has ascended into heaven, Jesus the Son of God, let us hold firmly to the faith we profess. (Hebrews 4:14)

He is the atoning sacrifice for our sins. (1 John 2:2)

Christ died and returned to life so that he might be the Lord of both the dead and the living. (Romans 14:9)

God the blessed and only Ruler, the King of kings and Lord of lords. (1 Timothy 6:15) sustaining all things by his powerful word. After he had provided purification for sins, he sat down at the right hand of the Majesty in heaven. (Hebrews 1:3)

The Son is the radiance of God's glory and the exact representation of his being, sustaining all things by his powerful word.

the Lamb of God. (John 1:29)

Rose of Sharon (Song of Songs 2:1)

(Him) who is, and who was, and who is to come, and from the seven spirits before his throne, and from Jesus Christ, who is the faithful witness, the firstborn from the dead, and the ruler of the kings of the earth. (Revelation 1:4-5)

Jesus, who has entered on our behalf. He has become a high priest forever, in the order of Melchizedek. (Hebrews 6:19-20)

That which was from the beginning, which we have heard, which we have seen with our eyes, which we have looked at and our hands have touched—this we proclaim concerning the Word of life. (1 John 1:1)

Let them know that you, whose name is the LORD—that you alone are the Most High over all the earth. (Psalm 83:18)

We have this hope as an anchor for the soul, firm and secure. It enters the inner sanctuary behind the curtain.

The Son of Man came eating and drinking, and they say, 'Here is a glutton and a drunkard, a friend of tax collectors and sinners.' (Matthew 11:19)

The Father has sent his Son to be the Savior of the world. (1 John 4:14)

The Root and the bright Morning Star. (Revelation 22:16)

The bridegroom. (Matthew 9:15)

Chosen of God (1 Peter 2:4)

On that day there will be one LORD, and his name the only name. (Zechariah 14:9)

The LORD will be king over the whole earth.

The virgin will conceive and give birth to a son, and will call him Immanuel. (Isaiah 7:14)

Desire of all nations. (Haggai 2:7)

I lay a stone in Zion, a tested stone, a precious cornerstone for a sure foundation. (Isaiah 28:16)

(thanks be to God for his indescribable gift. (2 Corinthians 9:15)

God, the blessed and only Ruler, the King of kings and Lord of lords. (1 Timothy 6:15)

From everlasting to everlasting you are God. (Psalm 90:2)

The Lord is enthroned as King forever. (Psalm 29:10)

I am the true vine, and my Father is the gardener. (John 15:1)

(O)ur Lord Jesus, that great Shepherd of the sheep (Hebrews 13:20)

(The) Shepherd and Overseer of your souls (1 Peter 2:25)

(W)e have an advocate with the Father—Jesus Christ, the Righteous One. (1 John 2:1)

I am the Root and the Offspring of David, and the bright Morning Star. (Revelation 22:16)

As for God, his way is perfect. (Psalm 18:30)

Heir of all things (Hebrews 1:2)

Chief Shepherd (1 Peter 5:4)

Sceptre (Numbers 24:17)

Judge (Acts 10:42)

Yahweh

Interact 8.3
God Is Eternal

Explore what it means for us that God is eternal.

1. Discover what these Scriptures tell us about God. Write your answers below, along with your own thoughts and questions. Job 36:26; Psalm 90:2, 4; Isaiah 45:21, 46:9–10; 2 Peter 3:8

2. Consider two possibilities for what is eternal, or lasts forever. What difference does it make which you believe? MATTER IS ETERNAL or GOD IS ETERNAL

3. Compare and contrast the following pairs of statements:

Good guys finish last.
The first shall be last and the last first.

Only the fittest survive.
He who loses his life shall save it.

It's a dog-eat-dog world.
If your enemy is hungry, feed him.

4. How does the fact that God is eternal affect the statement pairs in question 3?

Continued on back →

Let God Be GOD

God Is Eternal continued

5. Explain why those who believe God is eternal have a stronger case for opposing rape, bigotry, murder, or any other deviant act.

6. When we sin, what happens if we repent? Does God remember our sins forever? Are they eternal too? See Psalm 103:11–12.

7. If God no longer remembers our sins after He forgives us, why can't we forget them too? Why do wrong actions of our past sometimes haunt us?

8. God is eternal, but we are temporal; we live in time, and time is limited. What are some tactics we can use to make better use of our time? See Psalm 39:4–6; Psalm 90:7–12; Ephesians 5:15–17; James 4:14–17.

9. An old song says that we should live "with eternity's values in view." What does this mean? How does each activity mentioned in Colossians 3:1–4 reflect "eternity's values"?

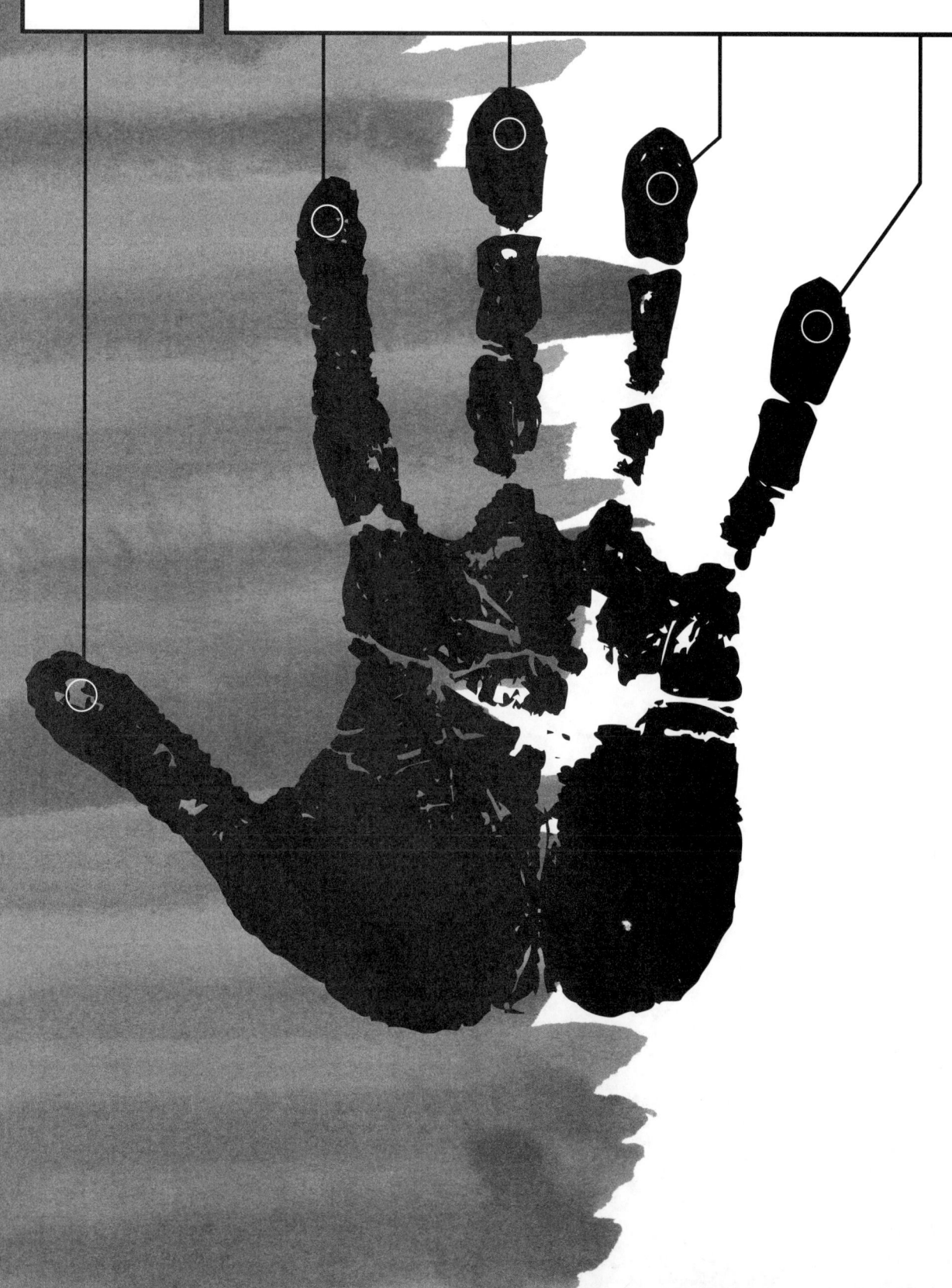

9

GOD Is Incomprehensible and Ineffable

Knowing the Unknowable

1. Look up the following Bible passages and be prepared to discuss them:

Ephesians 1:17b–19

Jeremiah 9:23–24

John 17:3

Philippians 3–8

2. How should God's incomprehensibility affect the way we study the Bible?

Yahweh   Power and might are in your hand. (2 Chronicles 20:6)

The Lord is gracious and compassionate, slow to anger and rich in love. (Psalm 145:8)

Holy, holy, holy is the Lord God Almighty, who was, and is, and is to come. (Revelation 4:8)

God is love. (1 John 4:16)

I am the first and the last. (Isaiah 44:6)   Just and true are your ways. (Revelation 15:3)

The Lord reigns (Psalm 93:1)   My ways are higher than your ways and my thoughts than your thoughts. (Isaiah 55:9)

Christ of God (Luke 9:20)   He does not treat us as our sins deserve. (Psalm 103:10)   The Lord do not change (Malachi 3:6)

Ever-present—Where can I flee from your presence? (Psalm 139:7)

Great is your faithfulness. (Lamentations 3:23)

Oh, the depth of the riches of the wisdom and knowledge of God! How unsearchable his judgments and his paths beyond tracing out! (Romans 11:33)

Righteousness and justice are the foundation of your throne; love and faithfulness go before you. (Psalm 89:14)

I am the Alpha and the Omega, the First and the Last, the Beginning and the End. (Revelation 22:13)   Give thanks to the Lord, for he is good; his love endures forever. (Psalm 118:1)

Lord of the sabbath (Mark 2:28)

Nothing in all creation is hidden from God's sight. (Hebrews 4:13)

Holy, holy, holy is the Lord Almighty. No one comes to the Father except through me. (John 14:6)   I AM (John 8:58)

I am the way and the truth and the life. (John 14:6)

The Lord is gracious and righteous; our God is full of compassion. (Psalm 116:5)   Taste and see that the Lord is good (Psalm 34:8)

In the beginning was the Word, and the Word was with God, and the Word was God. (John 1:1)

He is the true God. (1 John 5:20)   The Lord is good and his love endures forever. (Psalm 100:5)

The Lord works righteousness and justice for all the oppressed. (Psalm 103:6)

To God belong wisdom and power. (Job 12:13)

Your righteousness is everlasting. (Psalm 119:142)   And he will be called Wonderful Counselor, Mighty God, Everlasting Father, Prince of Peace. (Isaiah 9:6)

Jesus, the pioneer and perfecter of faith. (Hebrews 12:2)

For to us a child is born, to us a son is given, and the government will be on his shoulders. (Isaiah 9:6)

He is the atoning sacrifice for our sins. (1 John 2:2)   the Lamb of God (John 1:29)

Christ died and returned to life so that he might be the Lord of both the dead and the living. (Romans 14:9)

Therefore, since we have a great high priest who has ascended into heaven, Jesus the Son of God, let us hold firmly to the faith we profess. (Hebrews 4:14)

After he had provided purification for sins he sat down at the right hand of the Majesty in heaven. (Hebrews 1:3)

The Son is the radiance of God's glory and the exact representation of his being, sustaining all things by his powerful word. (Hebrews 1:3)

God, the blessed and only Ruler, the King of kings and Lord of lords (1 Timothy 6:15)

the bright Morning Star. (Revelation 22:16)

(H)im who is and who was, and who is to come, and from the seven spirits before his throne (Revelation 1:4)

name is the LORD—that you alone are the Most High over all the earth. (Psalm 83:18)

We have this hope as an anchor for the soul, firm and secure. It enters the inner sanctuary behind the curtain, where Jesus, who went before us, has entered on our behalf. He has become a high priest forever, in the order of Melchizedek. (Hebrews 6:19-20)

Rose of Sharon (Song of Songs 2:1)

That which was from the beginning, which we have heard, which we have seen with our eyes, which we have looked at and our hands have touched—this we proclaim concerning the Word of life. (1 John 1:1)

The Son of Man came eating and drinking, and they say, 'Here is a glutton and a drunkard, a friend of tax collectors and sinners.' (Matthew 11:19)

the Father has sent his Son to be the Savior of the world. (1 John 4:14)

I am the living bread that came down from heaven. (John 6:51)

I am with you always. (Matthew 28:20)

You alone are holy. (Revelation 15:4)

From everlasting to everlasting you are God. (Psalm 90:2)

The LORD will be king over the whole earth. On that day there will be one LORD, and his name the only name. (Zechariah 14:9)

The virgin will conceive and give birth to a son, and will call him Immanuel. (Isaiah 7:14)

Chosen of God (1 Peter 2:4)   a chosen and precious cornerstone for a sure foundation (Isaiah 28:16)

Thanks be to God for his indescribable gift! (2 Corinthians 9:15)

Desire of all nations (Haggai 2:7)

And we have seen and testify that the Father has sent his Son to be the Savior of the world. (1 John 4:14)

(O)ur Lord Jesus, that great Shepherd of the sheep (Hebrews 13:20)

The Lord is enthroned as King forever. (Psalm 29:10)

I am the true vine, and my Father is the gardener. (John 15:1)

(T)he Shepherd and Overseer of your souls (1 Peter 2:25)

(W)e have an advocate with the Father—Jesus Christ, the Righteous One. (1 John 2:1)

I am the Root and the Offspring of David, and the bright Morning Star. (Revelation 22:16)

As for God, his way is perfect. (Psalm 18:30)

I am the Chief Shepherd (1 Peter 5:4)

Heir of all things (Hebrews 1:2)   Judge (Acts 10:42)

Sceptre (Hebrews 1:8)   Yahweh

Interact 9.2
I Can Know God

My assigned psalms:_____

God's actions	God's character	Names or metaphors for God

Let God Be GOD

Yahweh

Power and might are in your hand. (2 Chronicles 20:6)

The Lord is gracious and compassionate, slow to anger and rich in love. (Psalm 145:8)

Holy, holy, holy is the Lord God Almighty, who was, and is, and is to come. (Revelation 4:8)

God is love. (1 John 4:16)

I am the first and the last. (Isaiah 44:6)

Just and true are your ways. (Revelation 15:3)

The Lord reigns (Psalm 93:1)

My ways are higher than your ways and my thoughts than your thoughts. (Isaiah 55:9)

He does not treat us as our sins deserve. (Psalm 103:10)

The Lord do not change. (Malachi 3:6)

Christ of God (Luke 9:20)

Ever-present—Where can I flee from your presence? (Psalm 139:7)

Great is your faithfulness. (Lamentations 3:23)

...his judgments, and his paths beyond tracing out! (Romans 11:33)

love and faithfulness go before you. (Revelation 22:13)

Lord of the Sabbath (Mark 2:28)

Oh, the depth of the riches of the wisdom and knowledge of God! How unsearchable his judgments, and his paths beyond tracing out! (Romans 11:33)

Righteousness and justice are the foundation of your throne; love and faithfulness go before you. (Psalm 89:14)

I am with you always. (Matthew 28:20)

I AM (John 8:58)

He is the true God. (1 John 5:20)

Nothing is hidden from God's sight. (Hebrews 4:13)

I am the Alpha and the Omega, the First and the Last, the Beginning and the End. (Revelation 22:13)

Give thanks to the Lord, for he is good; his love endures forever. (Psalm 118:1)

You alone are holy. (Revelation 15:4)

Lord of lords (Psalm 136:3)

Nothing is gracious in all creation

The Lord is gracious and righteous; our God is full of compassion. (Psalm 116:5)

I am the way and the truth and the life. No one comes to the Father except through me. (John 14:6)

Holy, holy, holy is the Lord Almighty. (Isaiah 6:3)

Taste and see that the Lord is good. (Psalm 34:8)

and the Word was God. (John 1:1) The Lord is good and his love endures forever. (Psalm 100:5)

Your righteousness is everlasting. (Psalm 119:142)

To God belong wisdom and power. (Job 12:13)

The Lord works righteousness and justice for all the oppressed. (Psalm 103:6)

In the beginning was the Word, and the Word was with God, and the Word was God.

And he will be called Wonderful Counselor, Mighty God, Everlasting Father, Prince of Peace. (Isaiah 9:6)

For to us a child is born, to us a son is given, and the government will be on his shoulders. (Isaiah 9:6)

he might be the Lord of both the dead and the living. (Romans 14:9)

He is the atoning sacrifice for our sins, and not only for ours but also for the sins of the whole world. (1 John 2:2)

Christ died and returned to life so that he might be the Lord of both the dead and the living.

the Lamb of God (John 1:29)

the bright Morning Star (Revelation 22:16)

the Majesty in heaven. (Hebrews 1:3)

The Son is the radiance of God's glory and the exact representation of his being, sustaining all things by his powerful word. (Hebrews 1:3)

God, the blessed and only Ruler, the King of kings and Lord of lords (1 Timothy 6:15)

the Ruler of the kings of the earth. (Revelation 1:5)

let us hold firmly to the faith we profess. (Hebrews 4:14)

a great high priest who has ascended into heaven, Jesus the Son of God (Hebrews 4:14)

Jesus, the pioneer and perfecter of faith. (Hebrews 12:2)

the faithful witness (Revelation 1:5)

After he had provided purification for sins, he sat down at the right hand of the Majesty in heaven. (Hebrews 1:3)

Rose of Sharon (Song of Songs 2:1)

That which was from the beginning, which we have heard, which we have seen with our eyes, which we have looked at and our hands have touched—this we proclaim concerning the Word of life. (1 John 1:1)

Him who is, and who was, and who is to come. (Revelation 1:4)

Let them know that you, whose name is the LORD—that you alone are the Most High over all the earth. (Psalm 83:18)

a high priest in the order of Melchizedek. (Hebrews 6:19-20)

Jesus, who went before us, has entered on our behalf. He has become a high priest... the inner sanctuary behind the curtain, which we have as an anchor for the soul, firm and secure. It enters (Hebrews 6:19-20)

And we have seen and testify that the Father has sent his Son to be the Savior of the world. (1 John 4:14)

The Son of Man came eating and drinking, and they say, 'Here is a glutton and a drunkard, a friend of tax collectors and sinners.' (Matthew 11:19)

God over all the whole earth. On that day there will be one LORD, and his name the only name. (Zechariah 14:9)

The LORD will be King over the whole earth. (Zechariah 14:9)

The virgin will conceive and give birth to a son, and will call him Immanuel. (Isaiah 7:14)

Chosen of God (1 Peter 2:4)

a righteous Branch, a King who will reign wisely and do what is just and right in the land. (Jeremiah 23:5)

Thanks be to God for his indescribable gift! (2 Corinthians 9:15)

See, I lay in Zion a stone, a tested stone, a precious cornerstone for a sure foundation. (Isaiah 28:16)

the Bridegroom (Matthew 9:15)

From everlasting to everlasting you are God. (Psalm 90:2)

Desire of all nations (Haggai 2:7)

The LORD is enthroned as King forever. (Psalm 29:10)

Our Lord Jesus, that great Shepherd of the sheep (Hebrews 13:20)

I am the true vine, and my Father is the gardener. (John 15:1)

the Shepherd and Overseer of your souls (1 Peter 2:25)

We have an advocate with the Father—Jesus Christ, the Righteous One. (1 John 2:1)

I am the Root and the Offspring of David, and the bright Morning Star. (Revelation 22:16)

As for God, his way is perfect. (Psalm 18:30)

Chief Shepherd (1 Peter 5:4)

Sceptre (Numbers 24:17)

Heir of all things (Hebrews 1:2)

Judge (Acts 10:42)

Yahweh

Interact 9.3

Picture a Person

Imagine a human being. Choose a characteristic for each of the categories in the list.

Age

Male or female

Height

Weight

Skin color

Hair color

Hair length

Glasses?

Other facial features

Clothes

Shoes

Income

Car model

Education level

Personality

Talents

Health issues

Moral standards

Religion

Hobbies

Habits

Marital status

Occupation

Family members

Friends

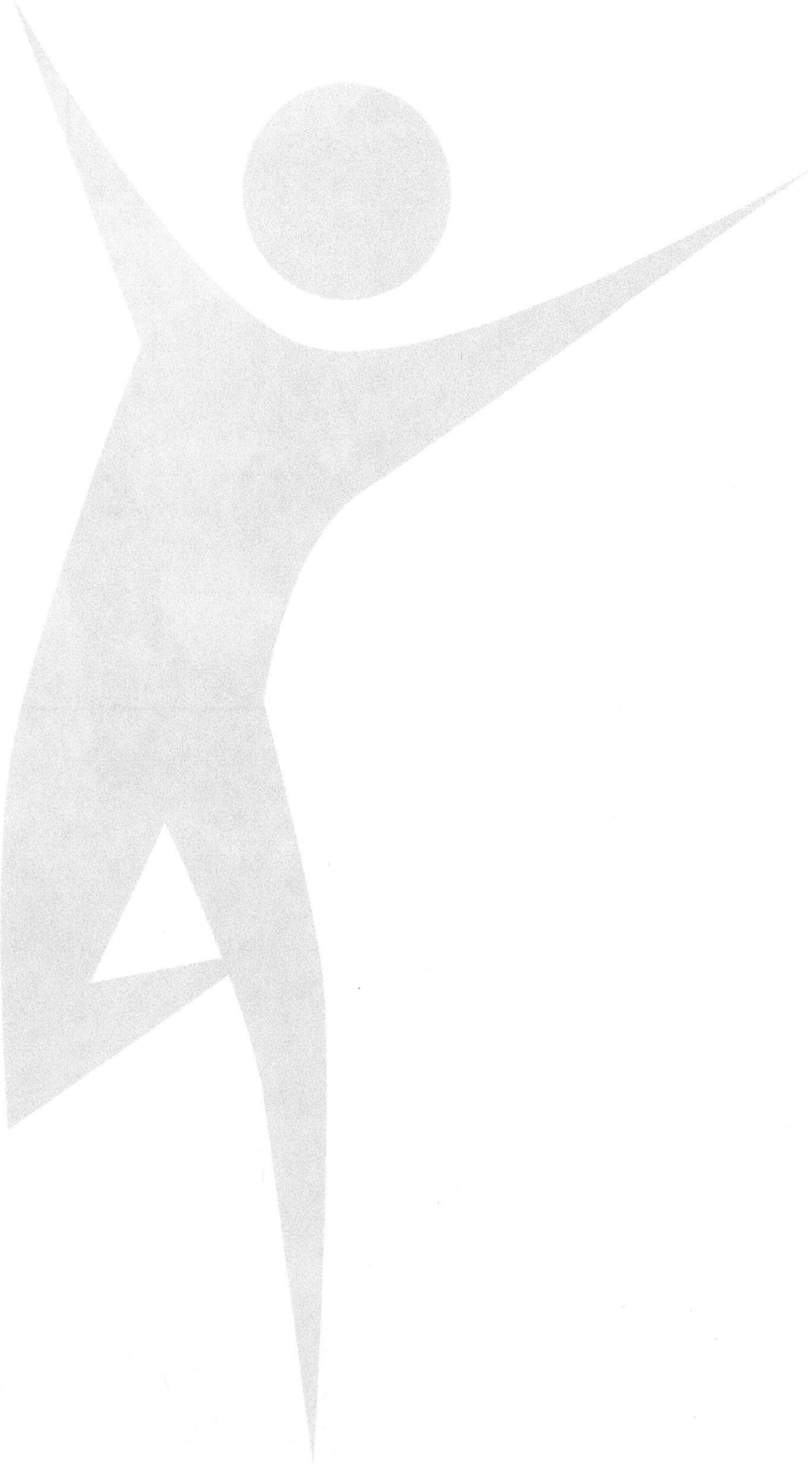

Yahweh

Power and might are in your hand. (2 Chronicles 20:6)

The Lord is gracious and compassionate, slow to anger and rich in love. (2 Chronicles...)

Holy, holy, holy is the Lord God Almighty, who was, and is, and is to come. (Revelation 4:8)

God is love. (1 John 4:16)

I am the first and the last. (Isaiah 44:6)

Just and true are your ways. (Revelation 15:3)

The Lord reigns (Psalm 93:1)

My ways are higher than your ways and my thoughts than your thoughts. (Isaiah 55:9)

He does not treat us as our sins deserve. (Psalm 103:10)

Christ of God (Luke 9:20)

Where can I flee from your presence? (Psalm 139:7)

I the Lord do not change (Malachi 3:6)

Ever-present—

Great is your faithfulness. (Lamentations 3:23)

Oh, the depth of the riches of the wisdom and knowledge of God! How unsearchable his judgments, and his paths beyond tracing out! (Romans 11:33)

Lord of the Sabbath (Mark 2:28)

I am with you always (Matthew 28:20)

Righteousness and justice are the foundation of your throne; love and faithfulness go before you. (Psalm 89:14)

I am the Alpha and the Omega, the First and the Last, the Beginning and the End. (Revelation 22:13)

Nothing in all creation is hidden from God's sight. (Hebrews 4:13)

Give thanks to the Lord, for he is good; his love endures forever. (Psalm 118:1)

You alone are holy (Revelation 15:4)

I AM (John 8:58)

The Lord is gracious and righteous; our God is full of compassion. (Psalm 116:5)

I am the way and the truth and the life. No one comes to the Father except through me. (John 14:6)

Holy, holy, holy is the Lord Almighty. (Isaiah 6:3)

Taste and see that the Lord is good (Psalm 34:8)

He is the true God. (1 John 5:20)

The Lord works righteousness and justice for all the oppressed. (Psalm 103:6)

In the beginning was the Word, and the Word was with God, and the Word was God. (John 1:1)

The Lord is good and his love endures forever. (Psalm 100:5)

Your righteousness is everlasting. (Psalm 119:142)

To God belong wisdom and power. (Job 12:13)

For to us a child is born, to us a son is given, and the government will be on his shoulders. And he will be called Wonderful Counselor, Mighty God, Everlasting Father, Prince of Peace. (Isaiah 9:6)

Jesus, the pioneer and perfecter of faith. (Hebrews 12:2)

the Lamb of God (John 1:29)

Christ died and returned to life so that he might be the Lord of both the dead and the living. (Romans 14:9)

Therefore, since we have a great high priest who has ascended into heaven, Jesus the Son of God, let us hold firmly to the faith we profess. (Hebrews 4:14)

He is the atoning sacrifice for our sins. (1 John 2:2)

The Son is the radiance of God's glory and the exact representation of his being, sustaining all things by his powerful word. After he had provided purification for sins, he sat down at the right hand of the Majesty in heaven. (Hebrews 1:3)

Rose of Sharon (Song of Songs 2:1)

(Him) who is, and who was, and who is to come (Revelation 1:4)

I am the living bread that came down from heaven. (John 6:51)

Let them know that you, whose name is the LORD—that you alone are the Most High over all the earth. (Psalm 83:18)

God, the blessed and only Ruler, the King of kings and Lord of lords (1 Timothy 6:15)

We have this hope as an anchor for the soul, firm and secure. It enters the inner sanctuary behind the curtain, where our forerunner, Jesus, has entered on our behalf. He has become a high priest forever, in the order of Melchizedek. (Hebrews 6:19-20)

the Root and the Offspring of David, and the bright Morning Star. (Revelation 22:16)

the Father has sent his Son to be the Savior of the world. (1 John 4:14)

Desire of all nations (Haggai 2:7)

The Son of Man came eating and drinking, and they say, 'Here is a glutton and a drunkard, a friend of tax collectors and sinners.' (Matthew 11:19)

a stone in Zion, a tested stone, a precious cornerstone for a sure foundation. (Isaiah 28:16)

Branch, a King who will reign wisely and do what is just and right in the land. (Jeremiah 23:5)

The LORD will be king over the whole earth. On that day there will be one LORD, and his name the only name. (Zechariah 14:9)

Chosen of God (1 Peter 2:4)

Thanks be to God for his indescribable gift! (2 Corinthians 9:15)

That which was from the beginning, which we have heard, which we have seen with our eyes, which we have looked at and our hands have touched—this we proclaim concerning the Word of life. (1 John 1:1)

From everlasting to everlasting you are God. (Psalm 90:2)

The virgin will conceive and give birth to a son, and will call him Immanuel. (Isaiah 7:14)

(O)ur Lord Jesus, that great Shepherd of the sheep (Hebrews 13:20)

The Lord is enthroned as King forever (Psalm 29:10)

I am the true vine, and my Father is the gardener. (John 15:1)

(The) Shepherd and Overseer of your souls (1 Peter 2:25)

(W)e have an advocate with the Father—Jesus Christ, the Righteous One. (1 John 2:1)

Root (Isaiah 11:10)

As for God, his way is perfect. (Psalm 18:30)

Heir of all things (Hebrews 1:2)

Chief Shepherd (1 Peter 5:4)

Sceptre (Numbers 24:17)

Judge (Acts 10:42)

Yahweh

Interact 9.4
Describing God's Love

The Bible often presents the same truth (or similar truths) in a variety of ways. The following passages all have something to say about God's love. Read each passage; then answer the question for that passage.

1. Statement. John 3:16, Romans 5:7–8, 1 John 4:16, 19.

What facts about God's love do you find in these passages?

2. Parable. Luke 15:11–32.

Jesus told this story. Many people see the father as God and the sons as His people. What can this story teach us about God's love?

3. Prophecy. Hosea 11:1–11.

In this prophecy, God talks to His people. What does this prophecy tell us about God's love for His people?

4. Poetry. Psalm 103

In this poem, David sings about God's love for His people. What does this poem tell us about God's love? How does David want us to respond to God's love?

5. History. Exodus 16.

God can show His love in historical accounts, even if the word *love* isn't mentioned! How does this historical passage show God's love?

Let God Be GOD

Yahweh

Power and might are in your hand. (2 Chronicles 20:6)

The Lord is gracious and compassionate, slow to anger and rich in love. (Psalm 145:8)

Holy, holy, holy is the Lord God Almighty, who was, and is, and is to come. (Revelation 4:8)

God is love. (1 John 4:16)

I am the first and the last. (Isaiah 44:5)

Just and true are your ways. (Revelation 15:3)

The Lord reigns (Psalm 93:1)

My ways are higher than your ways and my thoughts than your thoughts. (Isaiah 55:9)

He does not treat us as our sins deserve. (Psalm 103:10)

Christ of God (Luke 9:20)

Ever-present... Where can I flee from your presence? (Psalm 139:7)

the Lord do not change. (Malachi 3:6)

Great is your faithfulness. (Lamentations 3:23)

Oh, the depth of the riches of the wisdom and knowledge of God! How unsearchable his judgments, and his paths beyond tracing out! (Romans)

love and faithfulness go before you. (Psalm 89:14)

Righteousness and justice are the foundation of your throne;

Lord of the sabbath (Mark 2:28)

I am with you always. (Matthew 28:20)

I am the Alpha and the Omega, the First and the Last, the Beginning and the End. (Revelation 22:13)

Nothing in all creation is hidden from God's sight. (Hebrews 4:13)

You alone are holy. (Revelation 15:4)

Give thanks to the Lord, for he is good; his love endures forever. (Psalm 118:1)

Holy, holy, holy is the Lord Almighty. (Isaiah 6:3)

He is the true God. (1 John 5:20)

The Lord is gracious and righteous; our God is full of compassion. (Psalm 116:5)

I am the way and the truth and the life. No one comes to the Father except through me. (John 14:6)

I AM (John 8:58)

Taste and see that the Lord is good. (Psalm 34:8)

The Lord works righteousness and justice for all the oppressed. (Psalm 103:6)

The Lord is good and his love endures forever. (Psalm 100:5)

Wonderful Counselor, Mighty God, Everlasting Father, Prince of Peace. (Isaiah 9:6)

In the beginning was the Word, and the Word was with God, and the Word was God. (John 1:1)

Your righteousness is everlasting (Psalm 119:142)

To God belong wisdom and power. (Job 12:13)

For to us a child is born, to us a son is given; and the government will be on his shoulders. And he will be called

Jesus, the pioneer and perfecter of faith. (Hebrews 12:2)

the Lord of both the dead and the living. (Romans 14:9)

He is the atoning sacrifice for our sins and not only for ours but also for the sins of the whole world. (1 John 2:2)

Lamb of God (John 1:29)

the Majesty in heaven. (Hebrews 1:3)

Christ died and returned to life so that he might be the Lord of both the dead and the living.

After he had provided purification for sins he sat down at the right hand of

Therefore, since we have a great high priest who has ascended into heaven, Jesus the Son of God, let us hold firmly to the faith we profess. (Hebrews 4:14)

God, the blessed and only Ruler, the King of kings and Lord of lords (1 Timothy 6:15)

(Him) who is and who was, and who is to come

whose name is the LORD—that you alone are the Most High over all the earth. (Psalm 83:18)

and from the seven spirits before his throne, and

the Father has sent his Son to be the Savior of the world. (1 John 4:14)

which we have seen with our eyes, which we have looked at and our hands have touched. (1 John 1:1)

the inner sanctuary behind the curtain, where our forerunner, Jesus, has entered on our behalf. He has become a high priest forever, in the order of Melchizedek. (Hebrews 6:19-20)

Jesus Christ, who is the faithful witness, the firstborn from the dead, and the ruler of the kings of the earth. (Revelation 1:5)

the Lord will be one LORD, and his name the only name. (Zechariah 14:9)

The Son of Man came eating and drinking, and they say 'Here is a glutton and a drunkard, a friend of tax collectors and sinners.' (Matthew 11:19)

Desire of all nations (Haggai 2:7)

Here is a stone in Zion, a tested stone, a precious cornerstone for a sure foundation (Isaiah 28:16)

a king who will reign wisely (Jeremiah 23:5)

And we have seen and testify that the Father has sent his Son

The Son is the radiance of God's glory and the exact representation of his being, sustaining all things by his powerful word.

We have this hope as an anchor for the soul, firm and secure. It enters the

Let them know that you, whose name is the LORD

Rose of Sharon (Song of Songs 2:1)

That which was from the beginning, which we have heard, which we have seen

the bridegroom (Matthew 9:15)

Chosen of God (1 Peter 2:4)

Thanks be to God for his indescribable gift! (2 Corinthians 9:15)

the virgin will conceive and give birth to a son, and will call him Immanuel. (Isaiah 7:14)

The LORD will be king over the whole earth. On that day there will be one LORD

God, the blessed and only Ruler

From everlasting to everlasting you are God. (Psalm 90:2)

The Lord is enthroned as King forever. (Psalm 29:10)

(O)ur Lord Jesus, that great Shepherd of the sheep (Hebrews 13:20)

I am the true vine, and my Father is the gardener (John 15:1)

The Shepherd and Overseer of your souls. (1 Peter 2:25)

(W)e have an advocate with the Father—Jesus Christ, the Righteous One. (1 John 2:1)

the Root and the Offspring of David, and the bright Morning Star. (Revelation 22:16)

As for God, his way is perfect. (Psalm 18:30)

Heir of all things (Hebrews 1:2)

I am the Chief Shepherd (1 Peter 5:4)

Sceptre (Numbers 24:17)

Judge (Acts 10:42)

Yahweh

10

GOD **Is Omniscient and Omnipresent**

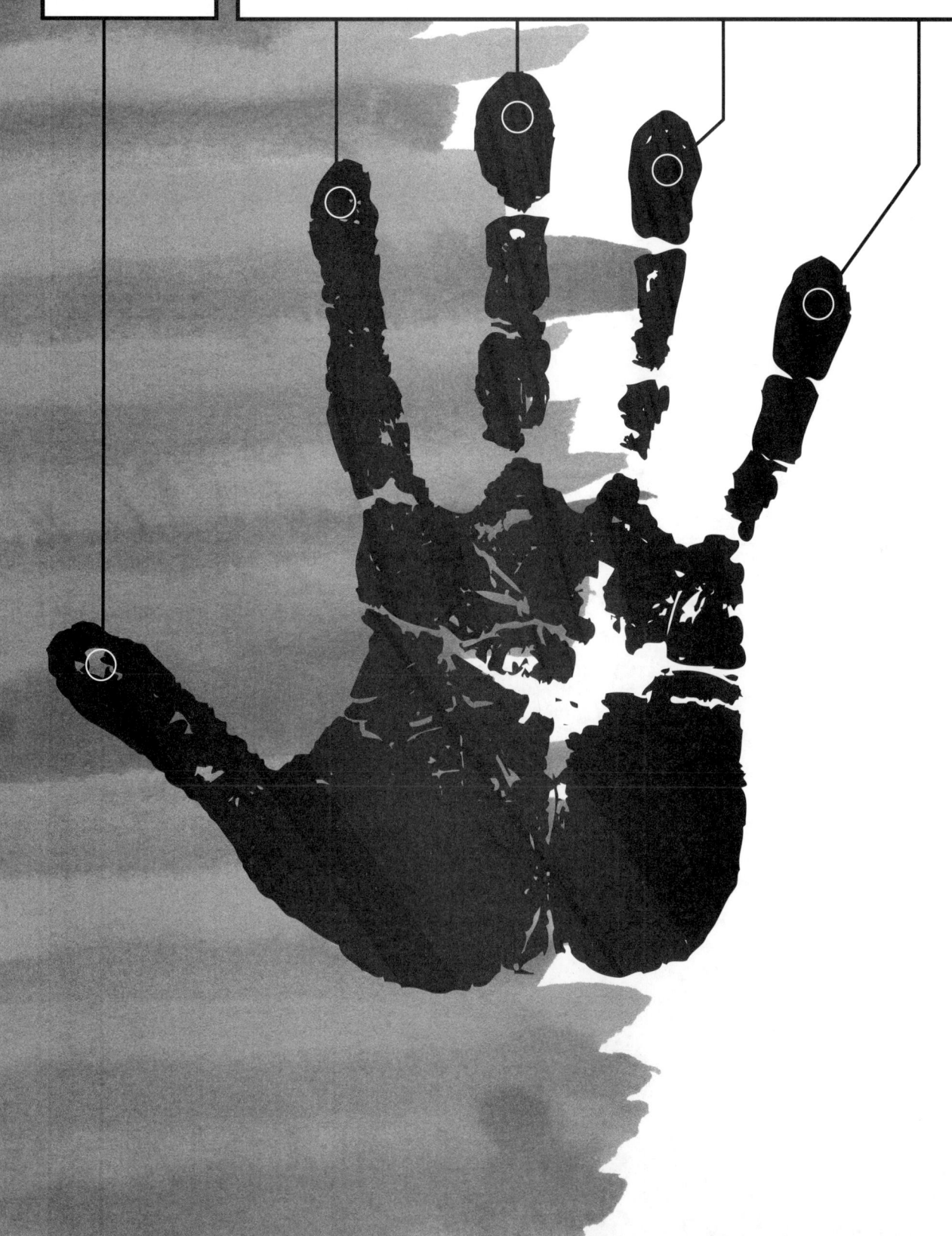

Interact 10.1
God Is Omniscient

Look up the Scripture verses and passages listed, and answer the questions. Feel free to write down any thoughts or questions you have as you work through this Interact.

1. Read Psalm 19:12–14, 1 Timothy 6:10–16, and Hebrews 4:12–13. What are some implications of God's knowing all our thoughts, motives, and intentions?

2. Read Genesis 3:9–13 in its context. Why did God ask Adam and Eve four questions in the garden? Didn't He know the answers?

3. What about the time when God sent angels to see about the situation in Sodom and Gomorrah? Didn't He know? (See Genesis 18:20–21.) Remember, God is communicating with humans.

4. Omniscience refers to knowledge. Brainstorm slogans, commercials, or other advertisements that use words such as *knowledge*, *brains*, or *school* to make a point. For example:

> The more you know, the more you'll grow.
> Be smart; stay in school.
> Don't waste a good brain.

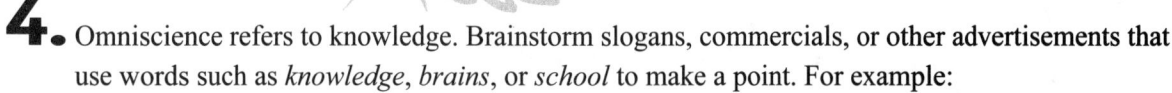

Let God Be GOD

Yahweh

Power and might are in your hand (2 Chronicles 20:6)

The Lord is gracious and compassionate, slow to anger and rich in love. (Psalm 145:8)

Holy, holy, holy is the Lord God Almighty, who was, and is, and is to come. (Revelation 4:8)

God is love. (1 John 4:16)

I am the first and the last. (Isaiah 44:6)

Just and true are your ways. (Revelation 15:3)

The Lord reigns (Psalm 93:1)

My ways are higher than your ways and my thoughts than your thoughts. (Isaiah 55:9)

He does not treat us as our sins deserve. (Psalm 103:10)

Christ of God (Luke 9:20)

Ever-present—Where can I flee from your presence? (Psalm 139:7)

Great is your faithfulness. (Lamentations 3:23)

Oh, the depth of the riches of the wisdom and knowledge of God! How unsearchable his judgments, and his paths beyond tracing out! (Romans 11:33)

Lord of the sabbath (Mark 2:28)

Righteousness and justice are the foundation of your throne; love and faithfulness go before you. (Psalm 89:14)

He is the true God. (1 John 5:20)

I am the Alpha and the Omega, the First and the Last, the Beginning and the End. (Revelation 22:13)

Nothing in all creation is hidden from God's sight. (Hebrews 4:13)

The Lord is gracious and righteous; our God is full of compassion. (Psalm 116:5)

Give thanks to the Lord, for he is good; his love endures forever. (Psalm 118:1)

You alone are holy. (Revelation 15:4)

I AM (John 8:58)

I am the way and the truth and the life. (John 14:6)

Holy, holy, holy is the Lord Almighty. (Isaiah 6:3)

No one comes to the Father except through me. (John 14:6)

In the beginning was the Word, and the Word was with God, and the Word was God. (John 1:1)

The Lord is good and his love endures forever. (Psalm 100:5)

Taste and see that the Lord is good. (Psalm 34:8)

He is the Lord of both the dead and the living. (Romans 14:9)

Jesus the Son of God, let us hold firmly to the faith we profess. (Hebrews 4:14)

To us a child is born, to us a son is given, and the government will be on his shoulders: And he will be called Wonderful Counselor, Mighty God, Everlasting Father, Prince of Peace. (Isaiah 9:6)

To God belong wisdom and power. (Job 12:13)

Your righteousness is everlasting. (Psalm 119:142)

The Lord works righteousness and justice for all the oppressed. (Psalm 103:6)

Jesus, the pioneer and perfecter of faith. (Hebrews 12:2)

He is the atoning sacrifice for our sins, and not only for ours but also for the sins of the whole world. (1 John 2:2)

The Lamb of God (John 1:29)

the bright Morning Star (Revelation 22:16)

After he had provided purification for sins, he sat down at the right hand of the Majesty in heaven. (Hebrews 1:3)

Christ died and returned to life so that he might be the Lord of both the dead and the living. (Romans 14:9)

The Son is the radiance of God's glory (Hebrews 1:3)

Rose of Sharon (Song of Songs 2:1)

That which was from the beginning, which we have heard, which we have seen with our eyes, which we have looked at and our hands have touched—this we proclaim concerning the Word of life. (1 John 1:1)

God, the blessed and only Ruler, the King of kings and Lord of lords (1 Timothy 6:15)

We have this hope as an anchor for the soul, firm and secure. It enters the inner sanctuary behind the curtain, where our forerunner, Jesus, has entered on our behalf. He has become a high priest forever, in the order of Melchizedek. (Hebrews 6:19-20)

the only name. (Acts 4:12)

the Most High (Luke 1:32)

And we have seen and testify that the Father has sent his Son to be the Savior of the world. (1 John 4:14)

Here is a glutton and a drunkard, a friend of tax collectors and sinners. (Matthew 11:19)

Desire of all nations (Haggai 2:7)

a stone in Zion, a tested stone, a precious cornerstone for a sure foundation. (Isaiah 28:16)

Branch, a King who will reign wisely and do what is just and right in the land. (Jeremiah 23:5)

Chosen of God (1 Peter 2:4)

Thanks be to God for his indescribable gift! (2 Corinthians 9:15)

The virgin will conceive and give birth to a son, and will call him Immanuel. (Isaiah 7:14)

The LORD will be king over the whole earth. (Zechariah 14:9)

from everlasting to everlasting you are God. (Psalm 90:2)

The Lord is enthroned as King forever. (Psalm 29:10)

(O)ur Lord Jesus, that great Shepherd of the sheep (Hebrews 13:20)

I am the true vine, and my Father is the gardener. (John 15:1)

(T)he Shepherd and Overseer of your souls (1 Peter 2:25)

(W)e have an advocate with the Father—Jesus Christ, the Righteous One. (1 John 2:1)

I am the Root and the Offspring of David, and the bright Morning Star. (Revelation 22:16)

As for God, his way is perfect. (Psalm 18:30)

Chief Shepherd (1 Peter 5:4)

Sceptre (Numbers 24:17)

Heir of all things (Hebrews 1:2)

Judge (Acts 10:42)

Yahweh

Interact 10.2
God Is Omnipresent

Answer the questions below. Add your own thoughts, insights, and examples.

1. List some of the ways in which we humans are limited by time and space.

2. What are some books, television shows, and movies that emphasize humanity's search for ways around time and space boundaries?

3. Why do people want to go beyond time and space limitations?

4. Read Psalm 139:1–12, Amos 9:2–4, Matthew 28:20, and Hebrews 13:5–6. List positive and negative aspects of God's omnipresence for humans.

Positive   Negative

Yahweh

Power and might are in your hand. (2 Chronicles 20:6)

The Lord is gracious and compassionate, slow to anger and rich in love. (Psalm 145:8)

Holy, holy, holy is the Lord God Almighty, who was, and is, and is to come. (Revelation 4:8)

God is love. (1 John 4:16)

I am the first and the last. (Isaiah 44:6)

Just and true are your ways. (Revelation 15:3)

The Lord reigns (Psalm 93:1)

My ways are higher than your ways and my thoughts than your thoughts. (Isaiah 55:9)

He does not treat us as our sins deserve. (Psalm 103:10)

the Lord do not change. (Malachi 3:6)

Christ of God (Luke 9:20)

Ever-present—Where can I flee from your presence? (Psalm 139:7)

Great is your faithfulness. (Lamentations 3:23)

Oh, the depth of the riches of the wisdom and knowledge of God! How unsearchable his judgments, and his paths beyond tracing out! (Romans 11:33)

Lord of the sabbath (Mark 2:28)

Righteousness and justice are the foundation of your throne; love and faithfulness go before you. (Psalm 89:14)

He is the true God. (1 John 5:20)

I am the Alpha and the Omega, the First and the Last, the Beginning and the End. (Revelation 22:13)

Nothing in all creation is hidden from God's sight. (Hebrews 4:13)

Give thanks to the Lord, for he is good; his love endures forever. (Psalm 118:1)

I AM (John 8:58)

I am with you always. (Matthew 28:20)

The Lord is gracious and righteous; our God is full of compassion. (Psalm 116:5)

I am the way and the truth and the life. (John 14:6)

Holy, holy, holy is the Lord Almighty. (Isaiah 6:3)

No one comes to the Father except through me. (John 14:6)

The Lord is good and his love endures forever. (Psalm 100:5)

Taste and see that the Lord is good. (Psalm 34:8)

The Lord works righteousness and justice for all the oppressed. (Psalm 103:6)

Your righteousness is everlasting. (Psalm 119:142)

To God belong wisdom and power. (Job 12:13)

In the beginning was the Word, and the Word was with God, and the Word was God. (John 1:1)

Wonderful Counselor, Mighty God, Everlasting Father, Prince of Peace. (Isaiah 9:6)

Jesus the pioneer and perfecter of faith. (Hebrews 12:2)

For to us a child is born, to us a son is given, and the government will be on his shoulders. And he will be called (Isaiah 9:6)

let us hold firmly to the faith we profess. (Hebrews 4:14)

He is the atoning sacrifice for our sins, and not only for ours but also for the sins of the whole world. (1 John 2:2)

Christ died and returned to life so that he might be the Lord of both the dead and the living. (Romans 14:9)

the Lamb of God (John 1:29)

Jesus, the Majesty in heaven. (Hebrews 1:3)

the firstborn from the dead and the ruler of the kings of the earth. (Revelation 1:5)

King of kings and Lord of lords (1 Timothy 6:15)

After he had provided purification for sins, he sat down at the right hand of the Majesty in heaven. (Hebrews 1:3)

He has become a high priest forever, in the order of Melchizedek. (Hebrews 6:19-20)

God, the blessed and only Ruler, the King of kings and Lord of lords (1 Timothy 6:15)

who has ascended into heaven.

The Son is the radiance of God's glory and the exact representation of his being, sustaining all things by his powerful word. (Hebrews 1:3)

Jesus Christ, who is the faithful witness, the firstborn from the dead. (Revelation 1:5)

name is the LORD—that you alone are the Most High over all the earth. (Psalm 83:18)

it enters the inner sanctuary behind the curtain, where our forerunner, Jesus, has entered on our behalf. (Hebrews 6:19-20)

Here is a glutton and a drunkard, a friend of tax collectors and sinners. (Matthew 11:19)

And we have seen and testify that the Father has sent his Son to be the Savior of the world. (1 John 4:14)

Therefore, since we have a great high priest who has ascended into heaven, Jesus the Son of God, let us hold firmly to the faith we profess.

Rose of Sharon (Song of Songs 2:1)

(H)im who is and who was, and who is to come.

Let them know that you, whose name is the LORD

we have this hope as an anchor for the soul, firm and secure.

(H)e will be one LORD, and his name the only name. (Zechariah 14:9)

The Son of Man (Matthew 9:6)

Bridegroom (Matthew 9:15)

Desire of all nations (Haggai 2:7)

a Branch, a King who will reign wisely and do what is just and right in the land. (Jeremiah 23:5)

a stone in Zion, a tested stone, a precious cornerstone for a sure foundation. (Isaiah 28:16)

Chosen of God (1 Peter 2:4)

thanks be to God for his indescribable gift! (2 Corinthians 9:15)

That which was from the beginning, which we have heard, which we have seen with our eyes, which we have looked at and our hands have touched—this we proclaim concerning the Word of life. (1 John 1:1)

From everlasting to everlasting you are God. (Psalm 90:2)

The LORD will be king over the whole earth. On that day there will be one LORD

The virgin will conceive and give birth to a son, and will call him Immanuel. (Isaiah 7:14)

(O)ur Lord Jesus, that great Shepherd of the sheep (Hebrews 13:20)

The Lord is enthroned as King forever. (Psalm 29:10)

I am the true vine, and my Father is the gardener. (John 15:1)

(T)he Shepherd and Overseer of your souls (1 Peter 2:25)

(W)e have an advocate with the Father—Jesus Christ, the Righteous One. (1 John 2:1)

I am the Root and the Offspring of David, and the bright Morning Star. (Revelation 22:16)

As for God, his way is perfect. (Psalm 18:30)

I am the Chief Shepherd (1 Peter 5:4)

Sceptre (Numbers 24:17)

Heir of all things (Hebrews 1:2)

Judge (Acts 10:42)

Yahweh

Interact 10.3
The "Gods" of My Life

Complete the following activities to find out about your personal "gods."

1. Rank your expenditures of time, energy, and money for each item listed. Rank them from 0 (lowest) to 10 (highest).

Item	Time	Energy	Money
Technology and media (television, radio, video games, Internet, music, texting, etc.)			
School, homework, reading, studying			
Stuff—crafts, collections, other possessions			
Sports, exercise, hobbies			
Friends			
My looks (clothes, hair, etc.)			
Making money			
Personal time and space, thinking and dreaming			
Family relationships			
Relationship with God (prayer, Bible reading/study, devotions, church activities, etc.)			

2. This evaluation reveals the following about me:

3. I plan to make these changes:

Let God Be GOD

Yahweh

Power and might are in your hand (2 Chronicles 20:6)

The Lord is gracious and compassionate, slow to anger and rich in love. (Psalm 145:8)

Holy, holy, holy is the Lord God Almighty, who was, and is, and is to come. (Revelation 4:8)

I am the first and the last. (Isaiah 44:6)

Just and true are your ways. (Revelation 15:3)

God is love. (1 John 4:16)

The Lord reigns (Psalm 93:1)

My ways are higher than your ways and my thoughts than your thoughts. (Isaiah 55:9)

Where can I flee from your presence? (Psalm 139:7)

He does not treat us as our sins deserve. (Psalm 103:10)

The Lord do not change. (Malachi 3:6)

Christ of God (Luke 9:20)

Ever-present—

Great is your faithfulness. (Lamentations 3:23)

...the riches of the wisdom and knowledge of God! How unsearchable his judgments, and his paths beyond tracing out! (Romans 11:33)

Lord of the sabbath (Mark 2:28)

Oh, the depth of the riches of the wisdom and knowledge of God!

Righteousness and justice are the foundation of your throne; love and faithfulness go before you. (Psalm 89:14)

the First and the Last, the Beginning and the End. (Revelation 22:13)

Nothing in all creation is hidden from God's sight. (Hebrews 4:13)

Give thanks to the Lord, for he is good; his love endures forever. (Psalm 118:1)

You alone are holy. (Revelation 15:4)

I am with you always. (Matthew 28:20)

I am the Alpha and the Omega

I am the way and the truth and the life. No one comes to the Father except through me. (John 14:6)

Holy, holy, holy is the Lord Almighty. (Isaiah 6:3)

In the beginning was the Word, and the Word was with God, and the Word was God. (John 1:1)

The Lord is good and his love endures forever. (Psalm 100:5)

Taste and see that the Lord is good (Psalm 34:8)

Wonderful Counselor, Mighty God, Everlasting Father, Prince of Peace. (Isaiah 9:6)

I AM (John 8:58)

He is the true God. (1 John 5:20)

The Lord is gracious and righteous; our God is full of compassion. (Psalm 116:5)

To God belong wisdom and power. (Job 12:13)

The Lord works righteousness and justice for all the oppressed. (Psalm 103:6)

Your righteousness is everlasting. (Psalm 119:142)

I am the living bread that came down from heaven. (John 6:51)

For to us a child is born, to us a son is given, and the government will be on his shoulders. And he will be called Wonderful Counselor, Mighty God, Everlasting Father, Prince of Peace. (Isaiah 9:6)

the Lord of both the dead and the living. (Romans 14:9)

the Lord who has ascended into heaven, Jesus the Son of God, let us hold firmly to the faith we profess. (Hebrews 4:14)

He is the atoning sacrifice for our sins (1 John 4:10)

God, the blessed and only Ruler, the King of kings and Lord of lords (1 Timothy 6:15)

He is the Lord—that you alone are the Most High over all the earth. (Psalm 83:18)

and he might be the Lord of both the dead and the living.

the Son is the radiance of God's glory and the exact representation of his being, sustaining all things by his powerful word. After he had provided purification for sins, he sat down at the right hand of the Majesty in heaven. (Hebrews 1:3)

Christ died and returned to life so that he might be the Lord of both the dead and the living. (Romans 14:9)

Therefore, since we have a great high priest who has ascended into heaven, Jesus the Son of God, let us hold firmly to the faith we profess. (Hebrews 4:14)

The Son is the radiance of God's glory (Hebrews 1:3)

Rose of Sharon (Song of Songs 2:1)

That which was from the beginning, which we have heard, which we have seen with our eyes, which we have looked at and our hands have touched—this we proclaim concerning the Word of life. (1 John 1:1)

Let them know that you, whose name is the LORD—that you alone are the Most High over all the earth. (Psalm 83:18)

The LORD will be king over the whole earth. On that day there will be one LORD, and his name the only name. (Zechariah 14:9)

from everlasting to everlasting you are God. (Psalm 90:2)

The virgin will conceive and give birth to a son, and will call him Immanuel. (Isaiah 7:14)

(O)ur Lord Jesus, that great Shepherd of the sheep (Hebrews 13:20)

I am the true vine, and my Father is the gardener. (John 15:1)

(T)he Shepherd and Overseer of your souls (1 Peter 2:25)

(W)e have an advocate with the Father—Jesus Christ, the Righteous One. (1 John 2:1)

the Root and the Offspring of David, and the bright Morning Star. (Revelation 22:16)

As for God, his way is perfect. (Psalm 18:30)

Chief Shepherd (1 Peter 5:4)

Heir of all things (Hebrews 1:2)

Judge (Acts 10:42)

Sceptre

Yahweh

the Lamb of God (John 1:29)

Jesus, the pioneer and perfecter of faith. (Hebrews 12:2)

the bright Morning Star (Revelation 22:16)

the Majesty in heaven (Hebrews 1:3)

Chosen of God (1 Peter 2:4)

...thanks be to God for his indescribable gift! (2 Corinthians 9:15)

the Lord is good and his love endures forever. (Psalm 34:8)

Son of Man (Matthew 9:6)

Bridegroom (Matthew 9:15)

the firstborn from the dead, and the ruler of the kings of the earth. (Revelation 1:5)

the Lamb of God (John 1:29)

the King of kings and Lord of lords (1 Timothy 6:15)

Desire of all nations (Haggai 2:7)

"Here is a glutton and a drunkard, a friend of tax collectors and sinners." (Matthew 11:19)

And we have seen and testify that the Father has sent his Son to be the Savior of the world. (1 John 4:14)

I lay a stone in Zion, a tested stone, a precious cornerstone for a sure foundation. (Isaiah 28:16)

The LORD is enthroned as King forever. (Psalm 29:10)

a King who will reign wisely (Jeremiah 23:5)

Branch (Jeremiah 23:5)

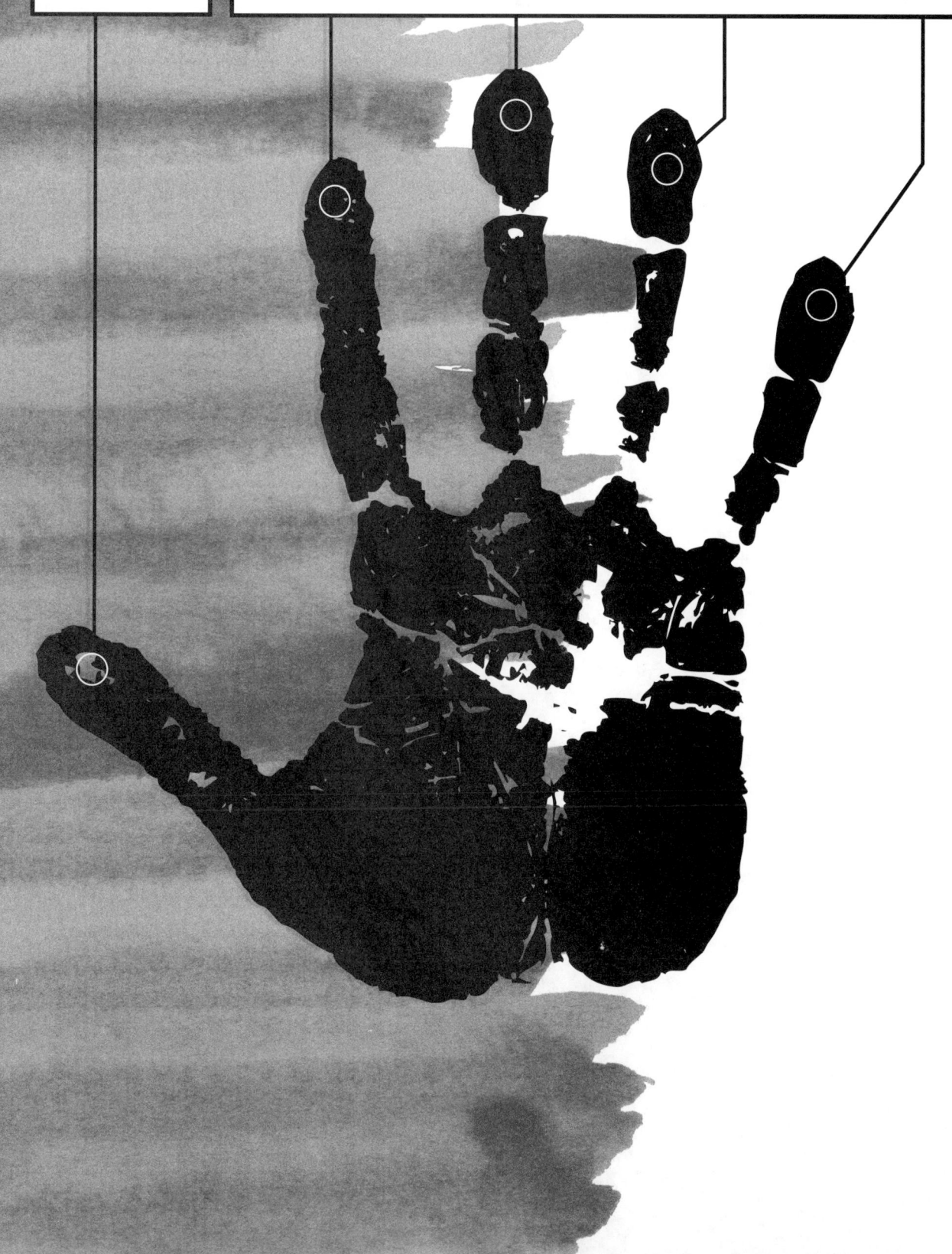

11

GOD Is Omnipotent

Interact 11.1
God Is Omnipotent

Look up each Bible passage and summarize what it says about God's power.

Job 26:7–14

Psalm 29:3–9

Psalm 68:32–35

Psalm 89:8–13

Jeremiah 10:12–13

Daniel 4:34–35

Habakkuk 3:3–6

Let God Be GOD

Yahweh

Power and might are in your hand. (2 Chronicles 20:6)

The Lord is gracious and compassionate, slow to anger and rich in love. (Psalm 145:8)

Holy, holy, holy is the Lord God Almighty, who was, and is, and is to come. (Revelation 4:8)

God is love. (1 John 4:16)

I am the first and the last. (Isaiah 44:6)

Just and true are your ways. (Revelation 15:3)

The Lord reigns (Psalm 93:1)

My ways are higher than your ways and my thoughts than your thoughts. (Isaiah 55:9)

Christ of God (Luke 9:20)

Where can I flee from your presence? (Psalm 139:7)

He does not treat us as our sins deserve (Psalm 103:10)

(I the Lord do not change (Malachi 3:6)

Ever-present—

Great is your faithfulness. (Lamentations 3:23)

Oh, the depth of the riches of the wisdom and knowledge of God! How unsearchable his judgments, and his paths beyond tracing out! (Romans 11:33)

Lord of the sabbath (Mark 2:28)

I am with you always. (Matthew 28:20)

Righteousness and justice are the foundation of your throne; love and faithfulness go before you. (Psalm 89:14)

He is the true God. (1 John 5:20)

I am the Alpha and the Omega, the First and the Last, the Beginning and the End. (Revelation 22:13)

You alone are holy. (Revelation 15:4)

Nothing in all creation is hidden from God's sight. (Hebrews 4:13)

Give thanks to the Lord, for he is good; his love endures forever. (Psalm 118:1)

I AM (John 8:58)

The Lord is gracious and righteous; our God is full of compassion. (Psalm 116:5)

Holy, holy, holy is the Lord Almighty. (Isaiah 6:3)

No one comes to the Father except through me. (John 14:6)

I am the living bread that came down from heaven. (John 6:51)

The Lord works righteousness and justice for all the oppressed. (Psalm 103:6)

I am the way and the truth and the life. (John 14:6)

Taste and see that the Lord is good (Psalm 34:8)

To God belong wisdom and power. (Job 12:13)

In the beginning was the Word, and the Word was with God, and the Word was God. (John 1:1)

The Lord is good and his love endures forever. (Psalm 100:5)

Your righteousness is everlasting. (Psalm 119:142)

Wonderful Counselor, Mighty God, Everlasting Father, Prince of Peace. (Isaiah 9:6)

Jesus the pioneer and perfecter of faith (Hebrews 12:2)

For to us a child is born, to us a son is given, and the government will be on his shoulders. And he will be called Wonderful Counselor, Mighty God, Everlasting Father, Prince of Peace. (Isaiah 9:6)

Christ died and returned to life so that he might be the Lord of both the dead and the living. (Romans 14:9)

He is the atoning sacrifice for our sins, and not only for ours but also for the sins of the whole world. (1 John 2:2)

After he had provided purification for sins, he sat down at the right hand of the Majesty in heaven. (Hebrews 1:3)

God, the blessed and only Ruler, the King of kings and Lord of lords (1 Timothy 6:15)

the Son of God

Jesus Christ, who is the faithful witness, the firstborn from the dead, and the ruler of the kings of the earth. (Revelation 1:5)

the Lamb of God (John 1:29)

Therefore, since we have a great high priest who has ascended into heaven, Jesus the Son of God, let us hold firmly to the faith we profess. (Hebrews 4:14)

The Son is the radiance of God's glory and the exact representation of his being, sustaining all things by his powerful word. (Hebrews 1:3)

whose name is the LORD—that you alone are the Most High over all the earth. (Psalm 83:18)

Here is a glutton and a drunkard, a friend of tax collectors and sinners. (Matthew 11:19)

the Father has sent his Son to be the Savior of the world. (1 John 4:14)

And we have seen and testify

Rose of Sharon (Song of Songs 2:1)

(Him) who is and who was, and who is to come

Let them know that you, whose name is the LORD

We have this hope as an anchor for the soul, firm and secure. It enters the inner sanctuary behind the curtain, where our forerunner, Jesus, has entered on our behalf. He has become a high priest forever, in the order of Melchizedek. (Hebrews 6:19-20)

which we have looked at and our hands have touched

The Son of Man came eating and drinking, and they say (Matthew 11:19)

Bridegroom (Matthew 9:15)

Chosen of God (1 Peter 2:4)

Desire of all nations (Haggai 2:7)

(I lay) a stone in Zion, a tested stone, a precious cornerstone for a sure foundation in the land. (Isaiah 28:16)

Branch, a King who will reign

Son of David, a righteous (Branch)

Thanks be to God for his indescribable gift! (2 Corinthians 9:15)

That which was from the beginning, which we have heard (1 John 1:1)

The LORD will be king over the whole earth. On that day there will be one LORD, and his name the only name. (Zechariah 14:9)

God, the blessed and only Ruler

From everlasting to everlasting you are God. (Psalm 90:2)

The virgin will conceive and give birth to a son, and will call him Immanuel. (Isaiah 7:14)

The Lord is enthroned as King forever. (Psalm 29:10)

(O)ur Lord Jesus, that great Shepherd of the sheep (Hebrews 13:20)

I am the true vine, and my Father is the gardener. (John 15:1)

(The) Shepherd and Overseer of your souls (1 Peter 2:25)

the Righteous One. (1 John 2:1)

(We) have an advocate with the Father—Jesus Christ, the Righteous One. (1 John 2:1)

the Root and the Offspring of David, and the bright Morning Star. (Revelation 22:16)

As for God, his way is perfect. (Psalm 18:30)

Heir of all things (Hebrews 1:2)

Chief Shepherd (1 Peter 5:4)

Sceptre (Numbers 24:17)

Judge (Acts 10:42)

Yahweh

Interact 11.2
God's Creative Power

Look up the Bible passages and answer the questions. Feel free to write your own thoughts as you meditate on what you discover.

1. Read Psalm 96:4–6. What comparisons does the psalmist make between God and false gods?

2. Read Isaiah 40:12–17, 21–26. What does the natural world reveal about God? How does God compare with other sources of power?

3. Read Acts 17:24–28. How does God expect us to respond to His creative power?

4. Read 1 Corinthians 8:4–8. What are some false gods we encounter today? How should we respond to the attractions of false gods?

Yahweh

Power and might are in your hand. (2 Chronicles 20:6)

The Lord is gracious and compassionate, slow to anger and rich in love. (Psalm 145:8)

Holy, holy, holy is the Lord God Almighty, who was, and is, and is to come. (Revelation 4:8)

God is love. (1 John 4:16)

I am the first and the last. (Isaiah 44:6)

Just and true are your ways. (Revelation 15:3)

The Lord reigns (Psalm 93:1)

My ways are higher than your ways and my thoughts than your thoughts. (Isaiah 55:9)

Christ of God (Luke 9:20)

Where can I flee from your presence? (Psalm 139:7)

He does not treat us as our sins deserve. (Psalm 103:10)

I the Lord do not change (Malachi 3:6)

Ever-present.

Great is your faithfulness. (Lamentations 3:23)

of God! How unsearchable his judgments, and his paths beyond tracing out! (Romans 11:33)

Righteousness and justice are the foundation of your throne; love and faithfulness go before you. (Psalm 89:14)

Lord of the Sabbath (Mark 2:28)

Oh, the depth of the riches of the wisdom and knowledge

I am with you always. (Matthew 28:20)

I am the Alpha and the Omega, the First and the Last, the Beginning and the End. (Revelation 22:13)

is hidden from God's sight. (Hebrews 4:13)

You alone are holy. (Revelation 15:4)

He is the true God. (1 John 5:20)

The Lord is full of compassion. (Psalm 116:5)

Give thanks to the Lord, for he is good: his love endures forever. (Psalm 118:1)

Holy, holy, holy is the Lord Almighty. (Isaiah 6:3)

I AM (John 8:58)

Nothing in all creation

I am the way and the truth and the life. No one comes to the Father except through me. (John 14:6)

and the Word was God. (John 1:1)

Taste and see that the Lord is good. (Psalm 34:8)

The Lord is gracious and righteous; our God is full of compassion. (Psalm 116:5)

In the beginning was the Word, and the Word was with God,

The Lord is good and his love endures forever. (Psalm 100:5)

Wonderful Counselor, Mighty God, Everlasting Father, Prince of Peace. (Isaiah 9:6)

I am the living bread that came down from heaven. (John 6:51)

The Lord works righteousness and justice for all the oppressed. (Psalm 103:6)

To God belong wisdom and power. (Job 12:13)

Your righteousness is everlasting. (Psalm 119:142)

For to us a child is born, to us a son is given, and the government will be on his shoulders. And he will be called Wonderful Counselor,

Christ died and returned to life so that he might be the Lord of both the dead and the living. (Romans 14:9)

Jesus the Son of God, let us hold firmly to the faith we profess. (Hebrews 4:14)

He is the atoning sacrifice for our sins, and not only for ours but also for the sins of the whole world. (1 John 2:2)

the Lamb of God (John 1:29)

Jesus, the pioneer and perfecter of faith. (Hebrews 12:2)

After he had provided purification for sins, he sat down at the right hand of the Majesty in heaven. (Hebrews 1:3)

sustaining all things by his powerful word. (Hebrews 1:3)

the faithful witness, the firstborn from the dead, and the ruler of the kings of the earth. (Revelation 1:5)

a high priest forever, in the order of Melchizedek. (Hebrews 6:20)

God, the blessed and only Ruler, the King of kings and Lord of lords (1 Timothy 6:15)

is the LORD—that you alone are the Most High over all the earth. (Psalm 83:18)

The Son is the radiance of God's glory and the exact representation of his being, (Hebrews 1:3)

(him who is and who was and who is to come, (Revelation 1:4)

which we have seen with our eyes, which we have looked at and our hands have touched. (1 John 1:1)

and his name the only name. (Zechariah 14:9)

the Father has sent his Son to be the Savior of the world. (1 John 4:14)

And we have seen and testify that

the inner sanctuary behind the curtain, where our forerunner, Jesus, has entered on our behalf. He has become a high priest

We have this hope as an anchor for the soul, firm and secure. It enters

Therefore, since we have a great high priest who has ascended into heaven, Jesus the Son of God

"Here is a glutton and a drunkard, a friend of tax collectors and sinners." (Matthew 11:19)

the Son of Man came eating and drinking, and they say,

Desire of all nations (Haggai 2:7)

we proclaim concerning the Word of life. (1 John 1:1)

the messenger of the covenant, whom you desire, will come. (Malachi 3:1)

a righteous Branch, a King who will reign wisely and do what is just and right in the land. (Jeremiah 23:5)

Hail, a stone in Zion, a tested stone, a precious cornerstone for a sure foundation. (Isaiah 28:16)

I will raise up to David

Chosen of God (1 Peter 2:4)

Thanks be to God for his indescribable gift! (2 Corinthians 9:15)

That which was from the beginning, which we have heard,

God, the blessed and only Ruler

The LORD will be king over the whole earth. (Psalm 90:2)

From everlasting to everlasting you are God.

The virgin will conceive and give birth to a son, and will call him Immanuel. (Isaiah 7:14)

The Lord is enthroned as King forever. (Psalm 29:10)

(O)ur Lord Jesus, that great Shepherd of the sheep (Hebrews 13:20)

I am the true vine, and my Father is the gardener. (John 15:1)

Rose of Sharon (Song of Songs 2:1)

(T)he Shepherd and Overseer of your souls. (1 Peter 2:25)

We have an advocate with the Father—Jesus Christ, the Righteous One. (1 John 2:1)

Root and the Offspring of David, and the bright Morning Star. (Revelation 22:16)

As for God, his way is perfect. (Psalm 18:30)

Heir of all things (Hebrews 1:2)

Judge (Acts 10:42)

Yahweh

Chief Shepherd (1 Peter 5:4)

Sceptre (Numbers 24:17)

Interact 11.3
Miracles of Jesus

Look up the Scripture passages and answer the questions. Notice how Jesus' miracles demonstrate God's omnipotence.

1. Skim the Gospel of Mark and complete the chart.

Reference	Miracle	God has power over ...
1:25	Demoniac healing	Satan, demons
1:31		
1:41		
2:5		
3:5		
4:39		
5:8		
5:29		
5:41		
6:41		
6:48		
7:29		
7:34–35		
8:6		
8:25		
9:25		
10:52		
11:7		
11:14, 21		

2. Basing your answer on your study of Jesus' miracles, what are some areas in which Jesus showed God's power and authority?

Continued on back →

Let God Be GOD

3. A miracle is something only God can do. In other words, God steps into the affairs of humans, sets aside the natural order He created, and does something supernatural. What were some effects of Jesus' miracles, other than physical effects?

4. Can we command God to perform a miracle? (See 2 Corinthians 12:7–9.)

5. Does God ever perform a miracle today? If so, under what circumstances?

Interact 11.4
God's Power and Ours

Answer the following questions. Feel free to add your own questions and ideas.

1. Can God do anything? Can God do everything? Explain.

2. Can God create a rock so large He can't lift it?

3. The words *manipulation*, *intimidation*, *coercion*, and *acquisition* suggest ways in which humans sometimes try to exercise power. Look up any words you don't know, and find synonyms or related words. Think of a personal example for each, describing something you've done or something you've seen others do.

4. How does our human desire for power relate to God's omnipotence?

Part IV
GOD's Shared Attributes

Yahweh   Power and might are in your hand. (2 Chronicles 20:6)

The Lord is gracious and compassionate, slow to anger and rich in love.

Holy, holy, holy is the Lord God Almighty, who was, and is, and is to come. (Revelation 4:8)

God is love. (1 John 4:16)   I am the first and the last. (Isaiah 44:6)   Just and true are your ways. (Revelation 15:3)

The Lord reigns (Psalm 93:1)   My ways are higher than your ways and my thoughts than your thoughts. (Isaiah 55:9)

Christ of God (Luke 9:20)   Where can I flee from your presence? (Psalm 139:7)   He does not treat us as our sins deserve. (Psalm 103:10)   I the Lord do not change. (Malachi 3:6)

Ever-present—   Great is your faithfulness. (Lamentations 3:23)   knowledge of God! How unsearchable his judgments, and his paths beyond tracing out! (Romans 11:33)   I am with you always. (Matthew 28:20)   Lord of the sabbath (Mark 2:28)

Oh, the depth of the riches of the wisdom and   love and faithfulness go before you.

Righteousness and justice are the foundation of your throne; (Psalm 89:14)

He is the true God. (1 John 5:20)   is hidden from God's sight. (Hebrews 4:13) Lord, for he is good. (Revelation 22:13) You alone are holy. (Revelation 15:4)

I am the Alpha and the Omega, the First and the Last, the Beginning and the End. (Psalm 116:5) Give thanks to the Lord, to the Father except through me. (John 14:6)   I AM (John 8:58)

Nothing in all creation is full of compassion. (Psalm 103:8) I am the way and the truth and the life. No one comes to the Taste and see that the Lord is good. (Psalm 34:8)

The Lord is gracious and righteous; our God is and the Word was God. (John 1:1) The Lord is good and his love endures forever. (Psalm 100:5)

Your righteousness is everlasting. (Psalm 119:142) In the beginning was the Word, and he will be called Wonderful Counselor, Mighty God, Everlasting Father, Prince of Peace. (Isaiah 9:6)

To God belong wisdom and power. (Job 12:13) I am the Word was with God, and he will be the Lord of both the dead and the living. (Romans 14:9) The Lord is the Majesty in heaven. (Hebrews 1:3)

For to us a child is born, to us a son is given, and the government will be on his shoulders; Jesus, the pioneer and perfecter of faith. (Hebrews 12:2)

In the beginning was the Word, and the might be the Lord of both the dead and the living. Lamb of God (John 1:29) (Revelation 1:4-5)

Christ died and returned to life so that he (Him) who is, and who was, and who is to come, and from the seven spirits before his throne, the faithful witness, the firstborn from the dead and the ruler of the kings of the earth, bright Morning Star (Revelation 22:16)

The Son is the radiance of God's glory and the exact representation of his being, sustaining all things by his powerful word. After he had provided purification for sins, he sat down at the right hand of the Majesty in heaven. (Hebrews 1:3)

Therefore, since we have a great high priest who has ascended into heaven, Jesus the Son of God, let us hold firmly to the faith we profess. (Hebrews 4:14)

That which was from the beginning, which we have heard, which we have seen with our eyes, which we have looked at and our hands have touched— (1 John 1:1)

We have this hope as an anchor for the soul, firm and secure. It enters the inner sanctuary behind the curtain, where our forerunner, Jesus, has entered on our behalf. He has become a high priest forever, in the order of Melchizedek. (Hebrews 6:19-20)

Rose of Sharon (Song of Songs 2:1)   Let them know that you, whose name is the LORD—that you alone are the Most High over all the earth. (Psalm 83:18)   He is the atoning sacrifice for our sins, and not only for ours but also for the sins of the whole world. (1 John 2:2)

God, the blessed and only Ruler, the King of kings and Lord of lords. (1 Timothy 6:15)   And we have seen and testify that the Father has sent his Son to be the Savior of the world. (1 John 4:14)

The LORD will be king over the whole earth. On that day there will be one LORD, and his name the only name. (Zechariah 14:9)   this we proclaim concerning the Word of life. (1 John 1:1)

From everlasting to everlasting you are God. (Psalm 90:2)   The Son of Man came eating and drinking, and they say, 'Here is a glutton and a drunkard, a friend of tax collectors and sinners.' (Matthew 11:19)

The virgin will conceive and give birth to a son, and will call him Immanuel. (Isaiah 7:14)   Chosen of God (1 Peter 2:4)   Thanks be to God for his indescribable gift! (2 Corinthians 9:15)

(O)ur Lord Jesus, that great Shepherd of the sheep   I am the true vine, and my Father is the gardener. (John 15:1)

The Lord is enthroned as King forever. (Psalm 29:10)   (Hebrews 13:20)   See, I lay a stone in Zion, a tested stone, a precious cornerstone for a sure foundation. (Isaiah 28:16)   Desire of all nations (Haggai 2:7)

(T)he Shepherd and Overseer of your souls (1 Peter 2:25)   Kingdom (Matthew 9:15)   David a righteous Branch, a King who will reign wisely and do what is just and right in the land. (Jeremiah 23:5)

(W)e have an advocate with the Father—Jesus Christ, the Righteous One. (1 John 2:1)   I am the Root and the Offspring of David, and the bright Morning Star. (Revelation 22:16)

As for God, his way is perfect. (Psalm 18:30)

I am the Root and the Offspring of David, and the bright Morning Star. (Revelation 22:16)

Chief Shepherd (1 Peter 5:4)   Heir of all things (Hebrews 1:2)   Judge (Acts 10:42)

Sceptre (Numbers 24:17)   Yahweh

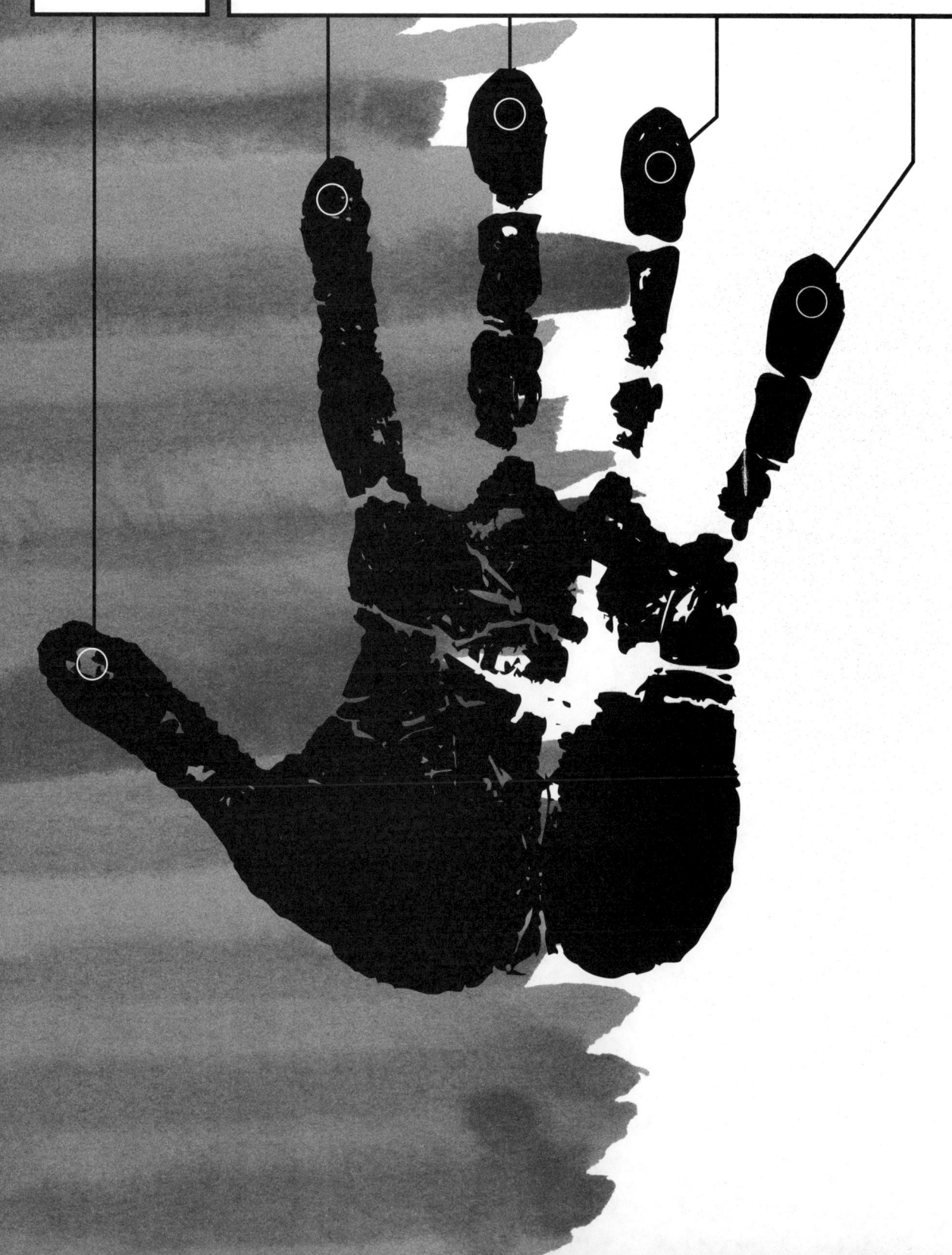

12

GOD Is Good

Interact 12.1
God Is Good

1. The following Bible passages talk about the goodness of God. As you read each passage, write *why* the author says God is good. (Look for actions of God that show He is good; also look for other attributes that the writers link to God's goodness.)

Genesis 18:25

Deuteronomy 32:3–4

1 Chronicles 16:34

2 Chronicles 5:13, 7:3

Ezra 3:10–11

Psalm 25:4–10

Psalm 34:8

Psalm 54:6

Psalm 86:5

Psalm 100:4–5

Psalm 106:1

Psalm 107:1

Psalm 116:1–7

Continued on back →

Let God Be GOD

Interact 12.1

God Is Good continued

Psalm 118:1, 29

Psalm 119:68

Psalm 135:3

Psalm 136:1

Nahum 1:7

Mark 10:18, Luke 18:19

John 10:11–15

1 Peter 2:2–3

2. According to these passages, how should we respond to the fact that God is good? (You may have to look in the surrounding verses to find a response.)

Interact 12.2

God Is Benevolent

In Matthew 5:45, Jesus describes God this way: "He causes his sun to rise on the evil and the good, and sends rain on the righteous and the unrighteous." Psalm 145:17 says, "The Lord is righteous in all his ways and loving toward all he has made."

God is good. One of the ways He shows His goodness is by the way He takes care of all He has made—everything in creation, including us! We call this attribute *benevolence*.

1. Choose one of these passages:

Job 38:39–39:30; Psalm 104; Psalm 116; Psalm 139:1–18; Psalm 145

2. Read the passage several times, thinking about what it says about God. Especially look for evidence of God's benevolence.

3. Write a paragraph to summarize what the passage says about God's benevolence.

4. Share your discoveries with other students.

Let God Be GOD

Yahweh

Power and might are in your hand. (2 Chronicles 20:6)

The Lord is gracious and compassionate, slow to anger and rich in love. (Psalm 145:8)

Holy, holy, holy is the Lord God Almighty, who was, and is, and is to come. (Revelation 4:8)

God is love (1 John 4:16)

I am the first and the last. (Isaiah 44:6)

Just and true are your ways. (Revelation 15:3)

The Lord reigns (Psalm 93:1)

My ways are higher than your ways and my thoughts than your thoughts. (Isaiah 55:9)

He does not treat us as our sins deserve. (Psalm 103:10)

I the Lord do not change (Malachi 3:6)

Christ of God (Luke 9:20)

Ever-present— Where can I flee from your presence? (Psalm 139:7)

Great is your faithfulness. (Lamentations 3:23)

knowledge of God! How unsearchable his judgments, and his paths beyond tracing out! (Romans 11:33)

Lord of the sabbath (Mark 2:28)

Oh, the depth of the riches of the wisdom and knowledge

Righteousness and justice are the foundation of your throne; love and faithfulness go before you. (Psalm 89:14)

I am with you always. (Matthew 28:20)

He is the true God. (1 John 5:20)

I am the Alpha and the Omega, the First and the Last, the Beginning and the End. (Revelation 22:13) You alone are holy. (Revelation 15:4)

Nothing in all creation is hidden from God's sight. (Hebrews 4:13)

Give thanks to the Lord, for he is good: his love endures forever. (Psalm 118:1)

I AM (John 8:58)

our God is full of compassion. (Psalm 116:5)

I am the way and the truth and the life. No one comes to the Father except through me. (John 14:6)

Holy, holy, holy is the Lord Almighty. (Isaiah 6:3)

In the beginning was the Word, and the Word was with God, and the Word was God. (John 1:1)

Taste and see that the Lord is good. (Psalm 34:8)

The Lord is good and his love endures forever. (Psalm 100:5)

And he will be called Wonderful Counselor, Mighty God, Everlasting Father, Prince of Peace. (Isaiah 9:6)

The Lord is gracious and righteous; our God is full of compassion. (Psalm 116:5)

The Lord works righteousness and justice for all the oppressed. (Psalm 103:6)

Christ died and returned to life so that he might be the Lord of both the dead and the living. (Romans 14:9)

let us hold firmly to the faith we profess. (Hebrews 4:14)

the pioneer and perfecter of faith. (Hebrews 12:2)

He is the atoning sacrifice for our sins, and not only for ours but also for the sins of the whole world. (1 John 2:2)

To God belong wisdom and power. (Job 12:13)

Your righteousness is everlasting. (Psalm 119:142)

For to us a child is born, to us a son is given, and the government will be on his shoulders. And he will be called

The Son is the radiance of God's glory and the exact representation of his being, sustaining all things by his powerful word. After he had provided purification for sins, he sat down at the right hand of the Majesty in heaven. (Hebrews 1:3)

God, the blessed and only Ruler, the King of kings and Lord of lords (1 Timothy 6:15)

who has ascended into heaven, and who is at God's right hand (1 Peter 3:22)

We have this hope as an anchor for the soul, firm and secure. It enters the inner sanctuary behind the curtain, where our forerunner, Jesus, has entered on our behalf. He has become a high priest forever, in the order of Melchizedek. (Hebrews 6:19-20)

Let them know that you, whose name is the LORD—that you alone are the Most High over all the earth. (Psalm 83:18)

And we have seen and testify that the Father has sent his Son to be the Savior of the world. (1 John 4:14)

On that day there will be one LORD, and his name the only name. (Zechariah 14:9)

the Lamb of God (John 1:29)

the Root and the Offspring of David, and the bright Morning Star. (Revelation 22:16)

Rose of Sharon (Song of Songs 2:1)

That which was from the beginning, which we have heard, which we have seen with our eyes, which we have looked at and our hands have touched— this we proclaim concerning the Word of life. (1 John 1:1)

The LORD will be king over the whole earth.

From everlasting to everlasting you are God. (Psalm 90:2)

The virgin will conceive and give birth to a son, and will call him Immanuel. (Isaiah 7:14)

Chosen of God (1 Peter 2:4)

thanks be to God for his indescribable gift! (2 Corinthians 9:15)

Bridegroom (Matthew 9:15)

The Son of Man came eating and drinking, and they say, 'There is a glutton and a drunkard, a friend of tax collectors and sinners.' (Matthew 11:19)

Desire of all nations (Haggai 2:7)

I lay a stone in Zion, a tested stone, a precious cornerstone for a sure foundation in the land. (Isaiah 28:16)

the messenger of the covenant, whom you desire, will come. (Malachi 3:1)

David, a righteous Branch, a King who will reign wisely and do what is just and right in the land. (Jeremiah 23:5)

(O)ur Lord Jesus, that great Shepherd of the sheep (Hebrews 13:20)

The Lord is enthroned as King forever. (Psalm 29:10)

I am the true vine, and my Father is the gardener (John 15:1)

(T)he Shepherd and Overseer of your souls. (1 Peter 2:25)

We have an advocate with the Father—Jesus Christ, the Righteous One. (1 John 2:1)

As for God, his way is perfect. (Psalm 18:30)

I am the Root and the Offspring of David, and the bright Morning Star. (Revelation 22:16)

Chief Shepherd (1 Peter 5:4)

Sceptre (Numbers 24:17)

Heir of all things (Hebrews 1:2)

Judge (Acts 10:42)

Yahweh

Interact 12.3
Does God's Goodness Matter?

Listed below are several facts. After each fact you will find two statements. These statements represent two ways of interpreting those facts. Which statements make the most sense to you? How would you explain why they make sense?

Fact: Sometimes it rains; sometimes it doesn't.

1. Wind, moisture, temperature, and other factors combine to make rain. Often we can predict when and where it will rain, but sometimes we guess wrong. The whole process is random.

2. The patterns and movements we see on weather maps are evidence that the earth's systems have an order that God built into creation. Even if we can't exactly forecast every weather change, weather systems are generally predictable. This points to a Creator.

Fact: Animals come in a wide variety of sizes, colors, and shapes. They eat a wide variety of things. They live in a wide variety of conditions, from the frozen Arctic to the burning Sahara.

1. The variety we see is basically a result of random events and accidents.

2. This variety is evidence of God's great creativity and love of beauty. The more we learn about these creatures and understand how they live, the more we admire and appreciate God's generous provision.

Fact: When people go through hard times, some pray for God's help and some get through on their own.

1. All we have is ourselves. Pray if you want to, but there's no one there to help you.

2. God gives us the strength to make it, whether we admit it or not. Praying isn't being lazy; it's facing the fact that no matter how hard we try, we all need help.

Yahweh

Power and might are in your hand. (2 Chronicles 20:6)

The Lord is gracious and compassionate, slow to anger and rich in love. (Psalm 145:8)

Holy, holy, holy is the Lord God Almighty, who was, and is, and is to come. (Revelation 4:8)

I am the first and the last. (Isaiah 44:6)

Just and true are your ways. (Revelation 15:3)

God is love. (1 John 4:16)

The Lord reigns. (Psalm 93:1)

My ways are higher than your ways and my thoughts than your thoughts. (Isaiah 55:9)

He does not treat us as our sins deserve. (Psalm 103:10)

I the Lord do not change. (Malachi 3:6)

Christ of God (Luke 9:20)

Ever-present—Where can I flee from your presence? (Psalm 139:7)

Great is your faithfulness. (Lamentations 3:23)

Lord of the sabbath (Mark 2:28)

I am with you always. (Matthew 28:20)

Oh, the depth of the riches of the wisdom and knowledge of God! How unsearchable his judgments, and his paths beyond tracing out! (Romans 11:33)

Righteousness and justice are the foundation of your throne; love and faithfulness go before you. (Psalm 89:14)

He is the true God. (1 John 5:20)

I am the Alpha and the Omega, the First and the Last, the Beginning and the End. (Revelation 22:13)

Nothing in all creation is hidden from God's sight. (Hebrews 4:13)

Give thanks to the Lord, for he is good; his love endures forever. (Psalm 118:1)

You alone are holy (Revelation 15:4)

The Lord is gracious and righteous; our God is full of compassion. (Psalm 116:5)

I am the way and the truth and the life. No one comes to the Father except through me. (John 14:6)

Taste and see that the Lord is good (Psalm 34:8)

Holy, holy, holy is the Lord Almighty. (Isaiah 6:3)

The Lord works righteousness and justice for all the oppressed. (Psalm 103:6)

To God belong wisdom and power. (Job 12:13)

In the beginning was the Word, and the Word was with God, and the Word was God. (John 1:1)

The Lord is good and his love endures forever. (Psalm 100:5)

I AM (John 8:58)

And he will be called Wonderful Counselor, Mighty God, Everlasting Father, Prince of Peace. (Isaiah 9:6)

Your righteousness is everlasting. (Psalm 119:142)

For to us a child is born, to us a son is given, and the government will be on his shoulders. (Isaiah 9:6)

he might be the Lord of both the dead and the living. (Romans 14:9)

Jesus, the pioneer and perfecter of faith. (Hebrews 12:2)

great high priest who has ascended into heaven, Jesus the Son of God, let us hold firmly to the faith we profess. (Hebrews 4:14)

He is the atoning sacrifice for our sins, and not only for ours but also for the sins of the whole world. (1 John 2:2)

Christ died and returned to life so that he might be the Lord of both the dead and the living. (Romans 14:9)

The Son is the radiance of God's glory and the exact representation of his being, sustaining all things by his powerful word. After he had provided purification for sins, he sat down at the right hand of the Majesty in heaven. (Hebrews 1:3)

the Lamb of God (John 1:29)

the firstborn from the dead and the ruler of the kings of the earth. (Revelation 1:5)

Jesus, the bright Morning Star. (Revelation 22:16)

a high priest forever, in the order of Melchizedek. (Hebrews 6:19-20)

God, the blessed and only Ruler, the King of kings and Lord of lords (1 Timothy 6:15)

Let them know that you, whose name is the LORD—that you alone are the Most High over all the earth. (Psalm 83:18)

It enters the inner sanctuary behind the curtain, where our forerunner, Jesus, has entered on our behalf. He has become a high priest forever (Hebrews 6:19-20)

we have this hope as an anchor for the soul, firm and secure. (Hebrews 6:19)

Therefore, since we have a great high priest

Rose of Sharon (Song of Songs 2:1)

That which was from the beginning, which we have heard, which we have seen with our eyes, which we have looked at and our hands have touched—this we proclaim concerning the Word of life. (1 John 1:1)

The Son of Man came eating and drinking, and they say, 'Here is a glutton and a drunkard, a friend of tax collectors and sinners.' (Matthew 11:19)

the living bread that came down from heaven. (John 6:51)

the Father has sent his Son to be the Savior of the world. (1 John 4:14)

and we have seen and testify that

the bridegroom (Matthew 9:15)

Desire of all nations (Haggai 2:7)

a righteous Branch, a King who will reign wisely and do what is just and right in the land. (Jeremiah 33:15)

Chosen of God (1 Peter 2:4)

Thanks be to God for his indescribable gift! (2 Corinthians 9:15)

a stone in Zion, a tested stone, a precious cornerstone for a sure foundation. (Isaiah 28:16)

The LORD will be king over the whole earth. On that day there will be one LORD, and his name the only name. (Zechariah 14:9)

From everlasting to everlasting you are God. (Psalm 90:2)

The virgin will conceive and give birth to a son, and will call him Immanuel. (Isaiah 7:14)

(O)ur Lord Jesus, that great Shepherd of the sheep (Hebrews 13:20)

The LORD is enthroned as King forever. (Psalm 29:10)

I am the true vine, and my Father is the gardener. (John 15:1)

(T)he Shepherd and Overseer of your souls. (1 Peter 2:25)

(W)e have an advocate with the Father—Jesus Christ, the Righteous One. (1 John 2:1)

the Root and the Offspring of David, and the bright Morning Star. (Revelation 22:16)

As for God, his way is perfect. (Psalm 18:30)

Chief Shepherd (1 Peter 5:4)

Sceptre (Numbers 24:17)

Heir of all things (Hebrews 1:2)

Judge (Acts 10:42)

Yahweh

Reflecting God's Goodness

Look up the following Scripture passages. Complete the chart by answering the questions for each Scripture passage.

Scripture passage	Summarize what this passage says about good works.	Give specific ways we can fulfill the teachings in this passage.
Matthew 5:16		
Romans 12:9, 21		
Galatians 6:9–10		
Ephesians 2:10		
Colossians 1:10		
1 Thessalonians 5:15, 21–22		
2 Thessalonians 2:16–17		
Titus 2:7–8		
Hebrews 10:24		
Hebrews 13:16		
1 Peter 2:12, 15		
1 Peter 38–11		
1 Peter 4:19		

Yahweh

Power and might are in your hand. (2 Chronicles 20:6)

The Lord is gracious and compassionate, slow to anger and rich in love. (Psalm 145:8)

Holy, holy, holy is the Lord God Almighty, who was, and is, and is to come. (Revelation 4:8)

God is love. (1 John 4:16)

I am the first and the last. (Isaiah 44:6)

Just and true are your ways. (Revelation 15:3)

The Lord reigns (Psalm 93:1)

My ways are higher than your ways and my thoughts than your thoughts. (Isaiah 55:9)

He does not treat us as our sins deserve. (Psalm 103:10)

Christ of God (Luke 9:20)

Ever-present—Where can I flee from your presence? (Psalm 139:7)

the Lord do not change. (Malachi 3:6)

Great is your faithfulness. (Lamentations 3:23)

Oh, the depth of the riches of the wisdom and knowledge of God! How unsearchable his judgments, and his paths beyond tracing out! (Romans 11:33)

Lord of the sabbath (Mark 2:28)

Righteousness and justice are the foundation of your throne; love and faithfulness go before you. (Psalm 89:14)

I am with you always. (Matthew 28:20)

He is the true God (1 John 5:20)

I am the Alpha and the Omega, the First and the Last, the Beginning and the End. (Revelation 22:13)

You alone are holy. (Revelation 15:4)

Nothing in all creation is hidden from God's sight. (Hebrews 4:13)

Give thanks to the Lord, for he is good; his love endures forever. (Psalm 118:1)

I AM (John 8:58)

The Lord is gracious and righteous; our God is full of compassion. (Psalm 116:5)

Holy, holy, holy is the Lord Almighty. (Isaiah 6:3)

I am the way and the truth and the life. No one comes to the Father except through me. (John 14:6)

In the beginning was the Word, and the Word was with God, and the Word was God. (John 1:1)

The Lord is good and his love endures forever. (Psalm 100:5)

I am the living bread that came down from heaven. (John 6:51)

To God belong wisdom and power. (Job 12:13)

The Lord works righteousness and justice for all the oppressed. (Psalm 103:6)

And he will be called Wonderful Counselor, Mighty God, Everlasting Father, Prince of Peace. (Isaiah 9:6)

Taste and see that the Lord is good. (Psalm 34:8)

He is the Lord of both the dead and the living. (Romans 14:9)

Your righteousness is everlasting. (Psalm 119:142)

For to us a child is born, to us a son is given, and the government will be on his shoulders. (Isaiah 9:6)

After he had provided purification for sins, he sat down at the right hand of the Majesty in heaven. (Hebrews 1:3)

Jesus, the Pioneer and perfecter of faith. (Hebrews 12:2)

the Lamb of God (John 1:29)

He is the atoning sacrifice for our sins, and not only for ours but also for the sins of the whole world. (1 John 2:2)

Christ died and returned to life so that he might be the Lord of both the dead and the living. (Romans 14:9)

Therefore, since we have a great high priest who has ascended into heaven, Jesus the Son of God, let us hold firmly to the faith we profess. (Hebrews 4:14)

God, the blessed and only Ruler, the King of kings and Lord of lords (1 Timothy 6:15)

sustaining all things by his powerful word. (Hebrews 1:3)

The Son is the radiance of God's glory and the exact representation of his being (Hebrews 1:3)

Him who is, and who was, and who is to come. (Revelation 1:4)

whose name is the LORD—that you alone are the Most High over all the earth. (Psalm 83:18)

Rose of Sharon (Song of Songs 2:1)

We have this hope as an anchor for the soul, firm and secure. It enters the inner sanctuary behind the curtain, where Jesus, who went before us, has entered on our behalf. He has become a high priest forever, in the order of Melchizedek. (Hebrews 6:19-20)

the faithful witness, the firstborn from the dead and the ruler of the kings of the earth. (Revelation 1:5)

the Father has sent his Son to be the Savior of the world. (1 John 4:14)

The LORD will be king over the whole earth. On that day there will be one LORD, and his name the only name. (Zechariah 14:9)

That which was from the beginning, which we have heard, which we have seen with our eyes, which we have looked at and our hands have touched—this we proclaim concerning the Word of life. (1 John 1:1)

From everlasting to everlasting you are God. (Psalm 90:2)

The virgin will conceive and give birth to a son, and will call him Immanuel. (Isaiah 7:14)

The Son of Man came eating and drinking, and they say, 'Here is a glutton and a drunkard, a friend of tax collectors and sinners.' (Matthew 11:19)

Chosen of God (1 Peter 2:4)

Desire of all nations (Haggai 2:7)

Behold, a King who will reign wisely and do what is just and right in the land. (Jeremiah 23:5)

I lay a stone in Zion, a tested stone, a precious cornerstone for a sure foundation. (Isaiah 28:16)

And we have seen and testify that the Father has sent his Son to be the Savior of the world. (1 John 4:14)

Thanks be to God for his indescribable gift! (2 Corinthians 9:15)

(O)ur Lord Jesus, that great Shepherd of the sheep (Hebrews 13:20)

I am the true vine, and my Father is the gardener. (John 15:1)

The Lord is enthroned as King forever. (Psalm 29:10)

(T)he Shepherd and Overseer of your souls. (1 Peter 2:25)

(W)e have an advocate with the Father—Jesus Christ, the Righteous One. (1 John 2:1)

Root and the Offspring of David, and the bright Morning Star. (Revelation 22:16)

As for God, his way is perfect. (Psalm 18:30)

Heir of all things (Hebrews 1:2)

Judge (Acts 10:42)

Yahweh

Chief Shepherd (1 Peter 5:4)

Sceptre (Hebrews 1:8)

13

GOD **Is Wise and Truthful**

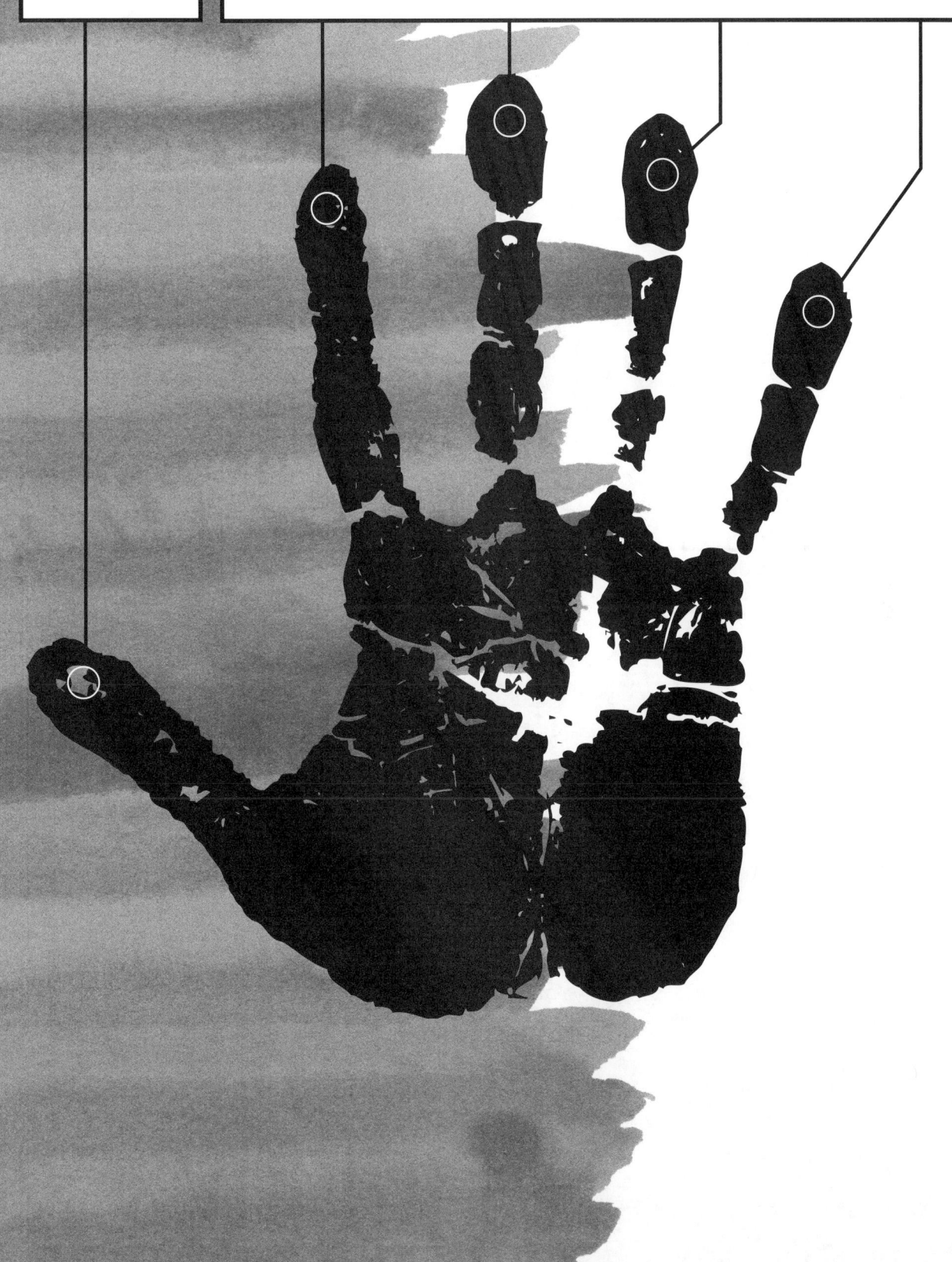

Interact 13.1
God Is Wise

Look up the following Scripture passages. After each one, make a note about how God shows His wisdom in that passage.

Hint: In some cases, you'll have to look at nearby passages in order to figure out what the passage is about.

Job 12:13

Psalm 104:24

Jeremiah 10:12

Daniel 2:20–21

Matthew 13:54

Romans 11:33

Romans 16:27

1 Corinthians 1:25

Ephesians 3:10

Let God Be GOD

Yahweh

Power and might are in your hand. (2 Chronicles 20:6)

The Lord is gracious and compassionate, slow to anger and rich in love. (Psalm 145:8)

Holy, holy, holy is the Lord God Almighty, who was, and is, and is to come. (Revelation 4:8)

God is love. (1 John 4:16)

I am the first and the last. (Isaiah 44:6)

Just and true are your ways. (Revelation 15:3)

The Lord reigns (Psalm 93:1)

My ways are higher than your ways and my thoughts than your thoughts. (Isaiah 55:9)

Christ of God (Luke 9:20)

Ever-present—Where can I flee from your presence? (Psalm 139:7)

He does not treat us as our sins deserve. (Psalm 103:10)

I the Lord do not change (Malachi 3:6)

Great is your faithfulness. (Lamentations 3:23)

Oh, the depth of the riches of the wisdom and knowledge of God! How unsearchable his judgments, and his paths beyond tracing out! (Romans 11:33)

I am with you always. (Matthew 28:20)

Lord of the sabbath (Mark 2:28)

Righteousness and justice are the foundation of your throne; love and faithfulness go before you. (Psalm 89:14)

I am the Alpha and the Omega, the First and the Last, the Beginning and the End. (Revelation 22:13)

Nothing in all creation is hidden from God's sight. (Hebrews 4:13)

He is the true God. (1 John 5:20)

The Lord is gracious and righteous; our God is full of compassion. (Psalm 116:5)

Give thanks to the Lord, for he is good; his love endures forever. (Psalm 118:1)

You alone are holy. (Revelation 15:4)

I AM (John 8:58)

The Lord works righteousness and justice for all the oppressed. (Psalm 103:6)

I am the way and the truth and the life. (John 14:6)

Holy, holy, holy is the Lord Almighty. (Isaiah 6:3)

No one comes to the Father except through me. (John 14:6)

Taste and see that the Lord is good. (Psalm 34:8)

I am the living bread that came down from heaven. (John 6:51)

To God belong wisdom and power. (Job 12:13)

Your righteousness is everlasting. (Psalm 119:142)

In the beginning was the Word, and the Word was with God, and the Word was God. (John 1:1)

And he will be called Wonderful Counselor, Mighty God, Everlasting Father, Prince of Peace. (Isaiah 9:6)

The Lord is good and his love endures forever. (Psalm 100:5)

For to us a child is born, to us a son is given, and the government will be on his shoulders. (Isaiah 9:6)

Christ died and returned to life so that he might be the Lord of both the dead and the living. (Romans 14:9)

Jesus the Son of God, let us hold firmly to the faith we profess. (Hebrews 4:14)

After he had provided purification for sins, he sat down at the right hand of the Majesty in heaven. (Hebrews 1:3)

The Son is the radiance of God's glory and the exact representation of his being, sustaining all things by his powerful word. (Hebrews 1:3)

He is the atoning sacrifice for our sins, and not only for ours but also for the sins of the whole world. (1 John 2:2)

the Lamb of God (John 1:29)

Jesus, the pioneer and perfecter of faith. (Hebrews 12:2)

God the blessed and only Ruler, the King of kings and Lord of lords (1 Timothy 6:15)

who is the faithful witness, the firstborn from the dead, and the ruler of the kings of the earth. (Revelation 1:5)

Let them know that you, whose name is the LORD—that you alone are the Most High over all the earth. (Psalm 83:18)

We have this hope as an anchor for the soul, firm and secure. It enters the inner sanctuary behind the curtain, where our forerunner, Jesus, has entered on our behalf. (Hebrews 6:19-20)

the Father has sent his Son to be the Savior of the world. (1 John 4:14)

Here is a glutton and a drunkard, a friend of tax collectors and sinners. (Matthew 11:19)

Desire of all nations (Haggai 2:7)

I lay a stone in Zion, a tested stone, a precious cornerstone for a sure foundation. (Isaiah 28:16)

a righteous Branch, a King who will reign wisely and do what is just and right in the land. (Jeremiah 23:5)

Bridegroom (Matthew 9:15)

The Son of Man came eating and drinking

Chosen of God (1 Peter 2:4)

Thanks be to God for his indescribable gift! (2 Corinthians 9:15)

The virgin will conceive and give birth to a son, and will call him Immanuel. (Isaiah 7:14)

God, the blessed and only Ruler. On that day there will be one LORD, and his name the only name. (Zechariah 14:9)

The LORD will be king over the whole earth. (Zechariah 14:9)

From everlasting to everlasting you are God. (Psalm 90:2)

(O)ur Lord Jesus, that great Shepherd of the sheep (Hebrews 13:20)

The Lord is enthroned as King forever. (Psalm 29:10)

I am the true vine, and my Father is the gardener. (John 15:1)

the Shepherd and Overseer of your souls (1 Peter 2:25)

(W)e have an advocate with the Father—Jesus Christ, the Righteous One. (1 John 2:1)

the Root and the Offspring of David, and the bright Morning Star. (Revelation 22:16)

As for God, his way is perfect. (Psalm 18:30)

I am the Root

Chief Shepherd (1 Peter 5:4)

Sceptre (Hebrews 1:8)

Heir of all things (Hebrews 1:2)

Judge (Acts 10:42)

Yahweh

Interact 13.2

God's Wisdom for Us

God shares His wisdom. "If any of you lacks wisdom, he should ask God, who gives generously to all without finding fault, and it will be given to him" (James 1:5). Though we can never be as wise as God, we can acquire wisdom from God.

Look up the following Scripture passages. Then fill in the chart with your answers. (Note: You may have to look in the surrounding verses in order to answer the questions.)

Scripture	Summarize the meaning of *wisdom* in this passage.	According to this passage, how does a person receive wisdom from God?
1 Kings 3:9		
1 Kings 4:29–34		
Psalm 37:30–31		
Psalm 90:12		
Psalm 111:10		
Proverbs 11:2		
Hosea 14:9		
Acts 6:3		
Acts 6:10		
Romans 16:19		
Ephesians 1:17		
Colossians 1:9		
Colossians 3:16		
2 Timothy 3:15		

Let God Be GOD

Yahweh Power and might are in your hand. (2 Chronicles 20:6)

The Lord is gracious and compassionate, slow to anger and rich in love. (Psalm 145:8)

Holy, holy, holy is the Lord God Almighty, who was, and is, and is to come. (Revelation 4:8)

God is love. (1 John 4:16) I am the first and the last. (Isaiah 44:6) Just and true are your ways. (Revelation 15:3)

The Lord reigns. (Psalm 93:1) My ways are higher than your ways and my thoughts than your thoughts. (Isaiah 55:9) He does not treat us as our sins deserve. (Psalm 103:10) (The Lord do not change. (Malachi 3:6)

Christ of God (Luke 9:20) Ever-present—Where can I flee from your presence? (Psalm 139:7)

Great is your faithfulness. (Lamentations 3:23) wisdom and knowledge of God! How unsearchable his judgments, and his paths beyond tracing out! (Romans 11:33) Lord of the sabbath (Mark 2:28)

Oh, the depth of the riches of the wisdom and I am with you always. (Matthew 28:20)

Righteousness and justice are the foundation of your throne; love and faithfulness go before you. (Psalm 89:14) I AM (John 6:58)

I am the Alpha and the Omega, the First and the Last, the Beginning and the End. (Revelation 22:13) You alone are holy. (Revelation 15:4)

He is the true God. (1 John 5:20) Nothing is hidden from God's sight. (Hebrews 4:13) Give thanks to the Lord, for he is good; his love endures forever. (Psalm 118:1)

Nothing in all creation is hidden from God's sight. I am the way and the truth and the life. No one comes to the Father except through me. (John 14:6) Taste and see that the Lord is good. (Psalm 34:8)

The Lord is gracious and righteous; our God is full of compassion. (Psalm 116:5) Holy, holy, holy is the Lord Almighty. (Isaiah 6:3)

Your righteousness is everlasting. (Psalm 119:142) In the beginning was the Word, and the Word was with God, and the Word was God. (John 1:1) The Lord is good and his love endures forever. (Psalm 100:5)

To God belong wisdom and power. (Job 12:13) And he will be called Wonderful Counselor, Mighty God, Everlasting Father, Prince of Peace. (Isaiah 9:6)

The Lord works righteousness and justice for all the oppressed. (Psalm 103:6) He is the Lord of both the dead and the living. (Romans 14:9) I am the living bread that came down from heaven. (John 6:51)

For to us a child is born, to us a son is given, and the government will be on his shoulders. (Isaiah 9:6) He is the atoning sacrifice for our sins. (1 John 2:2)

Christ died and returned to life so that he might be the Lord of both the dead and the living. (Romans 14:9) After he had provided purification for sins, he sat down at the right hand of the Majesty in heaven. (Hebrews 1:3)

The Son is the radiance of God's glory and the exact representation of his being, sustaining all things by his powerful word. (Hebrews 1:3) Jesus, the pioneer and perfecter of faith. (Hebrews 12:2)

That which was from the beginning, which we have heard, which we have seen with our eyes, which we have looked at and our hands have touched. (1 John 1:1) the Lamb of God (John 1:29) the bright Morning Star (Revelation 22:16)

Rose of Sharon (Song of Songs 2:1) Let us hold firmly to the faith we profess. (Hebrews 4:14)

We have this hope as an anchor for the soul, firm and secure. It enters the inner sanctuary behind the curtain. (Hebrews 6:19-20)

The LORD will be king over the whole earth. On that day there will be one LORD, and his name the only name. (Zechariah 14:9)

God, the blessed and only Ruler, the King of kings and Lord of lords. (1 Timothy 6:15)

(Him who) is and who was, and who is to come. (Revelation 1:8) The Son of Man came eating and drinking, and they say, 'Here is a glutton and a drunkard, a friend of tax collectors and sinners.' (Matthew 11:19)

From everlasting to everlasting you are God. (Psalm 90:2) The virgin will conceive and give birth to a son, and will call him Immanuel. (Isaiah 7:14)

the Father has sent his Son to be the Savior of the world. (1 John 4:14)

(I lay) a stone in Zion, a tested stone, a precious cornerstone for a sure foundation. (Isaiah 28:16)

David a righteous Branch, a King who will reign wisely and do what is just and right in the land. (Jeremiah 23:5)

Chosen of God (1 Peter 2:4) Thanks be to God for his indescribable gift! (2 Corinthians 9:15)

Desire of all nations (Haggai 2:7) And we testify that the Father has sent his Son to be the Savior of the world. (1 John 4:14)

(O)ur Lord Jesus, that great Shepherd of the sheep (Hebrews 13:20)

The Lord is enthroned as King forever. (Psalm 29:10)

I am the true vine, and my Father is the gardener. (John 15:1)

(The) Shepherd and Overseer of your souls. (1 Peter 2:25)

(W)e have an advocate with the Father—Jesus Christ, the Righteous One. (1 John 2:1)

I am the Root and the Offspring of David, and the bright Morning Star. (Revelation 22:16)

As for God, his way is perfect. (Psalm 18:30)

Chief Shepherd (1 Peter 5:4) Heir of all things (Hebrews 1:2) Judge (Acts 10:42)

I am the Root (Revelation 22:16) Scepter Yahweh

Interact 13.3
Becoming Wise

Your instructor will assign you one of the following chapters from Proverbs: 1, 2, 3, 4, 8, or 9.

Write your chapter number here: _____.

Read through the following questions. Then read your chapter several times. As you read your chapter, jot down answers to the questions. Write your answers on a separate sheet of paper.

After you have written answers to the questions, summarize the answers and transfer them to this Interact. Share your answer summaries with at least one other student.

Questions for your Proverbs chapter:

1. What synonyms did you find for *wisdom* or *wise*? What other words do these synonyms remind you of?

2. What antonyms did you find for *wisdom* or *wise*? What other words do these antonyms remind you of?

3. Why is wisdom important? What are some of the benefits of wisdom?

4. What warnings did you find?

5. What advice or guidance did you find regarding how to get wisdom?

6. How does the author link our wisdom with our relationship to God?

Let God Be GOD

Yahweh Power and might are in your hand. (2 Chronicles 20:6)

The Lord is gracious and compassionate, slow to anger and rich in love. (Psalm 145:8)

Holy, holy, holy is the Lord God Almighty, who was, and is, and is to come. (Revelation 4:8)

God is love. (1 John 4:16)   I am the first and the last. (Isaiah 44:6)   Just and true are your ways. (Revelation 15:3)

The Lord reigns (Psalm 93:1)   My ways are higher than your ways and my thoughts than your thoughts. (Isaiah 55:9)   He does not treat us as our sins deserve. (Psalm 103:10)   (the Lord do not change. (Malachi 3:6)

Christ of God (Luke 9:20)   Where can I flee from your presence? (Psalm 139:7)   Lord of the sabbath (Mark 2:28)

Ever-present—Where can I flee from your presence? (Psalm 139:7)   I am with you always (Matthew 28:20)

Great is your faithfulness. (Lamentations 3:23)   How unsearchable his judgments, and his paths beyond tracing out! (Romans 11:33)

Righteousness and justice are the foundation of your throne; love and faithfulness go before you. (Psalm 89:14)

Oh, the depth of the riches of the wisdom and knowledge of God's sight. (Hebrews 4:13)   End. (Revelation 22:13)   You alone are holy. (Revelation 15:4)

I am the Alpha and the Omega, the First and the Last, the Beginning and the   Give thanks to the Lord, for he is good, his love endures forever. (Psalm 118:1)   I AM (John 8:58)

Nothing in all creation is hidden from God's sight. (Psalm 116:5)   Holy, holy, holy is the Lord Almighty. (Isaiah 6:3)   Taste and see that the Lord is good (Psalm 34:8)

He is the true God. (1 John 5:20)   I am the way and the truth and the life.   No one comes to the Father except through me. (John 14:6)

The Lord is gracious and righteous; our God is full of compassion. (Psalm 103:6)   and the Word was God. (John 1:1)   The Lord is good and his love endures forever. (Psalm 100:5)

To God belong wisdom and power. (Job 12:13)   In the beginning was the Word, and the Word was with God,   Everlasting Father, Prince of Peace. (Isaiah 9:6)

The Lord works righteousness and justice for all the oppressed. (Psalm 103:6)   Jesus the Son of God, let us hold firmly to the faith we profess. (Hebrews 4:14)   Jesus the pioneer and perfecter of faith. (Hebrews 12:2)

Your righteousness is everlasting. (Psalm 119:142)   so that he might be the Lord of both the dead and the living. (Romans 14:9)   the Lamb of God (John 1:29)   Morning Star (Revelation 22:16)

For to us a child is born, to us a son is given, and the government will be on his shoulders.   He is the atoning sacrifice for our sins. (Psalm 83:18)   Jesus the Majesty in heaven. (Hebrews 1:3)

Christ died and returned to life so that he might be the Lord of both the dead and the living. (Romans 14:9)   And he will be called Wonderful Counselor, Mighty God,

Therefore, since we have a great high priest who has ascended into heaven, Jesus the Son of God, let us hold firmly to the faith we profess. (Hebrews 4:14)   high priest in the order of Melchizedek. (Hebrews 6:19-20)

The Son is the radiance of God's glory and the exact representation of his being, sustaining all things by his powerful word. After he had provided purification for sins, and not only for ours but also for the sins of the whole world. (1 John 2:2)

Rose of Sharon (Song of Songs 2:1)   Jesus Christ, who is the faithful witness, the firstborn from the dead, and the ruler of the kings of the earth. (Revelation 1:5)

That which was from the beginning, which we have heard, which we have seen with our eyes, which we have looked at and our hands have touched—this we proclaim concerning the Word of life. (1 John 1:1)

Let them know that you, whose name is the LORD—that you alone are the Most High over all the earth. (Psalm 83:18)   the Father has sent his Son to be the Savior of the world. (1 John 4:14)

We have this hope as an anchor for the soul, firm and secure. It enters the inner sanctuary behind the curtain, where our forerunner, Jesus, has entered on our behalf. He has become a high priest forever.

God, the blessed and only Ruler, the King of kings and Lord of lords. (1 Timothy 6:15)   And we have seen   (Matthew 11:19)

The LORD will be king over the whole earth. On that day there will be one LORD, and his name the only name. (Zechariah 14:9)   a friend of tax collectors and sinners. (Matthew 11:19)

We love him because he first loved us. (1 John 4:19)   The Son of Man came eating and drinking, and they say, 'Here is a glutton and a drunkard,

From everlasting to everlasting you are God. (Psalm 90:2)   Chosen of God (1 Peter 2:4)   Desire of all nations (Haggai 2:7)

God, the blessed and only Ruler.   Bridegroom (Matthew 9:15)   I will raise up for David a righteous Branch, a King who will reign wisely and do what is just and right in the land. (Jeremiah 23:5)

The virgin will conceive and give birth to a son, and will call him Immanuel. (Isaiah 7:14)   Thanks be to God for his indescribable gift! (2 Corinthians 9:15)

(O)ur Lord Jesus, that great Shepherd of the sheep (Hebrews 13:20)   The Lord is enthroned as King forever. (Psalm 29:10)

I am the true vine, and my Father is the gardener. (John 15:1)   a stone in Zion, a tested stone, a precious cornerstone for a sure foundation. (Isaiah 28:16)

(T)he Shepherd and Overseer of your souls (1 Peter 2:25)   The Shepherd and Overseer of your souls (1 Peter 2:25)

(W)e have an advocate with the Father—Jesus Christ, the Righteous One. (1 John 2:1)   the Righteous One. (1 John 2:1)

I am the Root and the Offspring of David, and the bright Morning Star. (Revelation 22:16)

As for God, his way is perfect. (Psalm 18:30)   As for God, his way is perfect. (Hebrews 1:2)

Chief Shepherd (1 Peter 5:4)   Heir of all things (Hebrews 1:2)   Judge (Acts 10:42)

Sceptre (Numbers 24:17)   Yahweh

Interact 13.4
My Wisdom Plan

Why it is important for me to acquire God's wisdom:

Ways my relationship to God affects how wise I become:

Obstacles to wisdom that I must remove from my life:

Specific activities and practices that will help develop godly wisdom in my life:

Yahweh

Power and might are in your hand. (2 Chronicles 20:6)

The Lord is gracious and compassionate, slow to anger and rich in love.

Holy, holy, holy is the Lord God Almighty, who was, and is, and is to come. (Revelation 4:8)

God is love. (1 John 4:16)

I am the first and the last. (Isaiah 44:6)

Just and true are your ways. (Revelation 15:3)

The Lord reigns. (Psalm 93:1)

My ways are higher than your ways and my thoughts than your thoughts. (Isaiah 55:9)

He does not treat us as our sins deserve. (Psalm 103:10)

I the Lord do not change. (Malachi 3:6)

Christ of God (Luke 9:20)

Where can I flee from your presence? (Psalm 139:7)

Ever-present—(Lamentations 3:23)

Great is your faithfulness. (Lamentations 3:23)

Oh, the depth of the riches of the wisdom and knowledge of God! How unsearchable his judgments, and his paths beyond tracing out! (Romans 11:33)

He is the true God. (1 John 5:20)

Righteousness and justice are the foundation of your throne; love and faithfulness go before you. (Psalm 89:14)

I am the Alpha and the Omega, the First and the Last, the Beginning and the End. (Revelation 22:13)

Lord of the Sabbath (Mark 2:28)

Nothing in all creation is hidden from God's sight. (Hebrews 4:13)

Give thanks to the Lord, for he is good; his love endures forever. (Psalm 118:1)

The Lord is gracious and righteous; our God is full of compassion. (Psalm 116:5)

You alone are holy. (Revelation 15:4)

I am the way and the truth and the life. (John 14:6)

Holy, holy, holy is the Lord Almighty. (Isaiah 6:3)

I AM. (John 8:58)

The Lord works righteousness and justice for all the oppressed. (Psalm 103:6)

In the beginning was the Word, and the Word was with God, and the Word was God. (John 1:1)

No one comes to the Father except through me. (John 14:6)

Taste and see that the Lord is good. (Psalm 34:8)

Your righteousness is everlasting. (Psalm 119:142)

I am the living bread that came down from heaven. (John 6:51)

The Lord is good and his love endures forever. (Psalm 100:5)

To God belong wisdom and power. (Job 12:13)

Jesus the Son of God, let us hold firmly to the faith we profess. (Hebrews 4:14)

He is the atoning sacrifice for our sins, and not only for ours but also for the sins of the whole world. (1 John 2:2)

Jesus, the pioneer and perfecter of faith. (Hebrews 12:2)

Wonderful Counselor, Mighty God, Everlasting Father, Prince of Peace. (Isaiah 9:6)

For to us a child is born, to us a son is given, and the government will be on his shoulders. And he will be called Wonderful Counselor, Mighty God, Everlasting Father, Prince of Peace. (Isaiah 9:6)

Christ died and returned to life so that he might be the Lord of both the dead and the living. (Romans 14:9)

God, the blessed and only Ruler, the King of kings and Lord of lords (1 Timothy 6:15)

The Son is the radiance of God's glory and the exact representation of his being, sustaining all things by his powerful word. After he had provided purification for sins, he sat down at the right hand of the Majesty in heaven. (Hebrews 1:3)

Therefore, since we have a great high priest who has ascended into heaven, Jesus the Son of God (Hebrews 4:14)

the Lamb of God (John 1:29)

the bright Morning Star. (Revelation 22:16)

Let them know that you, whose name is the LORD—that you alone are the Most High over all the earth. (Psalm 83:18)

We have this hope as an anchor for the soul, firm and secure. It enters the inner sanctuary behind the curtain, where our forerunner, Jesus, has entered on our behalf. He has become a high priest forever, in the order of Melchizedek. (Hebrews 6:19-20)

God, who is and who was and who is to come, the Almighty (Revelation 1:8)

The LORD will be king over the whole earth. On that day there will be one LORD, and his name the only name. (Zechariah 14:9)

The Son of Man came eating and drinking, and they say, 'Here is a glutton and a drunkard, a friend of tax collectors and sinners.' (Matthew 11:19)

And we have seen and testify that the Father has sent his Son to be the Savior of the world. (1 John 4:14)

Desire of all nations (Haggai 2:7)

Rose of Sharon (Song of Songs 2:1)

That which was from the beginning, which we have heard, which we have seen with our eyes, which we have looked at and our hands have touched—this we proclaim concerning the Word of life. (1 John 1:1)

Chosen of God (1 Peter 2:4)

the bridegroom (Matthew 9:15)

Behold, a King who will reign in righteousness (Isaiah 32:1)

So this is what the Sovereign LORD says: See, I lay a stone in Zion, a tested stone, a precious cornerstone for a sure foundation. (Isaiah 28:16)

From everlasting to everlasting you are God. (Psalm 90:2)

The virgin will conceive and give birth to a son, and will call him Immanuel. (Isaiah 7:14)

Thanks be to God for his indescribable gift! (2 Corinthians 9:15)

(O)ur Lord Jesus, that great Shepherd of the sheep (Hebrews 13:20)

The Lord is enthroned as King forever. (Psalm 29:10)

I am the true vine, and my Father is the gardener. (John 15:1)

(T)he Shepherd and Overseer of your souls. (1 Peter 2:25)

(W)e have an advocate with the Father—Jesus Christ, the Righteous One. (1 John 2:1)

I am the Root and the Offspring of David, and the bright Morning Star. (Revelation 22:16)

As for God, his way is perfect. (Psalm 18:30)

Chief Shepherd (1 Peter 5:4)

Sceptre (Numbers 24:17)

Judge (Acts 10:42)

Heir of all things (Hebrews 1:2)

Yahweh

Interact 13.5

God Is Truthful

Look up the following Scripture passages. Decide whether the passage is talking primarily about God's *person* or about His *words* or *both*, and check the appropriate box. Then add any notes or comments about why this information is important for us to know.

Scripture	Person or Words?	Notes
Psalm 25:5	☐ Person ☐ Words	
Psalm 33:4	☐ Person ☐ Words	
Psalm 119:142	☐ Person ☐ Words	
Isaiah 45:19	☐ Person ☐ Words	
Daniel 9:13	☐ Person ☐ Words	
John 14:6	☐ Person ☐ Words	
John 15:26	☐ Person ☐ Words	
John 16:13	☐ Person ☐ Words	
John 17:17	☐ Person ☐ Words	
Ephesians 1:13	☐ Person ☐ Words	
2 Timothy 2:25	☐ Person ☐ Words	
2 Timothy 4:4	☐ Person ☐ Words	
Titus 1:1	☐ Person ☐ Words	
James 1:18	☐ Person ☐ Words	
1 John 5:20	☐ Person ☐ Words	
Revelation 3:7	☐ Person ☐ Words	
Revelation 15:3	☐ Person ☐ Words	
Revelation 19:9	☐ Person ☐ Words	
Revelation 19:11	☐ Person ☐ Words	
Revelation 21:5	☐ Person ☐ Words	

Let God Be GOD

Yahweh

Power and might are in your hand. (2 Chronicles 20:6)

The Lord is gracious and compassionate, slow to anger and rich in love. (Psalm 145:8)

Holy, holy, holy is the Lord God Almighty, who was, and is, and is to come. (Revelation 4:8)

I am the first and the last. (Isaiah 44:6)

Just and true are your ways. (Revelation 15:3)

God is love. (1 John 4:16)

The Lord reigns (Psalm 93:1)

My ways are higher than your ways and my thoughts than your thoughts. (Isaiah 55:9)

Where can I flee from your presence? (Psalm 139:7)

He does not treat us as our sins deserve. (Psalm 103:10)

I the Lord do not change. (Malachi 3:6)

Christ of God (Luke 9:20)

Ever present...

Great is your faithfulness. (Lamentations 3:23)

Oh, the depth of the riches of the wisdom and knowledge of God! How unsearchable his judgments, and his paths beyond tracing out! (Romans 11:33)

He is the true God. (1 John 5:20)

Righteousness and justice are the foundation of your throne; love and faithfulness go before you. (Psalm 89:14)

I am the Alpha and the Omega, the First and the Last, the Beginning and the End. (Revelation 22:13)

Nothing in all creation is hidden from God's sight. (Hebrews 4:13)

The Lord is gracious and righteous; our God is full of compassion. (Psalm 116:5)

Give thanks to the Lord, for he is good; his love endures forever. (Psalm 118:1)

You alone are holy. (Revelation 15:4)

I am the way and the truth and the life. (John 14:6)

Holy, holy, holy is the Lord Almighty. (Isaiah 6:3)

I AM (John 8:58)

Lord of the sabbath (Mark 2:28)

I am with you always. (Matthew 28:20)

I am the living bread that came down from heaven. (John 6:51)

The Lord works righteousness and justice for all the oppressed. (Psalm 103:6)

To God belong wisdom and power. (Job 12:13)

In the beginning was the Word, and the Word was with God, and the Word was God. (John 1:1)

Taste and see that the Lord is good (Psalm 34:8)

No one comes to the Father except through me. (John 14:6)

Your righteousness is everlasting. (Psalm 119:142)

And he will be called Wonderful Counselor, Mighty God, Everlasting Father, Prince of Peace. (Isaiah 9:6)

The Lord is good and his love endures forever. (Psalm 100:5)

For to us a child is born, to us a son is given, and the government will be on his shoulders. (Isaiah 9:6)

Christ died and returned to life so that he might be the Lord of both the dead and the living. (Romans 14:9)

Jesus the Son of God, let us hold firmly to the faith we profess. (Hebrews 4:14)

He is the atoning sacrifice for our sins, and not only for ours but also for the sins of the whole world. (1 John 2:2)

After he had provided purification for sins, he sat down at the right hand of the Majesty in heaven. (Hebrews 1:3)

the faithful witness ... has entered on our behalf. He has become a high priest forever, in the order of Melchizedek. (Hebrews 6:19-20)

The Son is the radiance of God's glory and the exact representation of his being, sustaining all things by his powerful word. (Hebrews 1:3)

God, the blessed and only Ruler, the King of kings and Lord of lords (1 Timothy 6:15)

(Him) who is, and who was, and who is to come, and from the seven spirits before his throne (Revelation 1:4)

Jesus, the pioneer and perfecter of faith. (Hebrews 12:2)

He is the Lamb of God... (John 1:29)

whose name is the LORD—that you alone are the Most High over all the earth. (Psalm 83:18)

it enters the inner sanctuary behind the curtain, where our forerunner, Jesus, has entered on our behalf. (Hebrews 6:19-20)

which we have seen with our eyes, which we have looked at and our hands have touched (1 John 1:1)

the Father has sent his Son to be the Savior of the world. (1 John 4:14)

And we have seen and testify that the Father has sent his Son to be the Savior of the world. (1 John 4:14)

Here is a glutton and a drunkard, a friend of tax collectors and sinners. (Matthew 11:19)

Here is your king (Zechariah 9:9)

For the Son of Man came eating and drinking, and they say (Matthew 11:19)

this we proclaim concerning the Word of life. (1 John 1:1)

Desire of all nations (Haggai 2:7)

Branch, a King who will reign wisely and do what is just and right in the land. (Jeremiah 23:5)

a tested stone, a precious cornerstone for a sure foundation. (Isaiah 28:16)

Thanks be to God for his indescribable gift! (2 Corinthians 9:15)

Therefore, since we have a great high priest who has ascended into heaven, Jesus the Son of God (Hebrews 4:14)

The Son is the exact representation of God's glory (Hebrews 1:3)

We have this hope as an anchor for the soul, firm and secure. (Hebrews 6:19)

(In) him who is... whose name is the LORD (Psalm 83:18)

(Let) them know that you, whose name is the LORD (Psalm 83:18)

Rose of Sharon (Song of Songs 2:1)

That which was from the beginning, which we have heard, which we have seen with our eyes (1 John 1:1)

God, the blessed and only Ruler, the King of kings and Lord of lords (1 Timothy 6:15)

The LORD will be king over the whole earth. (Zechariah 14:9)

From everlasting to everlasting you are God. (Psalm 90:2)

The virgin will conceive and give birth to a son, and will call him Immanuel. (Isaiah 7:14)

Chosen of God (1 Peter 2:4)

The Son of Man came (Matthew 9:13)

On that day there will be one LORD, and his name the only name. (Zechariah 14:9)

(Our) Lord Jesus, that great Shepherd of the sheep (Hebrews 13:20)

I am the true vine, and my Father is the gardener (John 15:1)

The Lord is enthroned as King forever. (Psalm 29:10)

(The) Shepherd and Overseer of your souls (1 Peter 2:25)

(We have) an advocate with the Father—Jesus Christ, the Righteous One. (1 John 2:1)

I am the Root and the Offspring of David, and the bright Morning Star. (Revelation 22:16)

As for God, his way is perfect. (Psalm 18:30)

Chief Shepherd (1 Peter 5:4)

Sceptre (Hebrews 1:8)

Heir of all things (Hebrews 1:2)

Judge (Acts 10:42)

Yahweh

Interact 13.6

Reflecting God's Truthfulness

Look up the following Scripture passages. Complete the chart by answering the questions for each Scripture passage. (Note: You may want to look at the surrounding verses to get a better understanding of the passage.)

Scripture passage	Summarize what this passage says about reflecting God's truthfulness.	Give specific ways we can fulfill the teachings in this passage.
Psalm 15		
Proverbs 12:17		
Proverbs 22:17–21		
Proverbs 23:23		
Isaiah 59:14–15		
Zechariah 8:16–17		
Proverbs 11:1, 16:11		
John 19:35, 21:24		
1 Corinthians 13:6		
Ephesians 4:15, 25		
Ephesians 6:14		
Philippians 4:8		
1 John 1:1–3		
1 John 1:6		
1 John 3:18		
2 John 1–4		
3 John 3–4		

Let God Be GOD

Yahweh

Power and might are in your hand. (2 Chronicles 20:6)

The Lord is gracious and compassionate, slow to anger and rich in love.

Holy, holy, holy is the Lord God Almighty, who was, and is, and is to come. (Revelation 4:8)

God is love. (1 John 4:16)

I am the first and the last. (Isaiah 44:6)

Just and true are your ways. (Revelation 15:3)

The Lord reigns (Psalm 93:1)

My ways are higher than your ways and my thoughts than your thoughts. (Isaiah 55:9)

He does not treat us as our sins deserve. (Psalm 103:10)

I the Lord do not change. (Malachi 3:6)

Christ of God (Luke 9:20)

Ever-present—Where can I flee from your presence? (Psalm 139:7)

Oh, the depth of the riches of the wisdom and knowledge of God! How unsearchable his judgments, and his paths beyond tracing out! (Romans 11:33)

Lord of the Sabbath (Mark 2:28)

Great is your faithfulness. (Lamentations 3:23)

Righteousness and justice are the foundation of your throne; love and faithfulness go before you. (Psalm 89:14)

I am with you always. (Matthew 28:20)

I am the Alpha and the Omega, the First and the Last, the Beginning and the End. (Revelation 22:13)

Nothing in all creation is hidden from God's sight. (Hebrews 4:13)

You alone are holy. (Revelation 15:4)

He is the true God. (1 John 5:20)

The Lord is gracious and righteous; our God is full of compassion. (Psalm 116:5)

Give thanks to the Lord, for he is good; his love endures forever. (Psalm 118:1)

Holy, holy, holy is the Lord Almighty. (Isaiah 6:3)

I AM (John 8:58)

To God belong wisdom and power. (Job 12:13)

I am the way and the truth and the life. No one comes to the Father except through me. (John 14:6)

I am the living bread that came down from heaven. (John 6:51)

The Lord works righteousness and justice for all the oppressed. (Psalm 103:6)

In the beginning was the Word, and the Word was with God, and the Word was God. (John 1:1)

Taste and see that the Lord is good. (Psalm 34:8)

Your righteousness is everlasting. (Psalm 119:142)

I am the Lord of both the dead and the living. (Romans 14:9)

The Lord is good and his love endures forever. (Psalm 100:5)

For to us a child is born, to us a son is given, and the government will be on his shoulders. And he will be called Wonderful Counselor, Mighty God, Everlasting Father, Prince of Peace. (Isaiah 9:6)

Jesus, the pioneer and perfecter of faith. (Hebrews 12:2)

Christ died and returned to life so that he might be the Lord of both the dead and the living. (Romans 14:9)

God, the blessed and only Ruler, the King of kings and Lord of lords. (1 Timothy 6:15)

He is the atoning sacrifice for our sins, and not only for ours but also for the sins of the whole world. (1 John 2:2)

The Son is the radiance of God's glory and the exact representation of his being, sustaining all things by his powerful word. After he had provided purification for sins, he sat down at the right hand of the Majesty in heaven. (Hebrews 1:3)

Him who is and who was, and who is to come. (Revelation 1:4-5)

Jesus, who is the faithful witness, the firstborn from the dead, and the ruler of the kings of the earth. (Revelation 1:5)

I am the bright Morning Star. (Revelation 22:16)

Let them know that you, whose name is the LORD—that you alone are the Most High over all the earth. (Psalm 83:18)

We have this hope as an anchor for the soul, firm and secure. It enters the inner sanctuary behind the curtain, where our forerunner, Jesus, has entered on our behalf. He has become a high priest forever, in the order of Melchizedek. (Hebrews 6:19-20)

We have heard, which we have seen with our eyes, which we have looked at and our hands have touched. (1 John 1:1)

The LORD will be king over the whole earth. On that day there will be one LORD, and his name the only name. (Zechariah 14:9)

The Son of Man came eating and drinking, and they say, 'Here is a glutton and a drunkard, a friend of tax collectors and sinners.' (Matthew 11:19)

Bridegroom (Matthew 9:15)

Chosen of God (1 Peter 2:4)

The Father has sent his Son to be the Savior of the world. (1 John 4:14)

This we proclaim concerning the Word of life. (1 John 1:1)

The usual way; they came and worshiped him... (Matthew 28:9)

I am the Root and Offspring of David... (Revelation 22:16)

I lay a stone in Zion, a tested stone, a precious cornerstone for a sure foundation. (Isaiah 28:16)

And we have seen and testify that the Father has sent his Son to be the Savior of the world. (1 John 4:14)

Desire of all nations (Haggai 2:7)

In those days a King who will reign wisely. (Jeremiah 23:5)

Righteous Branch, a King who will reign wisely and do what is just and right in the land. (Jeremiah 23:5)

Therefore, since we have a great high priest who has ascended into heaven, Jesus the Son of God, let us hold firmly to the faith we profess. (Hebrews 4:14)

God the blessed and only Ruler, the King of kings and Lord of lords. (1 Timothy 6:15)

Thanks be to God for his indescribable gift! (2 Corinthians 9:15)

That which was from the beginning, which we have heard. (1 John 1:1)

From everlasting to everlasting you are God. (Psalm 90:2)

The virgin will conceive and give birth to a son, and will call him Immanuel. (Isaiah 7:14)

The Lord is enthroned as King forever. (Psalm 29:10)

(O)ur Lord Jesus, that great Shepherd of the sheep (Hebrews 13:20)

I am the true vine, and my Father is the gardener. (John 15:1)

(T)he Shepherd and Overseer of your souls (1 Peter 2:25)

(W)e have an advocate with the Father—Jesus Christ, the Righteous One. (1 John 2:1)

As for God, his way is perfect. (Psalm 18:30)

I am the Root and the Offspring of David, and the bright Morning Star. (Revelation 22:16)

I am the Chief Shepherd (1 Peter 5:4)

Heir of all things (Hebrews 1:2)

Sceptre (Numbers 24:17)

Judge (Acts 10:42)

Yahweh

14

GOD Is Holy and Righteous

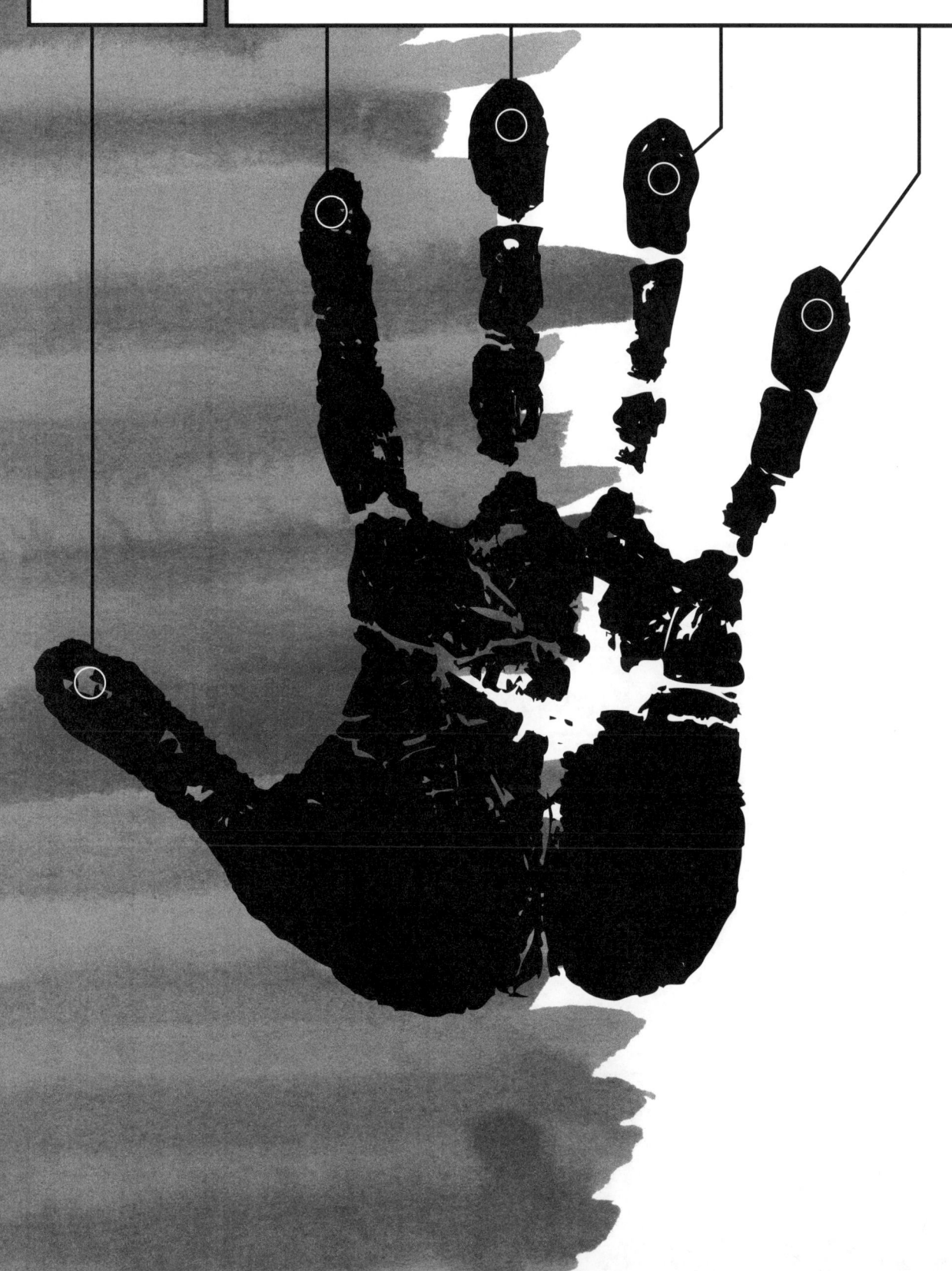

Interact 14.1
God Is Holy

Complete a Scripture search. Look up and read the passage assigned to you. Complete the Interact. For each passage, supply the following: The **problem** of the story; the teaching about God's **holiness**; the teaching about human **sinfulness**; and a specific, personal, and measurable **application** for your life today.

Leviticus 10:1–11

Problem

Holiness

Sinfulness

Application

Leviticus 24:10–23

Problem

Holiness

Sinfulness

Application

Continued on back →

Let God Be GOD

God Is Holy continued

Joshua 7

Problem

Holiness

Sinfulness

Application

2 Samuel 6:1–8

Problem

Holiness

Sinfulness

Application

Continued on next page →

Let God Be GOD

Interact 14.1

God Is Holy continued

Acts 5:1–11

Problem

Holiness

Sinfulness

Application

Acts 12:19–23

Problem

Holiness

Sinfulness

Application

Yahweh   Power and might are in your hand. (2 Chronicles 20:6)

The Lord is gracious and compassionate, slow to anger and rich in love.

Holy, holy, holy is the Lord God Almighty, who was, and is, and is to come. (Revelation 4:8)

God is love. (1 John 4:16)   I am the first and the last. (Isaiah 44:6)   Just and true are your ways. (Revelation 15:3)

The Lord reigns (Psalm 93:1)   My ways are higher than your ways and my thoughts than your thoughts. (Isaiah 55:9)

Christ of God (Luke 9:20)   Where can I flee from your presence? (Psalm 139:7)   He does not treat us as our sins deserve. (Psalm 103:10)   The Lord do not change (Malachi 3:6)

Ever-present—   How unsearchable his judgments, and his paths beyond tracing out! (Romans 11:33)   I am with you always (Matthew 28:20)

Great is your faithfulness. (Lamentations 3:23)   love and faithfulness go before you.   Lord of the sabbath (Mark 2:28)

On the depth of the riches of the wisdom and knowledge of God! How   (Revelation 22:13) You alone are holy. (Revelation 15:4)   I AM (John 8:58)

Righteousness and justice are the foundation of your throne; (Psalm 89:14)   Holy, holy, holy is the Lord Almighty. (Isaiah 6:3)   No one comes to the Father except through me. (John 14:6)   I am the living bread that come down from heaven. (John 6:51)

He is the true God (1 John 5:20)   God is full of compassion. (Psalm 116:5) Give thanks to the Lord, for he is good; his love endures forever. (Psalm 118:1)   Jesus, the pioneer and perfecter of faith. (Hebrews 12:2)

I am the Alpha and the Omega, the First and the Last, the Beginning and the End.   I am the way and the truth and the life. (John 14:6)   The Lord is good and his love endures forever. (Psalm 100:5)   Everlasting Father, Prince of Peace. (Isaiah 9:6)

Nothing in all creation is hidden from God's sight. (Hebrews 4:13)   and the Word was God. (John 1:1)   Taste and see that the Lord is good. (Psalm 34:8)

In the beginning was the Word, and the Word was with God,   the Son of God, let us hold firmly to the faith we profess. (Hebrews 4:14)   Wonderful Counselor, Mighty God,   the Lamb of God (John 1:29)

The Lord is gracious and righteous; our God is full of compassion. (Psalm 116:5)   Jesus the Son of both the dead and the living. (Romans 14:9)   He is the atoning sacrifice for our sins, and not only for ours but also for the sins of the whole world. (1 John 2:2)   Jesus, the bright Morning Star. (Revelation 22:16)

The Lord works righteousness and justice for all the oppressed. (Psalm 103:6)   And he will be the Lord of both the dead and the living. (Romans 14:9)   He is the atoning sacrifice for our sins, (1 Timothy 6:15)   After he had provided purification for sins, he sat down at the right hand of the Majesty in heaven. (Hebrews 1:3)

Your righteousness is everlasting. (Psalm 119:142)   who has ascended into heaven; Jesus the Son of God   (Zechariah 14:9) there is a glutton and a drunkard, a friend of tax collectors and sinners.   of Lord (Revelation 3:14)

To God belong wisdom and power. (Job 12:13)   a great high priest   He is the atoning sacrifice   the Root and the Offspring of David, and the bright Morning Star. (Revelation 22:16)

For to us a child is born; to us a son is given, and the government will be on his shoulders. And he will be called Wonderful Counselor, Mighty God, Everlasting Father, Prince of Peace. (Isaiah 9:6)   the Most High over all the earth. (Psalm 83:18)   He has entered on our behalf. He has become a high priest forever, in the order of Melchizedek. (Hebrews 6:19-20)

Christ died and returned to life so that he might be the Lord of both the dead and the living. (Romans 14:9)   the King of kings and Lord of lords (1 Timothy 6:15)   Here is a stone in Zion, a tested stone, a precious cornerstone for a sure foundation. (Isaiah 28:16)

The Son is the radiance of God's glory and the exact representation of his being, sustaining all things by his powerful word.   I am the Root and the offspring of David, whom you desire, will come. (Malachi 3:1)

Therefore, since we have a great high priest who has ascended into heaven, Jesus the Son of God, let us hold firmly to the faith we profess. (Hebrews 4:14)   the seven spirits before his throne   the Son of Man came eating and drinking and they say, (Matthew 11:19)

Rose of Sharon (Song of Songs 2:1)   (Him) who is, and who was, and who is to come,   It enters the inner sanctuary behind the curtain, where our forerunner, Jesus, has entered on our behalf. (Hebrews 6:19-20)   Desire of all nations (Haggai 2:7)

Let them know that you, whose name is the LORD—that you alone are the Most High over all the earth. (Psalm 83:18)   a King who will reign in righteousness and do what is just and right in the land. (Jeremiah 23:5)

We have this hope as an anchor for the soul, firm and secure. It enters   the Father has sent his Son to be the Savior of the world. (1 John 4:14)   And Lord who will reign in righteousness (Jeremiah 23:5)

God, the blessed and only Ruler, the King of kings and Lord of lords (1 Timothy 6:15)   his name the only name. (1 Peter 2:4)

That which was from the beginning, which we have heard, (1 John 1:1)   Chosen of God (1 Peter 2:4)   thanks be to God for his indescribable gift! (2 Corinthians 9:15)

The LORD will be king over the whole earth. (Zechariah 14:9)   On that day there will be one LORD, and his name the only name. (Zechariah 14:9)   The virgin will conceive and give birth to a son, and will call him Immanuel. (Isaiah 7:14)

from everlasting to everlasting you are God. (Psalm 90:2)   The Son of Man   The Lord is enthroned as King forever (Psalm 29:10)

(O)ur Lord Jesus, that great Shepherd of the sheep (Hebrews 13:20)

I am the true vine, and my Father is the gardener (John 15:1)

(T)he Shepherd and Overseer of your souls. (1 Peter 2:25)

(W)e have an advocate with the Father—Jesus Christ, the Righteous One. (1 John 2:1)

I am the Root and the Offspring of David, and the bright Morning Star. (Revelation 22:16)

As for God, his way is perfect. (Psalm 18:30)

Chief Shepherd (1 Peter 5:4)   Heir of all things (Hebrews 1:2)

Sceptre (Numbers 24:17)   Judge (Acts 10:42)

Yahweh

Interact 14.2
God Is Righteous

Look up the following Scripture passages and answer the questions. Be prepared to discuss your answers in class.

1. Once in a while, the Bible describes certain people as righteous. According to these verses, why are some people called righteous?

Genesis 18:22–25	
Exodus 9:27	
1 Samuel 24:17	
Psalm 15:1–2	
Psalm 97:10–12	
Psalm 103:17–18	
Psalm 112:1–9	
Proverbs 16:12	

2. Righteousness is an attribute of God. According to these verses, how does God show that He is righteousness?

Psalm 7:9	
Psalm 31:1	
Psalm 51:14	
Psalm 65:5	
Psalm 116:5	
Psalm 119:40	
Psalm 143:1, 11	
Isaiah 45:23–25	

3. Read these New Testament verses and answer the questions.

Matthew 5:20	
Luke 5:31–32	
Luke 18:9	
John 17:25	
Romans 1:17	
Romans 3:10	
Romans 3:20–22	
Romans 4:13	
2 Corinthians 5:21	
Philippians 3:8–9	

What kind of righteousness does God demand of us? How is it possible for us to have that kind of righteousness? What makes it possible for us to be righteous? Why is it dangerous to assume that we're righteous when we're not?

Yahweh

Power and might are in your hand. (2 Chronicles 20:6)

The Lord is gracious and compassionate, slow to anger and rich in love. (Psalm 145:8)

Holy, holy, holy is the Lord God Almighty, who was, and is, and is to come. (Revelation 4:8)

God is love. (1 John 4:16)

I am the first and the last. (Isaiah 44:6)

Just and true are your ways. (Revelation 15:3)

The Lord reigns (Psalm 93:1)

My ways are higher than your ways and my thoughts than your thoughts. (Isaiah 55:9)

He does not treat us as our sins deserve. (Psalm 103:10)

Christ of God (Luke 9:20)

Ever-present—Where can I flee from your presence? (Psalm 139:7)

the Lord do not change. (Malachi 3:6)

Great is your faithfulness. (Lamentations 3:23)

How unsearchable his judgments, and his paths beyond tracing out! (Romans 11:33)

Oh, the depth of the riches of the wisdom and knowledge of God!

Lord of the sabbath (Mark 2:28)

Righteousness and justice are the foundation of your throne; love and faithfulness go before you. (Psalm 89:14)

I am the Alpha and the Omega, the First and the Last, the Beginning and the End. (Revelation 22:13)

Nothing in all creation is hidden from God's sight. (Hebrews 4:13)

I am with you always (Matthew 28:20)

He is the true God. (1 John 5:20)

Give thanks to the Lord, for he is good; his love endures forever. (Psalm 118:1)

The Lord is gracious and righteous; our God is full of compassion. (Psalm 116:5)

You alone are holy. (Revelation 15:4)

I am the way and the truth and the life. No one comes to the Father except through me. (John 14:6)

Holy, holy, holy is the Lord Almighty. (Isaiah 6:3)

I AM (John 8:58)

In the beginning was the Word, and the Word was with God, and the Word was God. (John 1:1)

Taste and see that the Lord is good (Psalm 34:8)

The Lord works righteousness and justice for all the oppressed. (Psalm 103:6)

I am the living bread that came down from heaven. (John 6:51)

The Lord is good and his love endures forever. (Psalm 100:5)

Your righteousness is everlasting (Psalm 119:142)

And he will be called Wonderful Counselor, Mighty God, Everlasting Father, Prince of Peace. (Isaiah 9:6)

To God belong wisdom and power (Job 12:13)

He is the atoning sacrifice for our sins, and not only for ours but also for the sins of the whole world. (1 John 2:2)

The Lord of both the dead and the living. (Romans 14:9)

Jesus the Son of God, let us hold firmly to the faith we profess. (Hebrews 4:14)

For to us a child is born, to us a son is given, and the government will be on his shoulders.

After he had provided purification for sins, he sat down at the right hand of the Majesty in heaven (Hebrews 1:3)

Christ died and returned to life so that he might be the Lord of both the dead and the living.

the Lamb of God (John 1:29)

Jesus, the pioneer and perfecter of faith. (Hebrews 12:2)

Therefore, since we have a great high priest who has ascended into heaven, Jesus

God, the blessed and only Ruler, the King of kings and Lord of lords (1 Timothy 6:15)

The Son is the radiance of God's glory and the exact representation of his being, sustaining all things by his powerful word.

let them know that you, whose name is the LORD—that you alone are the Most High over all the earth. (Psalm 83:18)

I am the Root and the Offspring of David, and the bright Morning Star. (Revelation 22:16)

Rose of Sharon (Song of Songs 2:1)

(him who is, and who was, and who is to come, and from the seven spirits before his throne,

which we have seen with our eyes, which we have looked at and our hands have touched. (Zechariah 14:9)

That which was from the beginning, which we have heard,

Jesus has entered on our behalf. He has become a high priest forever, in the order of Melchizedek. (Hebrews 6:19-20)

We have this hope as an anchor for the soul, firm and secure. It enters the inner sanctuary behind the curtain, where our forerunner, Jesus,

The Father has sent his Son to be the Savior of the world. (1 John 4:14)

this we proclaim concerning the Word of life. (1 John 1:1)

the firstborn from the dead, and the ruler of the kings of the earth. (Revelation 1:5)

Here is a glutton and a drunkard, a friend of tax collectors and sinners. (Matthew 11:19)

The LORD will be king over the whole earth. On that day there will be one LORD, and his name the only name. (Zechariah 14:9)

The Son of Man came eating and drinking, and they say, 'Here is

Desire of all nations (Haggai 2:7)

I will betroth you to me forever. (Hosea 2:19)

a righteous Branch, a King who will reign wisely and do what is just and right in the land. (Jeremiah 23:5)

I lay a stone in Zion, a tested stone, a precious cornerstone for a sure foundation. (Isaiah 28:16)

Thanks be to God for his indescribable gift! (2 Corinthians 9:15)

And we have seen and testify that the Father has sent his Son to be the Savior of the world. (1 John 4:14)

Chosen of God (1 Peter 2:4)

From everlasting to everlasting you are God. (Psalm 90:2)

The virgin will conceive and give birth to a son, and will call him Immanuel. (Isaiah 7:14)

The Lord is enthroned as King forever. (Psalm 29:10)

(O)ur Lord Jesus, that great Shepherd of the sheep (Hebrews 13:20)

I am the true vine, and my Father is the gardener. (John 15:1)

(The) Shepherd and Overseer of your souls. (1 Peter 2:25)

(W)e have an advocate with the Father—Jesus Christ, the Righteous One. (1 John 2:1)

I am the Root and the Offspring of David, and the bright Morning Star. (Revelation 22:16)

As for God, his way is perfect. (Psalm 18:30)

Chief Shepherd (1 Peter 5:4)

Sceptre (Numbers 24:17)

Heir of all things (Hebrews 1:2)

Judge (Acts 10:42)

Yahweh

15

GOD **Is Merciful and Just**

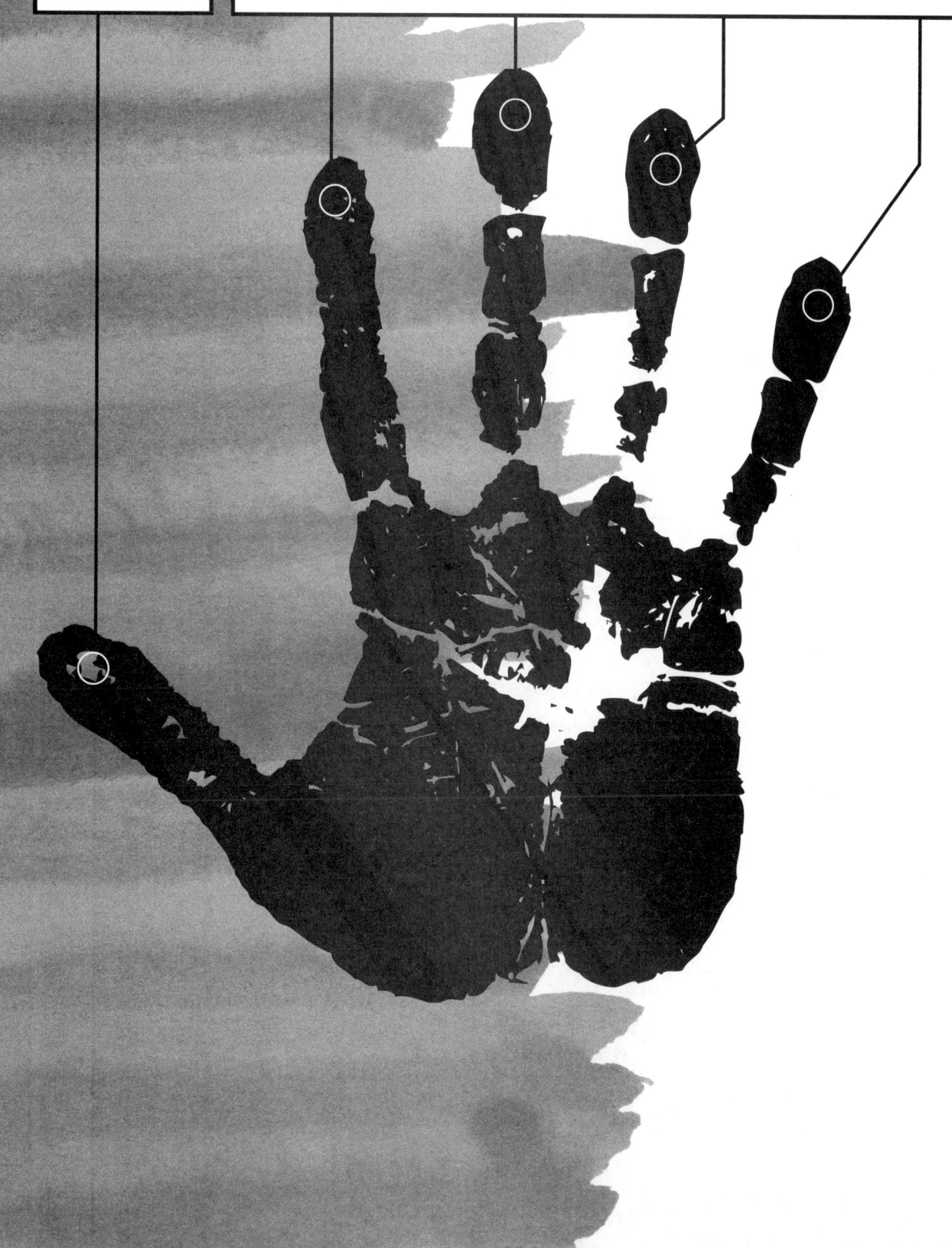

Interact 15.1

Old Testament Mercy

Read the Scripture passages and answer the questions.

1. What did Adam and Eve deserve? (Genesis 2:17)

What did Adam and Eve receive? (Genesis 3:17–24)

2. What did Cain deserve? (Genesis 4:10–12)

What did Cain receive? (Genesis 4:13–16)

3. What did humans deserve? (Genesis 6:5–7)

What did humans receive? (Genesis 6:3, 8)

4. What did the Amorites deserve? (Genesis 15:16)

What did the Amorites receive? (Genesis 15:16)

5. What did Ahab deserve? (1 Kings 21:17–26)

What did Ahab receive? (1 Kings 21:27–29)

6. What do believers deserve? (Psalm 103:10)

What do believers receive? (Psalm 103:11–14)

Let God Be GOD

Yahweh

Power and might are in your hand. (2 Chronicles 20:6)

The Lord is gracious and compassionate, slow to anger and rich in love. (Psalm 145:8)

Holy, holy, holy is the Lord God Almighty, who was, and is, and is to come. (Revelation 4:8)

God is love. (1 John 4:16) I am the first and the last. (Isaiah 44:6) Just and true are your ways. (Revelation 15:3)

The Lord reigns. (Psalm 93:1)

My ways are higher than your ways and my thoughts than your thoughts. (Isaiah 55:9)

He does not treat us as our sins deserve. (Psalm 103:10)   (the Lord do not change) (Malachi 3:6)

Christ of God (Luke 9:20)

Where can I flee from your presence? (Psalm 139:7)   I am with you always. (Matthew 28:20)

Ever-present   Great is your faithfulness. (Lamentations 3:23)

How unsearchable his judgments, and his paths beyond tracing out! (Romans 11:33)   Lord of the sabbath (Mark 2:28)

Oh, the depth of the riches of the wisdom and knowledge of God!

Righteousness and justice are the foundation of your throne; love and faithfulness go before you. (Psalm 89:14)

...is hidden from God's sight. (Hebrews 4:13)

I am the Alpha and the Omega, the First and the Last, the Beginning and the End. (Revelation 22:13)   You alone are holy. (Revelation 15:4)

He is the true God. (1 John 5:20)   Give thanks to the Lord, for he is good; his love endures forever. (Psalm 118:1)   I AM (John 8:58)

Nothing in all creation is hidden from God's sight. (Hebrews 4:13)

I am the way and the truth and the life. No one comes to the Father except through me. (John 14:6)

Holy, holy, holy is the Lord Almighty. (Isaiah 6:3)   I am living bread that came down from heaven. (John 6:51)

The Lord is gracious and righteous; our God is full of compassion. (Psalm 116:5)   Taste and see that the Lord is good (Psalm 34:8)

In the beginning was the Word, and the Word was with God, and the Word was God. (John 1:1)   The Lord is good and his love endures forever. (Psalm 146)   The Lord is good (Psalm 100:5)

...will be called Wonderful Counselor, Mighty God, Everlasting Father, Prince of Peace. (Isaiah 9:6)

To God belong wisdom and power. (Job 12:13)

The Lord works righteousness and justice for all the oppressed. (Psalm 103:6)

Jesus the Son of God, let us hold firmly to the faith we profess. (Hebrews 4:14)

...the Lord of both the dead and the living. (Romans 14:9)

And the government will be on his shoulders. And he will be called Wonderful Counselor, Mighty God...

He is the atoning sacrifice for our sins, and not only for ours but also for the sins of the whole world. (1 John 2:2)

the pioneer and perfecter of faith. (Hebrews 12:2)   Jesus   the Majesty in heaven. (Hebrews 1:3)

After he had provided purification for sins, he sat down at the right hand of the Majesty in heaven. (Hebrews 1:3)

the Lamb of God (John 1:29)   the faithful witness, the firstborn from the dead and the ruler of the kings of the earth. (Revelation 1:5)

Your righteousness is everlasting. (Psalm 119:142)

For to us a child is born, to us a son is given, and the government will be on his shoulders, so that he might be the Lord...

Christ died and returned to life so that he might be the Lord of both the dead and the living. (Romans 14:9)

The Son is the radiance of God's glory and the exact representation of his being, sustaining all things by his powerful word. (Hebrews 1:3)

Rose of Sharon (Song of Songs 2:1)

God, the blessed and only Ruler, the King of kings and Lord of lords (1 Timothy 6:15)   Him who is and who was, and who is to come (Revelation 1:4)

whose name is the LORD, and his name the only name. (Zechariah 14:9)

Let them know that you, whose name is the LORD—that you alone are the Most High over all the earth. (Psalm 83:18)

We have this hope as an anchor for the soul, firm and secure. It enters the inner sanctuary behind the curtain, where our forerunner, Jesus, has entered on our behalf. He has become a high priest forever, in the order of Melchizedek. (Hebrews 6:19-20)

the Father has sent his Son to be the Savior of the world. (1 John 4:14)   and we have put our trust

The Son of Man came eating and drinking, and they say, 'Here is a glutton and a drunkard, a friend of tax collectors and sinners.' (Matthew 11:19)

Desire of all nations (Haggai 2:7)   ...lay a stone in Zion, a tested stone, a precious cornerstone for a sure foundation (Isaiah 28:16)

...will reign... and do what is just and right in the land. (Jeremiah 23:5)   Chosen of God (1 Peter 2:4)

Thanks be to God for his indescribable gift. (2 Corinthians 9:15)

That, which was from the beginning, which we have heard, which we have seen with our eyes...

The LORD will be king over the whole earth. On that day there will be one LORD, and his name the only name. (Zechariah 14:9)

From everlasting to everlasting you are God. (Psalm 90:2)   The virgin will conceive and give birth to a son, and will call him Immanuel. (Isaiah 7:14)

The Lord is enthroned as King forever. (Psalm 29:10)

(O)ur Lord Jesus, that great Shepherd of the sheep (Hebrews 13:20)

I am the true vine, and my Father is the gardener. (John 15:1)

(T)he Shepherd and Overseer of your souls (1 Peter 2:25)

(W)e have an advocate with the Father—Jesus Christ, the Righteous One. (1 John 2:1)

...the Root and the Offspring of David, and the bright Morning Star. (Revelation 22:16)

As for God, his way is perfect. (Psalm 18:30)

I am the Root and the Offspring of David, and the bright Morning Star. (Revelation 22:16)

Heir of all things (Hebrews 1:2)   Judge (Acts 10:42)

Chief Shepherd (1 Peter 5:4)   Sceptre   Yahweh

Interact 15.2
Justice and Mercy

Read Isaiah 58 and 59 once without stopping. Then go back and read selected verses and answer these questions.

1. Why did the people think themselves religious? (58:1–3)

2. What specific items did the Lord identify in the people's conduct that showed their religion to be corrupt? (58:3–14)

3. What did the Lord identify as actions that would demonstrate true religion? (58:6–14)

4. What would be the results if the actions listed for question 3 were followed? (58:8–14)

5. List metaphors, similes, and other word pictures that God uses to describe the people's sin. (59:1–11) Why are these word pictures used?

6. Underline the word *justice* in Isaiah 59:1–15. List the words that parallel *justice*. (For example, in verse 4: "No one calls for justice; no one pleads his case with integrity.") Why are these other words important?

Continued on back →

Let God Be GOD

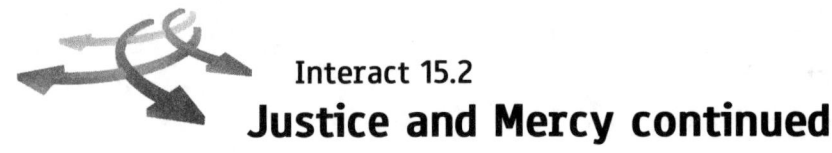

Justice and Mercy continued

7. List specific offenses in 59:12–15. Paraphrase the verses or describe the offenses in your own words, showing how they apply to our lives today. (For example, for "rebellion and treachery against the Lord" in verse 13, you might say, "We know what is right and refuse to do it. We plot. We find ways to get around God's standards of righteousness."

Interact 15.3
New Testament Justice

1. After reading each of the following passages from Matthew, circle the appropriate topic and write a word or phrase relating what Jesus said about *anger*, *justice*, or *hell*.

5:21–22 _____

7:1–2 _____

7:13–14 _____

10:28 _____

11:20–24 _____

12:35–37 _____

13:47–51 _____

16:21–23 _____

18:6 _____

21:18–22 _____

21:33–46 _____

25:28–30 _____

2. Why doesn't God punish evil and evildoers now?

Let God Be GOD

Yahweh Power and might are in your hand. (2 Chronicles 20:6)

The Lord is gracious and compassionate, slow to anger and rich in love. (Psalm 145:8)

Holy, holy, holy is the Lord God Almighty, who was, and is, and is to come. (Revelation 4:8)

God is love. (1 John 4:16) I am the first and the last. (Isaiah 44:6) Just and true are your ways. (Revelation 15:3)

The Lord reigns (Psalm 93:1) My ways are higher than your ways and my thoughts than your thoughts. (Isaiah 55:9) He does not treat us as our sins deserve. (Psalm 103:10) I the Lord do not change. (Malachi 3:6)

Christ of God (Luke 9:20) Ever-present—Where can I flee from your presence? (Psalm 139:7) I am with you always. (Matthew 28:20) Lord of the Sabbath (Mark 2:28)

Great is your faithfulness. (Lamentations 3:23) unsearchable his judgments, and his paths beyond tracing out! (Romans 11:33)

Oh, the depth of the riches of the wisdom and knowledge of God! How love and faithfulness go before you. (Psalm 89:14)

Righteousness and justice are the foundation of your throne; love and faithfulness go before you. (Psalm 89:14)

He is the true God. (1 John 5:20) I am the way and the truth and the life. No one comes to the Father except through me. (John 14:6) Taste and see that the Lord is good. (Psalm 34:8)

I am the Alpha and the Omega, the First and the Last, the Beginning and the End. (Revelation 22:13) You alone are holy. (Revelation 15:4)

Nothing in all creation is hidden from God's sight. (Hebrews 4:13) Give thanks to the Lord, for he is good; his love endures forever. (Psalm 118:1) I AM (John 8:58)

In the beginning was the Word, and the Word was with God, and the Word was God. (John 1:1) The Lord is good and his love endures forever. (Psalm 100:5)

The Lord is gracious and righteous; our God is full of compassion. (Psalm 116:5) I am the Son of God. (John 10:36) Holy, holy, holy is the Lord Almighty. (Isaiah 6:3) Everlasting Father, Prince of Peace. (Isaiah 9:6)

The Lord works righteousness and justice for all the oppressed. (Psalm 103:6) And he will be called Wonderful Counselor, Mighty God,

Your righteousness is everlasting. (Psalm 119:142) Jesus the Son of God (Hebrews 4:14) He is the atoning sacrifice for our sins, and not only for ours but also for the sins of the whole world. (1 John 2:2)

To God belong wisdom and power. (Job 12:13) I am the living bread that came down from heaven. (John 6:51)

For to us a child is born, to us a son is given, and the government will be on his shoulders. (Isaiah 9:6) He is powerful, for he had provided purification for sins, he sat down at the right hand of the Majesty in heaven. (Hebrews 1:3)

Christ died and returned to life so that he might be the Lord of both the dead and the living. (Romans 14:9) Jesus, the pioneer and perfecter of faith. (Hebrews 12:2)

Therefore, since we have a great high priest who has ascended into heaven, Jesus the Son of God, let us hold firmly to the faith we profess. (Hebrews 4:14) the Lamb of God (John 1:29) the Root and the Offspring of David, and the bright Morning Star. (Revelation 22:16)

The Son is the radiance of God's glory and the exact representation of his being, sustaining all things by his powerful word. (Hebrews 1:3) the firstborn from the dead, and the ruler of the kings of the earth. (Revelation 1:5)

God, the blessed and only Ruler, the King of kings and Lord of lords. (1 Timothy 6:15) He has become a high priest forever, in the order of Melchizedek. (Hebrews 6:20)

Let them know that you, whose name is the LORD—that you alone are the Most High over all the earth. (Psalm 83:18)

Rose of Sharon (Song of Songs 2:1) We have this hope as an anchor for the soul, firm and secure. It enters the inner sanctuary behind the curtain, (Hebrews 6:19-20) I am the Root and the Offspring of David. (Revelation 22:16)

That which was from the beginning, which we have heard, which we have seen with our eyes, which we have looked at and our hands have touched. (1 John 1:1) Here is a glutton and a drunkard, a friend of tax collectors and sinners. (Matthew 11:19)

God, the blessed and only Ruler, the King of kings and Lord of lords. (1 Timothy 6:15) and his name the only name. (Zechariah 14:9)

The LORD will be King over the whole earth. On that day there will be one LORD, and his name the only name. (Zechariah 14:9) the Father has sent his Son to be the Savior of the world. (1 John 4:14)

From everlasting to everlasting you are God. (Psalm 90:2) The Son of Man came eating and drinking, (Matthew 9:15) Desire of all nations (Haggai 2:7) And we have seen and testify that the Father has sent his Son to be the Savior of the world. (1 John 4:14)

The virgin will conceive and give birth to a son, and will call him Immanuel. (Isaiah 7:14) Chosen of God (1 Peter 2:4) Righteous Branch, a King who will reign wisely and do what is just and right in the land. (Jeremiah 23:5)

(O)ur Lord Jesus, that great Shepherd of the sheep (Hebrews 13:20) The Lord is enthroned as King forever. (Psalm 29:10) a stone in Zion, a tested stone, a precious cornerstone for a sure foundation. (Isaiah 28:16)

I am the true vine, and my Father is the gardener. (John 15:1) Thanks be to God for his indescribable gift! (2 Corinthians 9:15)

(T)he Shepherd and Overseer of your souls. (1 Peter 2:25)

(W)e have an advocate with the Father—Jesus Christ, the Righteous One. (1 John 2:1) Our Lord Jesus, the bright Morning Star. (Revelation 22:16)

(I am the) Root and the Offspring of David, and the bright Morning Star. (Revelation 22:16) As for God, his way is perfect. (Psalm 18:30)

Chief Shepherd (1 Peter 5:4) Heir of all things (Hebrews 1:2) Judge (Acts 10: 42)

Sceptre (Numbers 24:17) Yahweh

16

GOD Is Long-Suffering and Loving

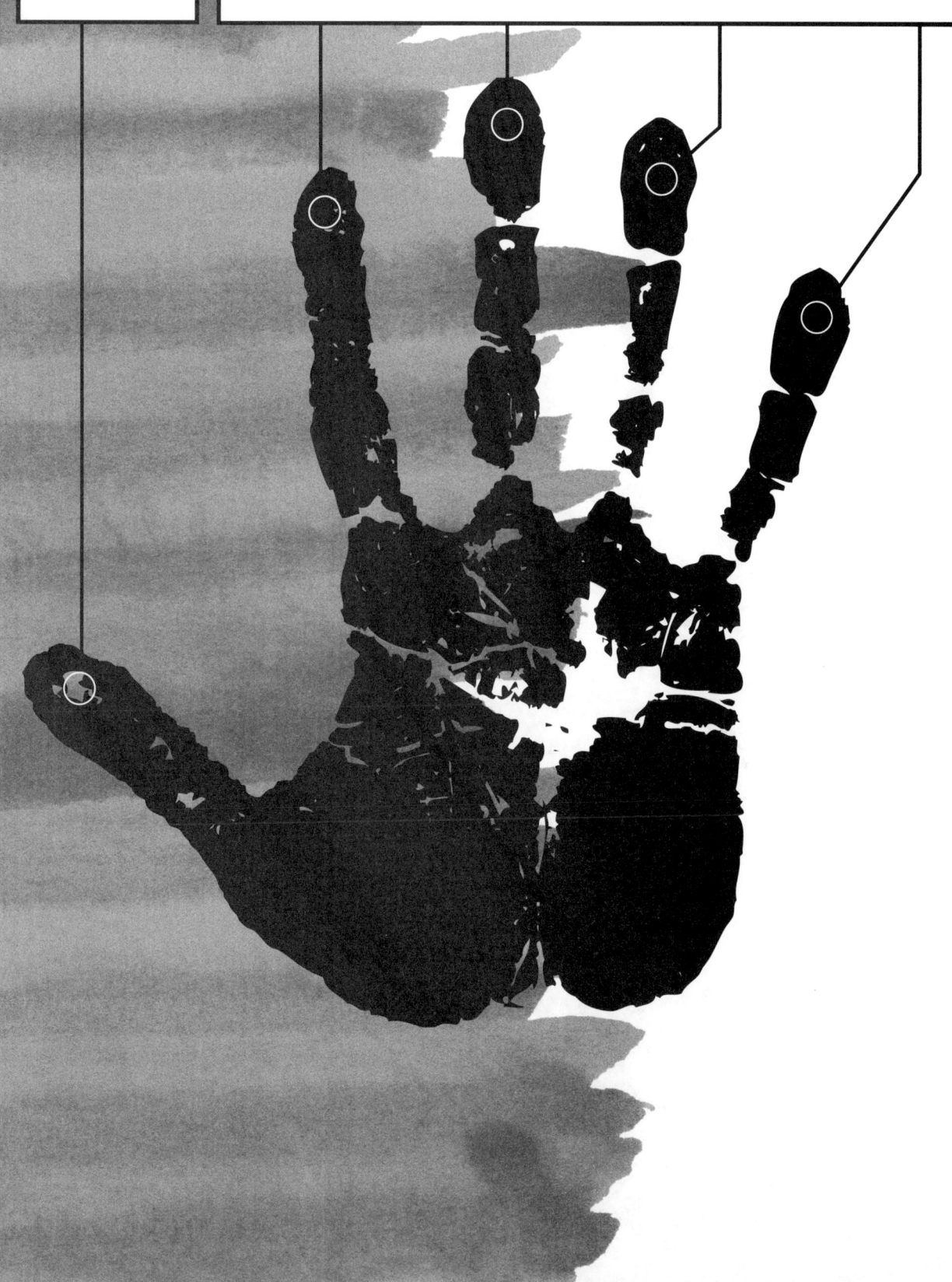

Interact 16.1
God's Wrath

Read each section of Scripture and record what it says about God's judgment and wrath.

The Lord Judges

Deuteronomy 32:35–36

2 Thessalonians 1:5–10

2 Peter 3:8–10

Revelation 20:11–15

The Lord's Wrath

Isaiah 34:8

Isaiah 61:2

Romans 1:18–23

Hebrews 10:28–31

Let God Be GOD

Yahweh

Power and might are in your hand (2 Chronicles 20:6)

The Lord is gracious and compassionate, slow to anger and rich in love. (Psalm 145:8)

Holy, holy, holy is the Lord God Almighty, who was, and is, and is to come.

Just and true are your ways. (Revelation 15:3)

God is love. (1 John 4:16)

The Lord reigns (Psalm 93:1)

I am the first and the last. (Isaiah 44:6)

My ways are higher than your ways and my thoughts than your thoughts. (Isaiah 55:9)

He does not treat us as our sins deserve. (Psalm 103:10)

I the Lord do not change (Malachi 3:6)

Christ of God (Luke 9:20)

Ever-present... Where can I flee from your presence? (Psalm 139:7)

Great is your faithfulness. (Lamentations 3:23)

Oh, the depth of the riches of the wisdom and knowledge of God! How unsearchable his judgments, and his paths beyond tracing out! (Romans 11:33)

I am with you always. (Matthew 28:20)

Lord of the sabbath (Mark 2:28)

Righteousness and justice are the foundation of your throne; love and faithfulness go before you. (Psalm 89:14)

I am the Alpha and the Omega, the First and the Last, the Beginning and the End. (Revelation 22:13)

Nothing in all creation is hidden from God's sight. (Hebrews 4:13)

The Lord is gracious and righteous; our God is full of compassion. (Psalm 116:5)

Give thanks to the Lord, for he is good; his love endures forever. (Psalm 118:1)

You alone are holy. (Revelation 15:4)

I AM (John 8:58)

I am the way and the truth and the life. (John 14:6)

Holy, holy, holy is the Lord Almighty. (Isaiah 6:3)

Taste and see that the Lord is good. (Psalm 34:8)

The Lord is good and his love endures forever. (Psalm 100:5)

He is the true God. (1 John 5:20)

Your righteousness is everlasting (Psalm 119:142)

The Lord works righteousness and justice for all the oppressed. (Psalm 103:6)

To God belong wisdom and power. (Job 12:13)

In the beginning was the Word, and the Word was with God, and the Word was God. (John 1:1)

No one comes to the Father except through me. (John 14:6)

I am the living bread that came down from heaven. (John 6:51)

And he will be called Wonderful Counselor, Mighty God, Everlasting Father, Prince of Peace. (Isaiah 9:6)

Jesus the Son of God, let us hold firmly to the faith we profess. (Hebrews 4:14)

After he had provided purification for sins he sat down at the right hand of the Majesty in heaven. (Hebrews 1:3)

He is the atoning sacrifice for our sins, and not only for ours but also for the sins of the whole world. (1 John 2:2)

The Lamb of God (John 1:29)

Jesus, the pioneer and perfecter of faith. (Hebrews 12:2)

For to us a child is born, to us a son is given, and the government will be on his shoulders. (Isaiah 9:6)

Christ died and returned to life so that he might be the Lord of both the dead and the living. (Romans 14:9)

a great high priest who has ascended into heaven, Jesus the Son of God (Hebrews 4:14)

God, the blessed and only Ruler, the King of kings and Lord of lords (1 Timothy 6:15)

who is to come, and from the seven spirits before his throne, and from Jesus Christ, who is the faithful witness, the firstborn from the dead, and the ruler of the kings of the earth. (Revelation 1:5)

the bright Morning Star (Revelation 22:16)

He has become a high priest forever, in the order of Melchizedek. (Hebrews 6:20)

The Son is the radiance of God's glory and the exact representation of his being (Hebrews 1:3)

Therefore, since we have a great high priest

We have this hope as an anchor for the soul, firm and secure. It enters the inner sanctuary behind the curtain, where our forerunner, Jesus, has entered on our behalf. He has become a high priest forever, in the order of Melchizedek. (Hebrews 6:19-20)

(Him) who is, and who was, and who is to come (Revelation 1:8)

whose name is the LORD—that you alone are the Most High over all the earth. (Psalm 83:18)

our hands have touched—this we proclaim concerning the Word of life. (1 John 1:1)

Here is a glutton and a drunkard, a friend of tax collectors and sinners. (Matthew 11:19)

And we have seen and testify that the Father has sent his Son to be the Savior of the world. (1 John 4:14)

Desire of all nations (Haggai 2:7)

(The one who is) speaking to you—I am he. (John 4:26)

Rose of Sharon (Song of Songs 2:1)

That which was from the beginning, which we have heard, which we have seen with our eyes, which we have looked at and our hands have touched

God, the blessed and only Ruler

On that day there will be one LORD, and his name the only name. (Zechariah 14:9)

The Son of Man came eating and drinking, and they say, 'Here is a glutton...' (Matthew 11:19)

Chosen of God (1 Peter 2:4)

I have set my King on Zion, my holy hill (Psalm 2:6)

See, I lay a stone in Zion, a tested stone, a precious cornerstone for a sure foundation. (Isaiah 28:16)

Thanks be to God for his indescribable gift! (2 Corinthians 9:15)

The LORD will be king over the whole earth. (Psalm 90:2)

The virgin will conceive and give birth to a son, and will call him Immanuel. (Isaiah 7:14)

From everlasting to everlasting you are God.

The Lord is enthroned as King forever. (Psalm 29:10)

(O)ur Lord Jesus, that great Shepherd of the sheep (Hebrews 13:20)

I am the true vine, and my Father is the gardener. (John 15:1)

(T)he Shepherd and Overseer of your souls (1 Peter 2:25)

(W)e have an advocate with the Father—Jesus Christ, the Righteous One. (1 John 2:1)

I am the Root and the Offspring of David, and the bright Morning Star. (Revelation 22:16)

As for God, his way is perfect. (Psalm 18:30)

Chief Shepherd (1 Peter 5:4)

Sceptre (Numbers 24:17)

Judge (Acts 10:42)

Heir of all things (Hebrews 1:2)

Yahweh

Interact 16.2
God's Long-Suffering

Read the following Scripture passages and complete the activities. Be prepared to discuss your answers.

1. Read Romans 2:1–11. Note any information you find regarding God's justice and patience. What further facts can we infer from what this passage teaches?

2. Read all the verses below; then answer the questions.
  Exodus 34:6–7; Isaiah 48:9; Psalm 30:5; Psalm 78:38; 2 Peter 3:9; Psalm 30:5; and Psalm 103:8–10.

  What do we deserve?

  What do we receive?

  What do we forget?

  What do we expect?

3. Read the verses below; then write your first impression of God's long-suffering.
  Jeremiah 2:32; Jeremiah 4:22; Jeremiah 5:1; Jeremiah 5:30–31; and Jeremiah 35:12–19.

4. In 25 to 50 words, tell how you feel about God's long-suffering.

Let God Be GOD

Yahweh

Power and might are in your hand. (2 Chronicles 20:6)

The Lord is gracious and compassionate, slow to anger and rich in love. (Psalm 145:8)

Holy, holy, holy is the Lord God Almighty, who was, and is, and is to come. (Revelation 4:8)

God is love. (1 John 4:16)

I am the first and the last. (Isaiah 44:6)

Just and true are your ways. (Revelation 15:3)

The Lord reigns (Psalm 93:1)

My ways are higher than your ways and my thoughts than your thoughts. (Isaiah 55:9)

He does not treat us as our sins deserve. (Psalm 103:10)

the Lord do not change (Malachi 3:6)

Christ of God (Luke 9:20)

Ever-present—Where can I flee from your presence? (Psalm 139:7)

Great is your faithfulness. (Lamentations 3:23)

...love and faithfulness go before you. (Psalm 89:14)

Lord of the sabbath (Mark 2:28)

I am with you always (Matthew 28:20)

Oh, the depth of the riches of the wisdom and knowledge of God! How unsearchable his judgments, and his paths beyond tracing out! (Romans 11:33)

Righteousness and justice are the foundation of your throne; love and faithfulness go before you. (Psalm 89:14)

I AM (John 8:58)

He is the true God. (1 John 5:20)

I am the Alpha and the Omega, the First and the Last, the Beginning and the End. (Revelation 22:13)

Nothing in all creation is hidden from God's sight. (Hebrews 4:13)

Give thanks to the Lord, for he is good; his love endures forever. (Psalm 118:1)

You alone are holy. (Revelation 15:4)

The Lord is gracious and righteous; our God is full of compassion. (Psalm 116:5)

I am the way and the truth and the life. No one comes to the Father except through me. (John 14:6)

Taste and see that the Lord is good. (Psalm 34:8)

Holy, holy, holy is the Lord Almighty. (Isaiah 6:3)

The Lord is good and his love endures forever. (Psalm 100:5)

I am the living bread that came down from heaven. (John 6:51)

The Lord works righteousness and justice for all the oppressed. (Psalm 103:6)

In the beginning was the Word, and the Word was with God, and the Word was God. (John 1:1)

...called Wonderful Counselor, Mighty God, Everlasting Father, Prince of Peace. (Isaiah 9:6)

To God belong wisdom and power. (Job 12:13)

Your righteousness is everlasting. (Psalm 119:142)

For to us a child is born, to us a son is given, and the government will be on his shoulders.

Christ died and returned to life so that he might be the Lord of both the dead and the living. (Romans 14:9)

the Lamb of God (John 1:29)

He is the atoning sacrifice for our sins, and not only for ours but also for the sins of the whole world. (1 John 2:2)

The Son is the radiance of God's glory and the exact representation of his being (Hebrews 1:3)

...let us hold firmly to the faith we profess. (Hebrews 4:14)

Therefore, since we have a great high priest who has ascended into heaven, Jesus the Son of God

God, the blessed and only Ruler, the King of kings and Lord of lords (1 Timothy 6:15)

...sustaining all things by his powerful word. After he had provided purification for sins, he sat down at the right hand of the Majesty in heaven. (Hebrews 1:3)

the faithful witness, the firstborn from the dead and the ruler of the kings of the earth. (Revelation 1:5)

Jesus, the pioneer and perfecter of faith (Hebrews 12:2)

...name is the LORD—that you alone are the Most High over all the earth. (Psalm 83:18)

...where our forerunner, Jesus, has entered on our behalf. He has become a high priest forever, in the order of Melchizedek. (Hebrews 6:20)

this we proclaim concerning the Word of life (1 John 1:1)

...who has seen with our eyes, which we have looked at and our hands have touched

We have this hope as an anchor for the soul, firm and secure. It enters the inner sanctuary behind the curtain (Hebrews 6:19)

That which was from the beginning, which we have heard, which we have seen with our eyes (1 John 1:1)

Let them know that you, whose name is the LORD (Psalm 83:18)

On that day there will be one LORD, and his name the only name. (Zechariah 14:9)

The Son of Man came eating and drinking, and they say, 'Here is a glutton and a drunkard, a friend of tax collectors and sinners.' (Matthew 11:19)

...the Father has sent his Son to be the Savior of the world. (1 John 4:14)

And we have seen and testify that the Father has sent his Son to be the Savior of the world. (1 John 4:14)

Desire of all nations (Haggai 2:7)

The Righteous Branch, a King who will reign wisely and do what is just and right in the land. (Jeremiah 23:5)

See, I lay a stone in Zion, a tested stone, a precious cornerstone for a sure foundation. (Isaiah 28:16)

Chosen of God (1 Peter 2:4)

Bridegroom (Matthew 9:15)

Thanks be to God for his indescribable gift! (2 Corinthians 9:15)

The virgin will conceive and give birth to a son, and will call him Immanuel. (Isaiah 7:14)

From everlasting to everlasting you are God. (Psalm 90:2)

The LORD will be King over the whole earth.

Rose of Sharon (Song of Songs 2:1)

(O)ur Lord Jesus, that great Shepherd of the sheep (Hebrews 13:20)

The Lord is enthroned as King forever. (Psalm 29:10)

I am the true vine, and my Father is the gardener. (John 15:1)

(The) Shepherd and Overseer of your souls (1 Peter 2:25)

(W)e have an advocate with the Father—Jesus Christ, the Righteous One. (1 John 2:1)

As for God, his way is perfect. (Psalm 18:30)

I am the Root and the Offspring of David, and the bright Morning Star. (Revelation 22:16)

Heir of all things (Hebrews 1:2)

Chief Shepherd (1 Peter 5:4)

Sceptre (Numbers 24:17)

Judge (Acts 10:42)

Yahweh

Interact 16.3
God Is Love

1. The following Bible passages talk about the love of God. As you read each passage, write *why* the author says God is loving. (Look for actions of God that show He is loving; also look for other attributes that the writers link to God's love.)

Exodus 34:5–7

Deuteronomy 7:7–8

Deuteronomy 10:14–15

2 Chronicles 7:3

2 Chronicles 20:21

Ezra 3:11

Psalm 33:4–5

Psalm 36:5–10

Psalm 103:8

Psalm 145:8

Jeremiah 31:3

Continued on back →

Let God Be GOD

God Is Love continued

Lamentations 3:22–23

John 3:16

John 13:1

John 17:23–26

Romans 5:8

Romans 8:35–39

2 Corinthians 13:14

2. According to the passages below, how should we respond to the fact that God is love? (You may also find suggestions in the passages you looked at when answering the first question.)

Matthew 22:35–40; John 15:9–17; Ephesians 5:1–2; Philippians 2:1–2; and 1 John 4:16, 19

Let God Be GOD

Interact 16.4
Singing God's Love

The book of Psalms is a worship songbook. Read the following passages from Psalms. Beside each passage, make notes and comments about the verses. What does the psalm writer say about God's love? How does God's love make a difference in the writer's life? How can we live in God's love?

6:4

13:5

25:6–7

31:14–16

42:8

51:1

86:5

89:1–2

101:1

117:1–2

118:1–4

136:1–26

145:8

Let God Be GOD

Part V
Synthesis and Review

Yahweh   Power and might are in your hand. (2 Chronicles 20:6)

The Lord is gracious and compassionate, slow to anger and rich in love. (Psalm 145:8)

Holy, holy, holy is the Lord God Almighty, who was, and is, and is to come. (Revelation 4:8)

God is love. (1 John 4:16)   I am the first and the last. (Isaiah 44:6)   Just and true are your ways. (Revelation 15:3)

The Lord reigns (Psalm 93:1)   My ways are higher than your ways and my thoughts than your thoughts. (Isaiah 55:9)

Christ of God (Luke 9:20)   Where can I flee from your presence? (Psalm 139:7)   He does not treat us as our sins deserve. (Psalm 103:10)   The Lord do not change. (Malachi 3:6)

Ever-present—(Lamentations 3:23)   How unsearchable his judgments, and his paths beyond tracing out! (Romans 11:33)   I am with you always. (Matthew 28:20)   Lord of the Sabbath (Mark 2:28)

Great is your faithfulness. (Lamentations 3:23)   of God! How unsearchable   love and faithfulness go before you. (Psalm 89:14)   I AM (John 8:58)

Oh, the depth of the riches of the wisdom and knowledge   the foundation of your throne; love and faithfulness   I am the living bread that came down from heaven. (John 6:51)

Righteousness and justice are the foundation of your throne;   and the End, the Beginning and the End. (Revelation 22:13) You alone are holy. (Revelation 15:4)

He is the true God. (1 John 5:20)   Give thanks to the Lord, for he is good; his love endures forever. (Psalm 118:1)

I am the Alpha and the Omega, the First and the Last, the Beginning and the End   Holy, holy, holy is the Lord Almighty. (Isaiah 6:3)

Nothing in all creation is hidden from God's sight. (Hebrews 4:13)   Taste and see that the Lord is good. (Psalm 34:8)

The Lord is gracious and righteous; our God is full of compassion. (Psalm 116:5)   No one comes to the Father except through me. (John 14:6)

I am the way and the truth and the life. (John 14:6)   The Lord is good and his love endures forever. (Psalm 100:5)

The Lord works righteousness. (Psalm 103:6)   In the beginning was the Word, and the Word was with God, and the Word was God. (John 1:1)

To God belong wisdom and power. (Job 12:13)   And he will be called Wonderful Counselor, Mighty God, Everlasting Father, Prince of Peace. (Isaiah 9:6)

Your righteousness is everlasting. (Psalm 119:142)   and the Word was with God, and the Word was God.

For to us a child is born, to us a son is given, and the government will be on his shoulders.   He is the atoning sacrifice for our sins. (1 John 2:2)

Christ died and returned to life so that he might be the Lord of both the dead and the living. (Romans 14:9)   Jesus, the pioneer and perfecter of faith. (Hebrews 12:2)

The Son is the radiance of God's glory and the exact representation of his being, sustaining all things by his powerful word. After he had provided purification for sins, he sat down at the right hand of the Majesty in heaven. (Hebrews 1:3)

Therefore, since we have a great high priest who has ascended into heaven, Jesus the Son of God, let us hold firmly to the faith we profess. (Hebrews 4:14)   the Lamb of God (John 1:29)

Rose of Sharon (Song of Songs 2:1)   let them know that you, whose name is the LORD—that you alone are the Most High over all the earth. (Psalm 83:18)   Jesus, the high priest in the order of Melchizedek. (Hebrews 6:19-20)

That which was from the beginning, which we have heard, which we have seen with our eyes, which we have looked at and our hands have touched—this we proclaim concerning the Word of life. (1 John 1:1)   the bright Morning Star. (Revelation 22:16)

We have this hope as an anchor for the soul, firm and secure. It enters the inner sanctuary behind the curtain. (Hebrews 6:19)   He is a glutton and a drunkard, a friend of tax collectors and sinners. (Matthew 11:19)

God, the blessed and only Ruler, the King of kings and Lord of lords. (1 Timothy 6:15)   he Son of Man came eating and drinking, and they say, He is a glutton and a drunkard

The LORD will be king over the whole earth. On that day there will be one LORD, and his name the only name. (Zechariah 14:9)   the Father has sent his Son to be the Savior of the world. (1 John 4:14)

God, the blessed and only Ruler   And we have seen and testify that   Desire of all nations (Haggai 2:7)

from everlasting to everlasting you are God. (Psalm 90:2)   a stone in Zion, a tested stone, a precious cornerstone for a sure foundation. (Jeremiah 23:5)

The virgin will conceive and give birth to a son, and will call him Immanuel. (Isaiah 7:14)   and do what is just and right in the land. (Jeremiah 33:15)

(O)ur Lord Jesus, that great Shepherd of the sheep (Hebrews 13:20)   Chosen of God (1 Peter 2:4)   Thanks be to God for his indescribable gift! (2 Corinthians 9:15)

I am the true vine, and my Father is the gardener. (John 15:1)   The Lord is enthroned as King forever. (Psalm 29:10)

(T)he Shepherd and Overseer of your souls (1 Peter 2:25)   the Root and the Offspring of David, and the bright Morning Star. (Revelation 22:16)

(W)e have an advocate with the Father—Jesus Christ, the Righteous One. (1 John 2:1)   As for God, his way is perfect. (Psalm 18:30)

(I) am the Root and the Offspring of David   Heir of all things (Hebrews 1:2)

I am the Good Shepherd (1 Peter 5:4)   Chief Shepherd (1 Peter 5:4)   Judge (Acts 10:42)

Sceptre (Numbers 24:17)   Heir of all things   Yahweh

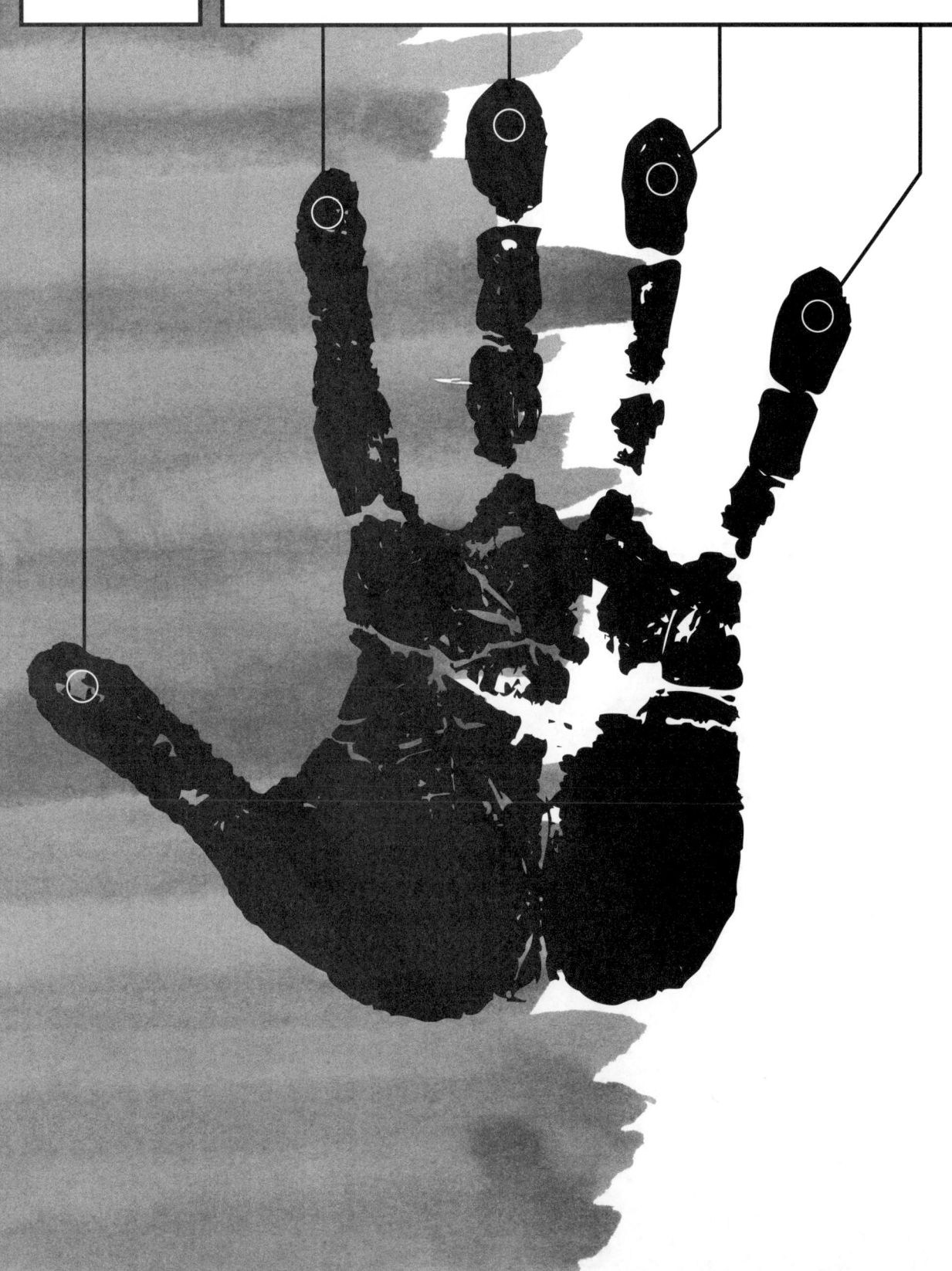

17

GOD'S ATTRIBUTES:
Complementary or Contradictory?

Complementary or Contradictory?

Complete this Interact by following the directions in each section.

1. Look up the following verses about God's love and God's hate. Write down the word or phrase that tells whom or what God loves or hates.

God's Love	God's Hate
Deuteronomy 4:32–38	**Proverbs 6:16–19**
Deuteronomy 7:7–9	**Isaiah 1:13–15**
Psalm 103:17	**Isaiah 61:8**
Psalm 119:64, 124	**Amos 5:21**
Psalm 146:8–0	**Psalm 5:4–6**
Malachi 1:2–3	**Psalm 11:4–6Z**

Continued on back →

Let God Be GOD

Complementary or Contradictory? continued

2. For each verse or passage listed below, write a phrase that indicates what, whom, and how we are to love or hate. (Remember that these verses represent only a few of many that could be cited.)

Our Love	Our Hate
Deuteronomy 10:9	Psalm 139:21
Deuteronomy 6:5	Psalm 119:128
Deuteronomy 10:12–13	Psalm 119:163

3. In the space below, write a short paragraph about the proper objects of our love and hate.